THE INDIAN CALIPHATE

IMRAN MULLA

The Indian Caliphate

*Exiled Ottomans and
the Billionaire Prince*

HURST & COMPANY, LONDON

First published in the United Kingdom in 2025 by
C. Hurst & Co. (Publishers) Ltd.,
New Wing, Somerset House, Strand, London, WC2R 1LA
© Imran Mulla, 2025
All rights reserved.

Distributed in the United States, Canada and Latin America by Oxford University Press, 546 Fifth Avenue, New York, NY 10036, United States of America.

The right of Imran Mulla to be identified as the author of this publication is asserted by him in accordance with the Copyright, Designs and Patents Act, 1988.

A Cataloguing-in-Publication data record for this book is available from the British Library.

ISBN: 9781805264248

EU GPSR Authorised Representative
Easy Access System Europe Oü, 16879218
Address: Mustamäe tee 50, 10621, Tallinn, Estonia
Contact Details: gpsr.requests@easproject.com, +358 40 500 3575

Printed and bound in Great Britain by Bell and Bain Ltd, Glasgow

www.hurstpublishers.com

For Amina.

CONTENTS

Note on Spelling and Titles	ix
Acknowledgements	xi
Introduction	1

PART ONE

1.	The Democrat Prince	9
2.	Anglicised Radicals	27
3.	'God Versus Man'	47
4.	The Last Caliphate	69
5.	Slings and Arrows	89

PART TWO

6.	An Oriental Dream	109
7.	'I Will Not Go Back to a Slave Country'	129
8.	'A Distinguished Son of Islam'	149
9.	Ottomans in Hyderabad	169
10.	The Caliphal Succession	187
	Epilogue	217

Notes	225
Bibliography	265
Index	271

NOTE ON SPELLING AND TITLES

In the late 1920s, Turkey (now Türkiye) adopted the Latin script as part of its lurch away from all things Ottoman. I have opted to use the spellings of Turkish names that were commonly used by English writers at the time and are likely to be easier for English readers, rather than their Turkish Latin counterparts: thus Abdulmejid instead of Abdülmecid, Durrushehvar rather than Dürrüşehvar and Niloufer over Nilüfer. When referring to modern Turkish writers, however, I follow the Turkish spelling.

In the Indian subcontinent in the early twentieth century, a single name could often be transliterated into English in several different ways—sometimes by the same person. I have chosen spellings rather arbitrarily and according to my own preferences—Mohamed Ali rather than Mohammed Ali, for example, or Sayyid Amir Ali instead of Syed Ameer Ali.

Finally, during the period in which the book is set, titles and honorifics were often heavily contested—Caliph Abdulmejid, for instance, didn't renounce his Caliphal title even after the Turkish government said it had stripped him of it. I deploy titles according to how people described themselves.

ACKNOWLEDGEMENTS

The idea for this book began in June 2023, in a conversation over Turkish tea late at night in Cambridge with Imad Ahmed, Moez Hayat and Adnan Mahmud. Adnan would later be of tremendous assistance with the Urdu primary sources, including helping me make sense of Prince Moazzam Jah's poetry. I am deeply grateful to Deniz Erdem and Burak Güzel for their help with the Ottoman Turkish material. James Wrathall, another close friend, was the best travel companion I could have wished for in India. Ayub Khan was wonderfully helpful in introducing me to new primary sources and sharing his profound knowledge of Hyderabadi history.

I am enormously grateful to Nawab Syed Ahmed Khan and his family, who hosted me in Hyderabad and showed me the many documents they have in their home, on the understanding that I could write whatever I liked. Maulana Shaukat Ali's grandson, Irfan Ali, generously sent me his father Khalid Ali's monumental biographical work on the Ali brothers (of which there are no published copies available). Imaan Irfan kindly arranged my interview with her grandmother Sultana Walajahi.

At Hurst, my deep thanks go to Michael Dwyer for taking the book on, and to Lara Weisweiller-Wu, Daisy Leitch, Letty Allen and Haitenlo Semy for doing such a wonderful job in turning the manuscript into the finished product. My thanks also go to my copyeditor Tom Feltham and proofreader Louise Tingle.

I am grateful to Middle East Eye for having published several pieces I wrote about the topics featured in these pages during various stages of my research. I first wrote about the last Caliph for Shafik Mandhai, a spectacular editor (and more importantly, a fellow native of Leicester). Nick Hunt not only magnificently edited two unreasonably long and unwieldy pieces on the subject, but also

ACKNOWLEDGEMENTS

played an invaluable role in helping me to develop and refine my ideas and approach to the book. I am hugely grateful to Ali Amir, Faisal Edroos, David Hearst, Daniel Hilton and Simon Hooper for teaching me a great deal about journalism and the world.

In late 2023 I contacted John Zubrzycki, whose work I heavily admired, completely out of the blue to share my book idea and ask for advice. He was more generous than any young writer could ever hope for, and without his assistance, knowledge and insight this book would not have been published. I am also extremely thankful to John Holmwood, one of the best thinkers I know, who reviewed an early draft of the manuscript and gave me vital feedback.

I credit Peter Oborne with turning me from a history student into a journalist (I hope he doesn't regret it). Over the past four years I have learnt an enormous amount from his knowledge, wisdom, unfailing generosity and deep integrity. Having initially encouraged me to write the book, Peter later reviewed an early draft and provided both ruthless criticism and important advice.

I could never sufficiently thank my parents, who have always been my greatest teachers and most revered role models. Considering the sheer number of books they read to me when I was two years old, it was perhaps always likely that I would eventually have a stab at writing one myself.

Finally, I am endlessly grateful to Amina Chowdhury, who was the first to read each rough and often incoherent chapter. Without her constant support, advice and passion, to say nothing of her fabulous research and editing, this book would never have been possible. Coincidentally, I married her a few days after submitting the manuscript.

INTRODUCTION

It was mid-morning but already forty degrees Celsius in the shade when the driver stopped his taxi and refused to continue any further. 'The car can't go on,' he proclaimed. 'There's no road.'

And so there wasn't. Around us the terrain stretched out, rocky and uneven. We were in Aurangabad, a district in India's western state of Maharashtra, and had in fact left any semblance of a road half a mile behind us. My travelling companion James and I looked at each other. We agreed: there was no way we would give up simply because of vehicular restrictions. We would have to leave the car and reach our destination on foot.

Twenty minutes later, James and I were in the wilderness and beginning to question our combined intelligence and decision-making capabilities. There was no sign of life ahead, neither humans nor—thankfully—animals, including sloth bears, which inhabit the region and have a reputation for aggression. I only learned that later. To our right, a treeline curved away into the distance, while to the left a dusty series of plateaus dominated the horizon. The sun beat down. We were low on water, having only brought a single, half-full bottle with us in another stroke of genius. I was vaguely on the lookout for snakes.

And then it appeared—the reason we were there. It was small at first, in the distance on a plateau, but unmistakable: a great mausoleum, around fifteen metres tall and eight metres wide, with a large Ottoman Turkish-style dome on top, latticed windows and archways on all four sides. We picked up the pace. The heat and potential deadly animals suddenly felt unimportant. As we drew closer, it became possible to distinguish the remains of a complex built around the mausoleum. Our excitement gave way to a quiet solemnity as we approached. The grey structure was tired and battered, although it still exuded a certain imperial grandeur.

Inside, the mausoleum was derelict. Walls were scrawled with graffiti, inane scribblings and the names of lovers drawn to the building for its isolation. Plaster, crumbled from the lower walls, was scattered across the bare floor. Melancholy and mystique hung around the building, and at its centre a small sunken pit marked where a grave should have been. It was empty.

Why was there an abandoned Ottoman tomb in the wilderness of western India? Trying to answer this was why we found ourselves there in May 2024. The man who had hoped to be buried in that mausoleum was one of the early twentieth century's most extraordinary and paradoxical figures: Abdulmejid II, holder of the title Caliph, which represented Islam's religious-political succession to the Prophet Muhammad. The final nominal leader of the Islamic world, Abdulmejid was a member of the House of Osman, the Ottoman dynasty, which had governed swathes of Europe, Asia and Africa for five centuries.

I first read about the last Caliph in November 2022, while I was reading history at Cambridge. There had recently been a surge of interest in Abdulmejid II because a collection of his artwork and letters had been put on display in an Istanbul exhibition.[1] To many readers today, however, the word Caliphate will evoke terrifying scenes of beheadings, brutal massacres and hostage videos. In 2013, a group of militants in Iraq and Syria described themselves as an Islamic State and claimed a Caliphate, asserting their leadership of the world's Muslims. The 'Islamic State of Iraq and Syria' (ISIS) was a group so horrific that even al-Qaeda, responsible for the attacks of 9/11, denounced it as extreme.[2] ISIS committed bloody war crimes, including a genocidal campaign against the region's Yazidi minority, and engineered a series of attacks on civilians in Western countries.[3] The group, at the time of writing hugely weakened, resolved the issue that barely any Muslims recognised it as a legitimate Caliphate by simply declaring Muslims who opposed it to be heretics.[4]

The spectre of the Caliphate has also been repeatedly invoked by Western governments themselves over the past few decades, as part of the American-led War on Terror. President George

INTRODUCTION

W. Bush, who illegally invaded Iraq in 2003, regularly declared that al-Qaeda aimed to establish a Caliphate. His vice president, Dick Cheney, likewise insisted that the group aimed to 're-create the old caliphate'. In Britain, my own country, the Conservative government's 'counter-extremism' programme branded Muslims extremist if they 'advocate a caliphate', defined extremely broadly as 'a pan-Islamic state encompassing many countries'.[5]

It is undeniable that the idea of the Caliphate continues to hold importance to many of the world's Muslims, representing as it does an ideal of Islamic unity and power.[6] The Ottoman Caliphs, however, would all have been outrageous heretics in the eyes of ISIS militants, and certainly don't fit the stereotype drawn up by hawkish Western governments and commentators. This was particularly true of Caliph Abdulmejid II, one of the most cultivated members of his dynasty. A talented painter, Francophile, amateur literary critic and classical music enthusiast, Abdulmejid was also devoted to Islam until his death.[7] Born and raised in the centre of Ottoman power, Istanbul, in 1868, he styled himself a 'democrat prince' and supported the Empire becoming a constitutional monarchy.

But after the First World War, the imperial edifice collapsed. By the time Abdulmejid was installed as Caliph in November 1922, a new Turkish state was being forged from the Ottoman Empire's ashes, and he became the first—and only—Caliph of modern Turkey. His destiny was exile: on 3 March 1924, the young Turkish Republic abolished Abdulmejid's title and bundled him and his family onto the Orient Express, headed for Switzerland. The demise of the 1,300-year-old Caliphate stunned the Islamic world, but what happened to the Caliph afterwards has been largely ignored by historians.

I was intrigued as to what Abdulmejid—who ended up in a seafront villa on the French Riviera—did in exile. It was hard to believe that he simply accepted his expulsion from Turkey. I spent months investigating and began to uncover an ambitious and ultimately failed plan to resurrect the Caliphate, a plan that involved one of the richest men in the world—at one point the richest. He was Osman Ali Khan, the seventh Nizam (ruler) of Hyderabad, a billionaire Indian Muslim prince and ruler of a modernising princely state the size of Italy, which claimed to be the successor polity to the mighty Mughal Empire and was under indirect British rule.[8]

I studied Ottoman eyewitness accounts of Abdulmejid's exile in France and spent hours in the British Library in London, itself an enduring product of the British Empire. There I trawled through hundreds of pages of unpublished documents brought from Hyderabad to England when the British left India. I found myself leafing through scores of letters, many marked as confidential, sent between the Nizam, Hyderabadi and British officials and the Ottoman exiles. They told how in 1931, Maulana Shaukat Ali, a legend of India's early independence movement against the British, successfully brokered a marriage between Abdulmejid's daughter Princess Durrushehvar and Prince Azam Jah, the Nizam's eldest son and heir apparent. The 1933-born son of the union, Prince Mukarram Jah, was both a member of the Ottoman dynasty and the designated next ruler of Hyderabad.

Loaded with political and civilisational significance, the alliance was part of a pro-Ottoman scheme which—through a congress in Jerusalem—helped establish the Palestinian struggle as a global Islamic cause. The union was opposed by Turkey and watched cautiously, often anxiously, by Britain. It brought together the Ottoman and Mughal legacies, the West and East of the Islamic world. And when the British left India in 1947, the Nizam aimed to make Hyderabad an independent state. If that had happened, Prince Mukarram Jah and his lineage would have been well placed to seek recognition from Muslim notables across the world and claim the Caliphal title once he became Nizam. Indeed, I have gathered strong evidence that this was Abdulmejid's wish before he died. But it was never to be. The British departure in August 1947 resulted in the creation of two unitary nation states, India and Pakistan. The new Indian government refused to accept the Nizam controlling a giant state in the middle of its territory and eventually invaded Hyderabad the following year.

But what if Partition had not occurred, and India had become a federation—an option that was on the table as late as 1946? Hyderabad could plausibly have become an autonomous, powerful and modernising princely state. Decades on, as ruler, Prince

INTRODUCTION

Mukarram Jah might have used his Ottoman lineage to claim the Caliphate, with a huge impact on global politics.

The Indian Caliphate is the tale of an idea, a scheme, a possibility that never came to pass. The signifier Indian refers to the subcontinent at large, not the modern nation state of India, and it certainly doesn't suggest that the Nizam of Hyderabad would have tried to conquer the entire subcontinent. I describe the scheme as Indian because it involved Indian Muslims outside of Hyderabad, and the Nizam's capital was widely recognised as home to the last flowering of Indo-Islamic culture. For the seat of the Caliphate to be in the Indian subcontinent might have risked religious conflict, certainly. But the Nizam would not have ruled outside Hyderabad, and Asaf Jahi rule usually amounted to tolerant pluralism. Meanwhile an Indian Caliphate could have made Hyderabad a focal point of the Islamic world.

This book is indebted to the serious work of countless historians and scholars over the decades. I aim to draw new links, tying events and people and themes together to reveal a new picture of this part of the twentieth century. I believe we have forgotten a significant chapter in global history. Bits and pieces can be found, scattered across books covering disparate disciplines. Yet the full story—stretching from London, Nice and Istanbul to Jerusalem, Bombay and Hyderabad—has never been told before. This book also seeks to paint real portraits of the people involved: how did they live and talk, how did they feel, how did they really see the world?

In one sense it is a tale of three worlds that collapsed and crumbled away; of the Ottoman Empire, the British Empire and an Indian princely state. But it also charts one of many attempts after the fall of the Ottomans to imagine a new political future for Muslims: as such it is a history that illuminates the extensive and often forgotten ties that exist between far-flung regions of the world. The Ottoman mausoleum in India stands as testament to the subcontinent's global importance—particularly its historical connections with the Middle East and position in the Islamic world. Today, the subcontinent is seen by Muslims as peripheral at best. Yet Sir Muhammad Iqbal felt able to proclaim that 'India is the greatest Muslim country in the world' in 1930. 'India is perhaps the only country in the world,' he argued, 'where Islam as a society is almost entirely due to the working of Islam as a culture inspired by a specific ethical ideal.'[9]

By this, he meant that Indian Muslims, the world's largest Muslim population, had no shared ethnicity or language. Only Islam encompassed them as a community. 'We have a duty towards Asia, especially Muslim Asia,' Iqbal maintained, since '70 millions of Muslims in a single country constitute a far more valuable asset to Islam than all the countries of Muslim Asia put together.'[10] And this was so even though Muslims were a minority. As many Hindu leaders then believed, Muslim politics could be a major boon to India's global position. This history reveals India to have been in many ways the epicentre of the Islamic world in the early twentieth century, a reality long since forgotten.

PART ONE

It is now for the Mussulman world alone, which has the exclusive right, to pass with full authority and in complete liberty upon this vital question.

– Caliph Abdulmejid II

I belong to two circles of equal size, but which are not concentric. One is India, and the other is the Muslim world... We as Indian Muslims came in both circles. We belong to these two circles, each of more than 300 millions, and we can leave neither.

– Maulana Mohamed Ali

1

THE DEMOCRAT PRINCE

The French travel writer Pierre Loti first met Prince Abdulmejid in 1910 in Istanbul, the great capital of the Ottoman Empire. The prince invited him to lunch at his palace in the secluded Camlica district, and Loti's account of the visit provides a vivid portrait of Abdulmejid and the world in which he lived. Loti found the prince's gardens, on top of a hill, to be a sort of 'secluded Eden'. The palace itself he thought was 'truly Oriental', where the walls of the vast, bright rooms were covered in blue and white tiles 'adorned with delicate, ancient designs.'[1] The rooms were furnished, however, 'with exquisite European taste'.[2]

Loti portrayed Abdulmejid himself, then aged forty-two, as a classic renaissance prince—and cosmopolitan to boot. A handsome man with bright, sharp eyes and a regal face, Abdulmejid sported a fabulous moustache. He customarily wore a European-style suit: as one ambassador in Istanbul remarked, 'when he is not wearing a fez, he looks like a well-bred Frenchman.'[3] Proficient not just in Ottoman Turkish, Arabic and Persian but also in French, which he particularly loved, Abdulmejid was given to 'shaking hands in the British manner' and was fond, his French guest soon found, of reciting Victor Hugo poems from memory.[4]

Loti, notoriously orientalist, was rather disappointed that lunch was served 'with all the refined modern customs,' and that red fez hats 'were (alas!) the only nod to the oriental'. He reported that the harem, the most intimate part of the palace, was guarded by 'affable eunuchs' in high-neck frock coats, like English clergymen.[5] Abdulmejid introduced Loti to one of his wives, Lady Shesuvar, who was twenty-nine years old and spoke French just as well as her husband. 'She has a grace that would make many princesses jealous,' Loti wrote, 'and a pleasant demeanour that instantly makes you feel at ease.' He first saw her dressed like a Parisian woman 'playing the cello in one of the salons alone, exquisitely interpreting a piece by Bach.'[6] As an avid Turcophile drawn to the exotic image of the Ottoman world, Loti was utterly fascinated by the prince and his world. He became firm friends with Abdulmejid and would go on to lobby on behalf of the Ottomans in France, as European attitudes hardened towards the Empire in the decade to come.

Abdulmejid was born in 1868. At the age of eight, his life was thrown into turmoil when the Young Ottomans, a band of reformers who aimed to turn the Empire into a liberal constitutional monarchy, launched a coup against his father, the reigning Sultan Abdulaziz, on 30 May 1876. They swiftly deposed him and installed his nephew, Prince Murad V, as the new Sultan. Murad, a constitutionalist, was the perfect choice for the reformers, but he was so paranoid people would suspect him of having conspired against Abdulaziz that he had a nervous breakdown. He was soon deemed unfit to govern and the Sultanate passed to his younger brother, Abdulmejid's cousin, who became Sultan Abdulhamid II on 1 September 1876.[7] A constitution was established and the next year a parliament opened. It seemed as though the Young Ottomans were getting their way.

But not for long: the next year, Abdulhamid dramatically dissolved parliament and began arresting dissenters. He also felt threatened by his cousins and nephews, and locked them up too. Abdulmejid spent the next twenty-eight years under house arrest. Loti wrote in his memoirs of his friend's plight: 'Along with Sultan Murad and all the other princes of imperial descent who could, directly or indirectly, lay claim to the throne, he was locked up... He was watched night and day by armed guards posted in front of the gilded doors.'[8] But this was not a difficult life, and Abdulmejid didn't undergo the rigorous imprisonment that was imposed on the deposed Murad V and his son. Though kept under surveillance, he was free to engage in all his artistic and intellectual pursuits.[9] And it was Abdulhamid's authoritarianism that made the young Abdulmejid the man he came to be.

Beethoven in the Harem

In his gilded conditions, the prince established himself as one of the first modern Turkish painters. In 1887 or 1888 he painted *Women in the Courtyard*, a depiction of a harem bath. 'In a large garden, by the fountains gushing out limpid water,' wrote a journalist describing the painting, 'was a group of odalisques, some in languid poses and some showing off their harmonious physiques and young, supple bodies, in front of their master, a pasha resting in the shade of a large tree, smoking a hookah.'[10] Most of the figures depicted are scantily clad; one is nude.[11] This was no traditional Ottoman miniature, but a modern painting in the school of orientalism, which was made up of Western painters who looked to the East for inspiration as European empires expanded.

Prince Abdulmejid produced other orientalist nude paintings. One half-finished work, which depicts the full figure of a naked woman, is entitled simply *Nude*.[12] Using naked women as models, so common in Europe, was forbidden at Istanbul's Academy of Fine Arts. Not so in some of the palaces.[13] Abdulmejid took after his father, Sultan Abdulaziz; the ruler had once acquired a painting by the French artist Charles Chaplin entitled *May Roses*, which featured a topless young woman gazing at herself in the mirror. Abdulmejid later produced a copy of it.[14]

There is a perplexing irony to this: here was an Ottoman prince with an intimate knowledge of the dynasty's inner life imitating art that reflected the wildest ideas European painters had about Islamic courts. Orientalist art portrayed the Islamic world as backwards, despotic and stifling, but also tantalising and erotic. Abdulmejid's work exhibits how in the late nineteenth century, many Ottoman elites internalised and even embraced European ideas about their own Empire.[15] These elites aspired to become Westernised, which they saw as civilised and modern. They sought to align their sensibilities with those of aristocratic Frenchmen, and saw themselves as superior to many of the supposedly backwards people of their Empire. The Arab world appeared almost as alien to some elite Ottoman men as it did to European colonialists.

This trend helps explain Abdulmejid's infatuation with French culture, and with orientalist painting. As the prince grew older, his views and sensibilities evolved. He became more comfortable in his Ottoman identity. In his later work, in the early 1900s, fantastical harem scenes gave way to authentic depictions of family life in the harem.[16] *Beethoven in the Harem*, painted in 1915, shows the prince listening to three women playing music. The violinist is his wife Shesuvar, while the most senior female servant is at the piano. The canvas also depicts a bust of Beethoven himself on a marble pedestal, and a bronze statue of the prince's father.[17]

A Polish tutor of the prince recalled that when Abdulmejid was twenty, he was considered 'so Europeanised' that paranoid Sultan Abdulhamid became suspicious, 'and it was not long before the secret police began to follow me as well.'[18] But in truth, Abdulmejid was never just a moderniser devoted to the imitation of European high culture. Instead he was in conversation with it, and attempted (like many other elite figures) to meld that culture with Ottoman and Islamic civilisation. He was deeply committed to Islam and throughout his adult life practised calligraphy, the most widespread form of Islamic art.[19] Abdulmejid saw himself as an Ottoman, European Muslim. His 1918 painting *Goethe in the Harem*, which depicts a woman in an Ottoman dress reclining with a copy of a Goethe book on her lap, indicates the nature of Abdulmejid's engagement with European culture—Goethe, a German writer, was himself famously interested in Islam and the East, and took inspiration from Hafez, the legendary Persian mystical poet.[20]

Nor was Abdulmejid apologetic or ashamed about his sensibilities, which he viewed as unproblematic from an Islamic perspective. 'This nation is capable of everything, but we cannot contribute to art in the Western sense,' he complained in an interview in the 1910s, since the ulema, Islamic jurists, prohibited painting living beings. Abdulmejid called for juridical reform so that such painting would be accepted.[21] He was keen that the European painting style would catch on, predicting that the Ottomans would one day have their own 'extraordinary masterpieces like the works of Raphael, Michelangelo, Titian, Leonardo da Vinci'. The problem, he identified, was that 'we lack the help and support of sovereigns, popes and wealthy men.'[22]

Cultural exchange was also important to him. He founded a society focused on countering negative Western views of Islam and the Ottomans, and patronised a diverse array of initiatives from the Armenian Women's Union to the Islamic Charitable Society and the Society of Islamic Education. His library included works in Turkish, Arabic, Persian, French and German.[23] Abdulmejid also gained considerable recognition in Europe for his work, more because of its novelty than its quality. A 1918 exhibition in Vienna, the first European exhibition of Turkish artists, showed four of his paintings.[24]

Adolphe Thalasso, a writer living between Paris and Istanbul, revered the prince for painting human figures, which he condescendingly wrote 'defied national prejudices' that were 'futile and ignorant'.[25] Meanwhile Abdulmejid hoped that the West would come to appreciate the cultures of Islamic civilisation; he praised, for instance, the famous Turkish painter Shevket Bey as 'a lover, a devotee, a poet of the works of Islam', whose paintings 'powerfully explain the works of Islam to Westerners.'[26]

The prince also loved music. Abdulmejid was an accomplished pianist, violinist and cellist—as well as a rumoured harpsichordist.[27] Here again, he was influenced by his father: Sultan Abdulaziz composed European-style classical music, and on his visits to Paris and London, where he liked to attend concerts, would be typically welcomed with performances of his own compositions.[28] Meanwhile Western musicians and composers came to Istanbul, including Franz Liszt.[29] Mozart, Beethoven, Brahms, Wagner and Chopin were all deeply interested in the Ottoman world and produced Turkish-style compositions.[30] A student of Liszt, who once visited Istanbul, even taught Abdulmejid music in the 1890s.[31]

Abdulmejid carried his love for music through his life. His private secretary Salih Keramet Nigar's mother was a talented poet. In November 1917 she found herself invited along with other members of Abdulmejid's inner circle to his mansion in Baglarbasi. Having initially planned to stay for one day, she found herself still at the mansion four nights later: 'Every night, amidst the prince's

13

precious paintings, an orchestra consisting of a piano, two violins, two alto violins, and two cellos played to an audience composed of artists, the prince and his companions, and six alternating servants,' she recalled. 'I was enraptured. I played and sang too, occasionally… We spent four days and four nights in this fashion.'[32]

Abdulmejid composed poetry as well, and was a literary enthusiast. Once, in 1908, the writer Ahmed Hikmet Bey, not particularly fond of the House of Osman, was dismayed to be sat next to the prince at the theatre. But he was soon won over by Abdulmejid's 'noble, majestic yet disarming smile' and extensive literary knowledge. Hikmet would become his chief chamberlain in 1919.[33] Intelligent and highly cultivated, Abdulmejid immersed himself in the arts to deal with his restrictive situation. Culture provided solace from the intractable political realities of his time. Necessarily reclusive, he was nonetheless cosmopolitan in outlook; enamoured by Europe yet devoted to Islam. Reflecting the Empire itself, he was a thoroughly paradoxical figure.

This was the man who would be the last Caliph of the Islamic world.

The Ottoman Caliphate

The Caliphate was one of the most significant institutions in world history. Existing in different forms for over a thousand years, it was central to Islam as a political institution that regarded itself as representing religious-political succession to the Prophet Muhammad—and leadership of the world's Muslims. After the Prophet's death, his close companion Abu Bakr became the first Caliph, his successor, in 632 CE, after being elected by a council of the Prophet's close companions. Three more companions would be elected to the role, and those first four Caliphs would come to be remembered by Sunnis, the majority Muslim sect, as Rashidun—rightly guided.[34]

Then, amid civil war, another companion, Mu'awiya, became Caliph in 661 and transformed the institution into a monarchy, appointing his son his successor.[35] Over the following centuries, the formative period of Islam which saw the monumental expansion of the Islamic Empire, the Caliphate was never uncontested: at times rival Muslim rulers laid claim to the title of Caliph. In the ninth century the Abbasid Caliphate dominated the Arabian peninsula as well as modern-day Iran, Iraq and Afghanistan; the following century a rival Fatimid Caliphate was declared in north Africa.[36] Minority sects often opposed the institution, yet the Caliphate was crucial to Islam's post-Prophetic history.

The Abbasids became so powerful that even far-flung Muslim rulers offered symbolic allegiance to the Caliph, including the Delhi Sultanate as far east as India.[37] From their capital in Baghdad, the Abbasids presided over what historians have often described as the medieval Golden Age of Islam—until the Mongols ravaged the capital in 1258 and brought the dynasty to its knees.

At this point the Caliphate that had been recognised by most Muslims lost political power, which would happen again after the collapse of the Ottoman Empire many centuries on. The Abbasid Caliphs remained as figureheads, but did not wield true political authority, which was held by a range of regional dynasties. This novel situation triggered a revolution in Islamic political thought.[38] With the Caliphate no longer corresponding to a grand and mighty Islamic Empire, ideas about it swirled around in new and unprecedented forms as regional Islamic dynasties rose and vied for power.

The House of Osman, a Turkish dynasty which began as a tribe in Anatolia, conquered its rivals and built up a mighty Empire throughout the fifteenth and sixteenth centuries. In 1512 the House of Osman, the Ottomans, laid claim to the Caliphate—a claim which grew stronger over the following decades as their Empire conquered the Islamic holy cities of Mecca, Medina and Jerusalem, as well as Baghdad, the former Abbasid capital. The Ottomans developed a narrative which claimed continuity between themselves and the Abbasid Caliphate: they contended that Ertugrul, the father of Osman, the eponymous founder of the dynasty, had been commissioned by the powerful Seljuk dynasty to defend the Abbasid realm.[39]

For decades, modern Western scholarship has held that the Caliphate was of minor importance to the Ottoman Empire until the nineteenth century, but more recent work has upended that idea. Hüseyin Yılmaz has shown in a recent monumental study that the

Caliphate 'became the linchpin of imperial ideology in the sixteenth century'.[40] The Ottomans reinvented the Caliphate into something substantively different, though with crucial elements in common, to previous Caliphates. The Caliph was now a mystical figure with deep spiritual and political power, a deputy or vicegerent of God—thus one of his titles was God's Shadow on Earth. This idea originated in sayings attributed to the Prophet, one of which was that 'the sultan is God's shadow on earth: every person who is wronged turns to him'.[41] The House of Osman projected itself as a dynasty appointed by God, with Ottoman rule the seal of the Caliphate, expected to last until the end of time. But this reconstituted Caliphate was only possible because of a dramatic shift in Islamic political thought.

The Caliphate had previously been defined by Sunni ulema (jurists). Their view, dominant throughout Islam's formative period, was that the Caliphate was an institution held by members of the Quraysh, the Prophet's tribe. This meant the Caliph needed to be an Arab, which posed an obvious difficulty for the non-Arab House of Osman. What could be done? In response to this predicament, in the Ottoman Empire the ulema ceased to lead the way in defining the Caliphate. Instead, the ruling dynasty promoted philosophers and sufis (roughly translated as mystics) who reconfigured the Caliphate 'outside the disciplinary confines of Islamic jurisprudence.'[42] Sufi orders took centre stage in fashioning mainstream Islamic political thought in the early modern period; thus in the fifteenth and sixteenth centuries Muslim dynasts were tutored by sufis who espoused esoteric mystical visions of rulership, as opposed to jurisprudential versions.[43] This didn't mean that the ulema were rejected—they continued to be involved in political thought, but were no longer the dominant authority.[44] The Ottoman Caliphate was to survive for 412 years, from 1512 until 1924.

Having taken Constantinople (now known as Istanbul), the centre of the Eastern Roman Empire, in 1453, the Ottomans simultaneously proclaimed themselves the inheritors of Byzantium and the ancient Romans—and Arabs, Persians, Indians and Turks alike recognised the Sultan to be the Roman Caesar. So too did many European writers, with some suggesting dubiously that the Ottomans were descended from the Trojans.[45] One sixteenth-century adviser to the Pope noted that the Sultan claimed the 'Empire of Rome', being the 'legitimate successor of the Emperor Constantine'. Being the Caesar co-existed neatly with being the Sultan and the Caliph.

Ottoman elites (as well as their Muslim counterparts as far away as in India) closely studied the *Akhlaq-i Jalali*, a masterpiece of political theory authored by Jalal-ud-Din Davvani (d.1506). Davvani described the 'Ruler' as 'distinguished by Divine support' to order the 'collective welfare' of his people. The ruler's law, he declared, must abide by the 'universal principles of the shari'at [Islamic law].' The ideal ruler, whose edicts preserve the principles of the Shari'a, is described as the 'Caliph of God', 'Shadow of God' and 'Deputy of the Prophet'.[46]

In the late sixteenth century, the Ottoman Chief Justice Qinalizadeh Ali Efendi even drew on ancient Greek philosophy to conceptualise the Caliph. He argued that Plato's concept of the 'Manager of the World' and Aristotle's 'Civic Man' were both, in fact, the same as the 'Caliph', who is 'distinguished by Divine support and upon whom is bestowed unending Divine accord such that he is able to order the welfare of the domain and also to perfect the souls of the people'. This was also, he noted, whom the Shi'as called the 'Imam'. Without this divinely guided Caliph, the figure envisaged by Plato and Aristotle, 'the corners of the built-up world will not be free from the cries of the oppressed and the laments of those seeking justice'.[47] The stakes were set high: the Caliphate was seen as necessary for the wellbeing of humanity.

Ottomans and Indians

The Indian subcontinent would play a pivotal role in the final years of the Ottoman Caliphate—and in its attempted revival, as we will see. As early as the sixteenth century, the Ottomans engaged with India, which was outside of their Empire. This was through conflict with the Portuguese, with whom they vied for trade dominance in the Indian Ocean. In 1538 an Ottoman armada laid siege to Diu, a Portuguese port in Gujarat, on India's west coast—where by that point a community of Ottoman traders lived. The siege failed, but shortly afterwards the Ottomans briefly took control of Surat, today still a major Indian commercial city, making it their main port of trade.[48]

Seydi Ali Reis (d. 1562–3), a daring Ottoman military commander who found himself in Gujarat in 1554, claimed in his travelogue that the Muslim rulers he met accepted the pre-eminence of the Ottomans in the Islamic world. 'We fervently hoped that God in his mercy would soon send an Ottoman fleet to Gujarat, to save this land for the Ottoman empire' from the 'infidels [the Portuguese]', the Muslims of Surat told him when he arrived there.[49] He describes how the Sultan of Gujarat 'assured me of his devotion to our glorious Padishah [Emperor]', Sultan Suleiman.[50]

In reality, Muslim rulers in India were largely unconcerned with Suleiman's grand claim to universal sovereignty. But they did nominally recognise the sultans as caliphs, including the rulers of the great Mughal Empire, which began in the sixteenth century.[51] While Mughal Emperors from Akbar onwards often liked to claim themselves as caliphs as part of a long list of mystical titles, it never entailed a genuine challenge to the Ottoman claim, but was usually an indication of indifference to the Ottomans. Thus a grey jade wine-cup made for the Emperor Jahangir in the early seventeenth century described him among other things as the 'Pearl-on-the-Stairway of Caliphal Succession and Emperorship'.[52] Why, thought the Mughal rulers, should they not employ such language? Their Empire was after all both richer and more populous than the Ottoman Empire. But this was just imperial grandstanding: the Ottomans, most Muslims believed, clearly held the Caliphate.

The tide of modernity

The Ottomans struggled to tackle the onset of modernity. The modernising states of Europe by the late eighteenth century were more expansive and powerful than states had ever been before. They strove to effectively surveil, manage, control and tax their populations. All this was challenging for an empire that was vast and decentralised, so that by the turn of the nineteenth century the Ottoman state lacked the strength and capacity enjoyed by the governments of the European colonial empires. The latter were ruled for the advantage of the metropole, whereas the Ottoman Empire represented an older imperial style that incorporated land and populations—and governed mostly at arm's length.

Sultan Mahmud II, girded in 1808, launched a series of reforms aimed at modernisation and centralisation.[53] In 1829, when the janissaries, the elite slave army, launched one of their customary mutinies, Mahmud crushed them with new armies equipped with modern artillery.[54] The state ballooned, while railways effectively collapsed the distance between far-flung regions, and telegrams enabled oversight of the Empire's peripheries. Augustus Slade, an Englishman who became an admiral in the Ottoman navy, observed the transformations with sorrow, and spoke of how in the old days an Ottoman 'paid no tithe' and 'travelled where he pleased without passports; no customs-house officer intruded… no police watched… His house was sacred.'[55] The modern world was different.

The Sultan that succeeded Mahmud, Abdulmejid I, brought in a series of liberalising policies known as the Tanzimat Period (Period of Reforms), from 1839 to 1876. The 1839 Gulhane (Rose-Chamber) Edict was declared by the Sultan to appease the British and secure aid with which to suppress a rebellion in Egypt. It introduced regular taxation and universal conscription—like modern European states.[56] It drew heavily from European liberalism, but was also distinctly Islamic, asserting the importance of the Shari'a. The edict can be seen not just as a force of liberalisation but also as an Islamic reformist reaction against Sultan Mahmud's centralising reforms.[57] An edict in 1856 went even further in cementing religious equality and freedom of religion.[58]

Europeanisation was visible in the urban landscape of Istanbul. Beginning in the eighteenth century with a series of new imperial mosques, Ottoman Sultans took to a new architectural style influenced by Europe. It has come to be known as Ottoman Baroque, often denigrated by historians as derivative, aping the West, the result of a 'faltering of cultural self-confidence', as Bernard Lewis put it, or else simply weird.[59] Ünver Rüstem disagrees, and sees in the Ottoman Baroque 'a sophisticated and conscious strategy to reaffirm the Ottoman state's position in an age when older aesthetic idioms had lost their relevance'. Its aim was to send a message both to Ottoman subjects and to the West—it allowed Istanbul to be both obviously Ottoman yet also 'globally resonant' and primed for diplomacy with European powers.[60] Thus the Sultan moved out of the Topkapi Palace, the old imperial dwelling, and built the resplendent Dolmabahce Palace on the European shore of the Bosphorus as a new heart for the Empire. The Dolmabahce's architects were Armenians educated in France, and it was unsurprisingly modelled on European palaces, prominently displayed on the city's landscape.[61]

As Istanbul looked increasingly like the great European capitals, sartorial transformations occurred too. Fashion trends flowed there from Paris—Ottoman gentlemen started in the 1820s to wear European trousers and a frock coat, donning the fez, a red top hat, instead of a turban.[62] They wore tailored suits and sat on dining chairs.[63] From among these elites, but partially in reaction to extreme Westernisation, came the Young Ottomans, a reformist movement that admired French thinkers associated with the French Revolution, like Rousseau and Voltaire. They wanted representative government (including a council of state and elected senate)—but also took Islam seriously and felt strongly that the Empire had to assert its Islamic identity.[64] The Sultan-Caliph derived authority from God, they believed, and also from a contract with the people. This vision of Ottomanism was also inclusive, being decidedly non-ethnic and enthusiastic about religious pluralism.[65]

In this period, the Caliphate was repeatedly reimagined. The Young Ottoman coup against Prince Abdulmejid's father Sultan Abdulaziz I in 1876, which resulted in Sultan Abdulhamid II coming to power, dramatically backfired when the new ruler not only abolished the constitution and parliament shortly after their introduction but also established a sort of personal rule, which involved placing Abdulmejid and the other princes under house arrest.[66] Sultan Abdulhamid, who enjoyed playing the piano and had a theatre built in his palace so that he could watch comic opera, asserted the idea of the Caliphate in a new way, promoting himself as a modern Caliph and ruler of the Islamic world.[67]

By then most of the world's Muslims had fallen under non-Muslim, European rule. The Ottoman Empire itself lost much of its European territory (including Romania, Serbia and Montenegro) in a war with Russia in 1877–8. This was devastating for the Ottomans and severely weakened their Empire. The majority of its people were now Muslims, setting the stage for Abdulhamid to significantly play up the Islamic nature of Ottoman rule. But the Sultan also aspired to have all the Muslims of the world, not just those in the Ottoman domains, declare loyalty to him as their Caliph.[68]

It was only with the collapse of Mughal power in the late eighteenth and nineteenth centuries that many Indian Muslims, chafing at their loss of sovereignty, turned seriously to the Ottomans. In the late eighteenth century the ruler of Mysore in the south, Tipu Sultan, having disavowed even nominal allegiance to the Mughal Emperor, recognised the Ottoman Caliph, and in return secured from the Ottomans a recognition of himself as an independent ruler.[69] Then in 1857, when a great rebellion that nearly collapsed British authority broke out, Britain secured a proclamation from Sultan Abdulmejid I urging Indian Muslims not to revolt. It had little impact.[70] Afterwards, though, with no Mughal Emperor, Indian Muslims began to look to the Caliph in Istanbul.

The Caliphate through European eyes

In response to Sultan Abdulhamid deploying the idea of the Caliphate to draw support from Muslims outside the Ottoman Empire, the British and French Empires in the late nineteenth and early twentieth centuries advanced their own conceptions of the Caliphate, to try to secure the loyalty of their Muslim subjects. This came with censorship. The British in India banned the import of Ottoman newspapers seen as dangerous. Pamphlets similarly deemed threatening were banned, and the Ottoman consul general Huseyin Kamil Efendi found his mission prematurely terminated by the government. In the Punjab, the British went so far as to ban the Turkish fez.[71]

In 1882 former diplomat Wilfred Scawen Blunt, later to be an adviser to Winston Churchill and one of Britain's most important thinkers on Islam, declared that the Caliphate question:

ought certainly to interest Englishmen, for on its solution the whole problem of Mussulman loyalty or revolt in India most probably depends, and though it would certainly be unwise, at the present moment, for an English Government to obtrude itself violently in a religious quarrel not yet ripe, much might be done in a perfectly legitimate way to influence the natural course of events and direct it to a channel favourable to British interests.[72]

The European powers decided to bolster and promote the claim by many Arab rulers that the Caliph had to be a member of the Quraysh, the Prophet's tribe. In the British case, retired civil servants who opposed the Ottomans took to the pages of English newspapers to advocate replacing the Sultan with the Arab Sharif of Mecca (conveniently under British rule) as Caliph. This dovetailed neatly with the agenda of many politicians in the Arab world who opposed the Ottomans.[73] Sultan Abdulhamid responded in a characteristic manner—he simply banned the publication of hadiths, prophetic sayings, which undercut Ottoman authority. 'England's aim is to transfer the Great Caliphate from Istanbul to Jidda in Arabia or to a place in Egypt,' the Sultan told an Ottoman journalist, 'and by keeping the Caliphate under her control to manage all the Muslims as she wishes.'[74]

The contest escalated in the 1880s, when European powers suspected an Ottoman conspiracy to support anti-colonial revolts in their own Empires. This gave rise to the term 'pan-Islamism' among European diplomats—the idea of Islamic politics, as represented by the idea of the Caliphate and by Muslims allying and expressing solidarity across national and imperial borders, was a clear threat to colonial interests. French scholar Carra de Vaux, thinking strategically, suggested that 'we should split the Muhamaddan world, and break its moral unity, taking advantage of the political and ethnic divisions that already exist in it.' The goal was to 'weaken Islam, make it restless, numb it, and render it forever incapable of great awakenings.'[75] De Vaux and others like him wanted to manipulate Islamic theology and legal scholarship to produce a version of Islam that would be conducive to colonial interests. The conceptual battle over the Caliphate was in effect a struggle to shape Islam in the modern world.

In the late nineteenth century, British imperial officials and intellectuals began describing the British Empire as a Muslim power—the 'greatest Mohammedan power'.[76] This bombastic claim was based on the fact that there were more Muslims in the British Empire than any other. While the Ottomans claimed the Caliphate on Islamic grounds and saw their rule in Islamic terms, for the British what mattered was the sheer *number* of Muslims they governed.[77] As Faisal Devji has argued, 'British discourse on Islam was shaped politically as well as conceptually by India, which was not only recognized from the nineteenth century as possessing the world's largest Muslim population, but was also of far greater political and strategic importance to Britain than the Middle East.' Thus India 'defined the Middle East's role in British political life'.[78]

Blunt envisioned Britain becoming a sort of successor to the declining Ottomans and the dead Mughal Empire, proclaiming that with the ultimate fall of the Ottomans 'there will no longer be any great Mussulman sovereignty in the world, and the Mohammedan population of India, already the wealthiest and most numerous, will then assume its full importance in the counsels of believers.' The English Crown, he wrote, should make 'itself in some sort the political head of Islam.'[79] Yet as colonial thinkers ruminated on how to reinvent Islam, great changes were afoot in the Ottoman capital itself—changes that ultimately created a radically new version of the Caliphate.

The constitutional Caliphate

Amid Abdulhamid's iron fisted rule in the 1880s, the Young Turks emerged. Quite different from the Young Ottomans, they were a political group aimed full-throatedly at Westernising the Empire, so as to make it modern, European and—in their view—civilised. At the same time, though, to achieve their goal of taking power the Young Turks had to work with the heterodox Bektashi sufi order and Rumi's Mevlevi order, among other diverse groups united by their opposition to Abdulhamid.[80] Their moment came in July 1908, which saw a constitutional revolution that forced Abdulhamid to reinstate the 1876 constitution and recall parliament.

THE INDIAN CALIPHATE

And so the Caliphate was reconstituted again. An older generation of historians presented the 1908 revolution as entirely Westernising and modernising, with little Islamic import. More recent scholarship has shown that this was far from the case—as Yakoob Ahmed has demonstrated, many ulema were immensely important players in the revolution, which ushered in a 'constitutional Caliphate'. While some defended Abdulhamid's absolutism, others argued that the new constitution was Islamically correct, and argued the point seriously.[81]

Sheikh-ul-Islam Cemaleddin Efendi, the chief jurisconsult of the Empire, sided with the revolutionaries at the most critical juncture. When the Sultan asked him to issue a legal ruling against the insurgents, the Sheikh-ul-Islam refused, telling a dismayed Abdulhamid to 'grant them the constitution because it is compatible with the honoured Sharia.' One foreign journalist remarked that it was largely due to Cemaleddin that the revolution was bloodless.[82]

The post-1908 order was unprecedented. In 1876 the Sultan still had the right to dismiss the constitution—a right he obviously made use of. But 1908 brought about a parliamentary constitutional monarchy in which the constitution was the 'requisite for the Caliphate'. This meant that the Caliph was made 'subservient and accountable' to the constitution, and parliament was given the power to hold the Caliph to account.[83] When a British reporter asked him whether Islam could possibly permit a constitutional government, the Sheikh-ul-Islam shocked him by replying, 'Permitted? [Islam] is more liberal than the Constitution itself... Our Law, rightly interpreted, is in accordance with the principles of representative government. The wisest men, chosen by the people are to direct the ruler, and if he rules without their consent he is going beyond his power.'[84] The influence of European liberal and democratic thought is easy to detect here—but so is a strong commitment to older Islamic political ideas of just governance and accountability.

Yet the Young Turks triggered a backlash. In April 1909 an armed uprising erupted in Istanbul, consisting of disgruntled soldiers and madrasa students.[85] It failed to topple the new order but was serious enough to turn the Young Turk government autocratic. They came to feel that Muslim 'reactionaries' were a deadly threat and deposed

Abdulhamid, sending him to house arrest in Salonica.[86] During the 1912–13 Balkan Wars, the Young Turks turned the Empire into a dictatorship, amid devastating turmoil and the brutal forced relocation of ethnic groups from one place to another. Balkan countries ethnically cleansed hundreds of thousands of Muslims, while the Ottomans did the same with Christians in their European territories.[87]

But for the princes, the revolution of 1908 could not be undone: it meant their liberation from confinement. For Abdulmejid this changed everything. From quietly working on his paintings and playing music with his friends he suddenly found himself out in the open. Under the new constitutional Caliphate, he could blossom in the public eye and transformed himself into a fashionable public figure. He advocated for constitutional monarchy and social reform, donating liberally to the Red Crescent charity and (in a signifier of his pluralistic disposition) the Armenian Women's Association.

Abdulmejid embraced the new order and transformed himself into a man of political importance, someone journalists turned to for commentary on current affairs. Astonishingly, not only did he produce a painting of Abdulhamid being removed from power, Abdulmejid even posed for a photo with the men who carried out the act.[88] The prince exploited the new situation by presenting himself as the persecuted victim of Abdulhamid's authoritarianism. He enthusiastically hailed the new constitutional arrangement and styled himself as 'the democrat prince', the member of the House of Osman 'who loves his homeland and his nation the most'. A doctor encountered Abdulmejid on a ferry once and asked him his thoughts on the new political order. Abdulmejid sighed: 'After thirty years in custody, could there be a happier outcome than our present state?'[89]

The prince had two children. His son Omer Faruk was born to his wife Shesuvar in 1898. When the boy was eleven, after the revolution, Abdulmejid sent him to Vienna to receive a European military education.[90] Abdulmejid also had a daughter, born to his third wife, Lady Atiye Mehisti, in 1914.[91] She was named Durrushehvar, meaning 'pearl of sultans'. The princess grew up in her father's house on the Asiatic shore of the Bosphorus, in the middle of a large park, perfect for the 'untiring activity of my young mind and body', as Durrushehvar later wrote.

By all measures, it was a happy childhood. 'I was a big vigorous child,' the princess recalled decades on, having inherited the 'strong physique' characteristic of the Ottoman imperial family. She had an English governess and a Turkish teacher. Durrushehvar was a product of Ottoman modernisation—and of the views and sensibilities of her father. 'I was not trained to become a meek, timid creature, a plaything, without individuality, as Westerners often picture us Moslem women to be.' Instead, she was 'allowed to reign supreme in the kingdom of my imagination'. This was despite Durrushehvar's lack of natural aptitude for her academic studies; she preferred to draw, like her father.

In those days, the women of the imperial family were able to walk freely in public parks—unthinkable in previous centuries. They could also drive and go shopping, as long as they wore a headscarf which would always be 'cut in accordance with the latest Paris fashion'.[92] But this was a world destined to soon collapse. The Empire was hurtling towards its demise, and as a ten-year-old, Durrushehvar would find herself banished from her beloved Istanbul. She would never come to terms with the loss. Hers was to be a life of exile, amid the crumbling of old orders.

2

ANGLICISED RADICALS

'It was love at first sight,' recalled Mohandas Karamchand Gandhi, known reverentially by most as the Mahatma (Great Soul), of his meeting the Ali brothers.[1] It was 1918 and the two had just been released from prison, following a four-year internment by the British Raj. Their crime was showing sympathy for the Ottoman Empire when it had become the enemy of Britain and war had broken out. To most Indians they were heroes; to Gandhi they were friends and allies. Today, the two brothers are typically caricatured as quirky pro-Ottoman Muslim campaigners or as early members of the Pakistan movement. But in truth, the Ali brothers helped shape the course of Indian history, although Mohamed Ali, the younger brother, died in 1930. Shortly afterwards, as we will see, the elder brother, Shaukat, would help determine the future of the House of Osman after the Empire's fall, nearly changing the course of global Islamic history. The vision and worldview that the Ali brothers developed are of central importance in understanding how that plan came about.

Shaukat Ali was born on 10 March 1873, the youngest of three children until on 10 December 1878, Mohamed Ali was born.[2] Their father Abdul, an official in the court of the Nawab of Rampur, died in 1880.[3] Their mother raised them, alongside her four other children. Abadi Bano Begum was no less extraordinary than her sons; later popularly known as Bi Amma, the mother of the anti-colonial struggle, she was made a widow aged only twenty-eight.[4] Yet she was determined to give her children the best in life—Shaukat and Mohamed were educated at the Muhammadan Anglo-Oriental

College at Aligarh, founded by the arch-modernist Sir Sayyid Ahmed Khan in 1875.[5] Khan and his institution represented a profound response to the reality of British rule in India—to train elite Indian Muslims into suave, suit-wearing, English-speaking gentlemen.[6]

Indians in England

After he left the college, Mohamed Ali headed to Britain in the late 1890s to receive an Oxford education. There he encountered and imbibed Englishness at its most upper-class and sophisticated, mingling with the English elites and learning their way of life. This wasn't unusual. The idea from the perspective of the British Raj was that elite Indians should go over to Britain, become civilised Englishmen in mannerisms and at heart, and go on to work in the Indian civil service as loyal servants of Empire. This, they thought, would contribute to the advancement of their Indian colony. But the scheme had unintended consequences that played a significant role in the Raj's ultimate downfall—it produced an entire generation of political radicals who would be some of India's most significant anti-colonial voices.

Gandhi spent time as a barrister in Britain and imbibed the culture; so too did the father of Pakistan, the talented lawyer Muhammad Ali Jinnah, who qualified as a barrister at Lincoln's Inn in London in 1895. Jawaharlal Nehru, who was to be the Indian Union's first prime minister, attended Trinity College, Cambridge, from 1907 to 1910. The poet-philosopher-politician Sir Muhammad Iqbal had been at Trinity too, where he studied philosophy in 1905. Their experiences in Britain transformed them. They came to feel that they fully understood Western, specifically British, culture—and realised, from interacting and making friends with English men and women, that they were equals and should be treated as such. It was small wonder that some of them began agitating against British imperial policies towards Indians and other colonised people—especially where British actions seemed not to live up to high-minded British ideals.

This disturbed the British government. By 1909, with around ninety Indian students at Cambridge, the prickly Secretary of State for India, Lord Morley, decided something had to be done. His fear was of 'the extremists, who nurse fanatic beliefs that they will someday drive us out of India', and his proposed solution was to tell the Masters of Cambridge's colleges to set a strict limit (two, to be precise) on the number of Indians who could come to take civil service and law exams each year. The Master of Downing College, Professor Frederick Marsh, thought this violated the British tradition of fair play and flatly refused, saying it would be an unjustifiable 'rebuff' to Indian students.[7]

Mohamed Ali was one of the radicals the British government was concerned had emerged from the Oxbridge crucible. He was at Lincoln College, founded in 1427, during his four Oxford years. Colleges were more than just accommodation for their students: they were entire communities. Lincoln consisted of a series of small courtyards. In a small room with an aerial window Ali lived and slept; in the Gothic dining hall, on long tables with benches, he had his daily meals. He studied in the beautiful college library.[8]

And Ali thrived on Oxford's intense educational regimen. The college rector William Warde Fowler judged that one paper he wrote on *Macbeth* 'could not have been written by anyone but a man of ability, capable of thinking for himself'.[9] As an Indian Ali was a minority, but this was far from a negative experience. Elements of student life posed challenges for his Islamic sensibilities, like Oxford's infamous drinking culture; in Lincoln's dining hall he and his friend Abdul Wahid would pretend to drink, to please their peers, but 'did not swallow the ale'.[10] They fasted sometimes, and one day decided to pray together, but realised that the walls of Ali's room were plastered in pictures, to which prostrating would be idolatrous. Having diligently removed all of the pictures, it then dawned on the two that they had no idea where Mecca, the direction of prayer, was—and proceeded to toss a coin to decide where to pray towards. 'When that was done,' Abdul Wahid later remembered, 'we were, both of us, so much impressed by the humorous side of the situation, that we found it difficult to regain the right religious mood of sobriety and calm resignation.' Ali also had a Qur'an on his bookshelf, and when he read it he 'could not be induced to close it for some hours'. But mostly it stood on his shelf, like an ornament.¹¹

He also learned ballroom dancing, and participated in it with tremendous enthusiasm. Romance he discovered by way of a girl called Ethel from Yorkshire. The two met and became friends; that friendship blossomed into love, although it 'did not go beyond a kiss under the mistletoe', in Ali's words.¹² Shaukat Ali's late grandson Khalid Ali produced an extraordinary book on the brothers in 2011, drawn from his unmatched access to primary sources. His own son, Irfan Ali, very generously gave me access to the work, which at time of writing isn't in print. It provides an extraordinary insight into the inner lives of the men. Khalid Ali noted that Muslims in South Asia tend to 'bristle at the slightest reference to their heroes' interest in wine, pork, and women. This self-induced censorship disregards truth and even drains the sap of humanity from their lives.' Mohamed Ali, by contrast, was 'incapable of such dissimulation'.¹³

A love of England, and of individual English people they knew, helped shape the worldview of the brothers, even as they campaigned against British rule in India. Shaukat used to tease Mohamed for having 'a soft corner in your heart for that place called Oxford.' But Shaukat himself admitted that even 'if it becomes my duty to kill the first Englishman I come across, if he happens to have blue eyes, my knife will not work; because I shall think of the eyes of Theodore Beck', who had been the principal at Aligarh.¹⁴

Mohamed Ali returned to India in December 1901 and arrived in Lucknow in an English suit, with a short beard and a distinguished moustache. He was a dandy, and his 'considerable baggage included a chest of hair oils, creams and perfumes, and he used to devote the better part of an hour to a rather elaborate grooming.' Shaukat Ali thought this rather effeminate.¹⁵ At that time the older brother was an officer in the Opium Department of the princely state of Baroda, in modern-day Gujarat.¹⁶ Mohamed Ali took after his brother for a while, but began dabbling in writing while in the job, offering columns to the *Times of India*. When the state officials were all warned not to express any politically radical opinions, he took it as a cue to leave.¹⁷

ANGLICISED RADICALS

'They only live who dare'

In the early 1910s the brothers transformed themselves into a mixture of journalists and political activists, launching two newspapers in two languages: an Urdu weekly, *Hamdard*, and an English paper called *The Comrade*.[18] The latter they launched in 1910 in Calcutta. Its motto exemplified their approach:

> Stand upright, speak thy thought, declare
> The truth thou hast that all may share.
> Be bold, proclaim it everywhere;
> They only live who dare![19]

The Comrade quickly became a vehicle for the Ali brothers to advocate Hindu-Muslim unity in the face of British colonialism. The magazine rapidly took off in popularity, to the consternation of British officials. It published articles not just on India but on issues worldwide: 'The pogroms of Russia and the no less heinous exhibition of anti-Semitic feeling in the rest of Europe show that Europe is not very far removed from the days of Inquisition and the massacre of St. Bartholomew,' Mohamed Ali thundered from the publication's pages.[20]

He was a born politician. Ali was embedded both in elite Indian Muslim politicking and in the Hindu-dominated secular Congress Party, which advocated for increased Indian political rights. He was there in Dhaka, in Bengal, in 1906 when the All-India Muslim League was founded, and would later become its president; in 1920 he would found a Muslim university, Jamia Millia Islamia, which is in operation to this day. He would even be elected president of the Congress in 1923.[21]

Shaukat Ali has been largely overshadowed in history by his brother, five years his junior. Mohamed was the ideas man; Shaukat was more practically minded. He was also famously hot-headed. A British official in Allahabad was once sent to negotiate with the brothers over a dispute they had with the railway authorities, and found that the younger brother was calm and 'ready to argue'. Shaukat, by contrast, 'added quite unnecessarily that if I insulted him he would knock me down and kept shaking his fist not far off my face.'[22]

But he was tremendously popular with nearly all who knew him. The *Egyptian Gazette* would describe an older Shaukat Ali in 1931:

> [He is] one of the most picturesque leaders of the world. Big in every physical sense, he is bluff and hearty… His face is impressive. Like everything about him, it is big. Piercing eyes glare out from under the huge bushy eyebrows and over a jutting nose. A large mobile mouth is half hidden in the commencement of a grey beard, which juts out truculently on the rock of a chin. Very ready to talk on anything connected with Moslem affairs, words issue in an unending stream tumbling over one another in their anxiety to be heard.[23]

The brothers brought about a sea change in the operation of the Muslim League, which was avowedly loyal to the British Crown, by encouraging the organisation to be more assertive. In 1913 Mohamed Ali and the League's secretary Sayyid Wazir Hasan went to England to try to gain an audience with the government on various issues Muslims were concerned about, although ministers declined to meet them.[24] Ali attended a suffragette meeting, at which the famous suffragette Charlotte Despard expressed her surprise at the presence there of an Indian man—and, more shockingly still, a Muslim. Ali informed her he had six good reasons to be interested in the movement: his mother, his wife and his four daughters, 'little sturdy suffragettes'. While in London, he also met the renowned poet Wilfrid Blunt, who condemned British policy abroad and the authoritarianism of rule in India, and had dinner with H. G. Wells—now famous as the author of *The Time Machine*—and his wife.[25]

Most significantly of all, though, he encountered Muhammad Ali Jinnah, then practising as a lawyer, and successfully entreated him to join the League. Jinnah and the Ali brothers influenced the League into backing self-government for India in March 1913, a significant lurch towards the Congress's approach. This was the prelude to a pact declaring Hindu-Muslim unity with the Congress in 1916.[26] Around that time, the Ali brothers underwent a dramatic fashion change which made them appear to have more in common with the masses, swapping Savile Row suits for astrakhan caps, flowing robes and growing beards.[27]

Mohamed Ali was deeply concerned with inequality. 'One class of men rolling in wealth or enjoying high positions, and another steeped in poverty to the very lips—poverty sordid and graceless; great pleasures existing side by side with great misery and pain'; these all stunted human progress, he believed. At heart he was a democrat, and admired Britain's constitutional monarchy, since to the English the King was nothing more 'than the embodiment of their national identity' as opposed to an overpowering despot.[28] And he was deeply committed to ethnic and religious tolerance. He wanted all groups to unite in the pursuit of 'creature comforts' and 'the disappearance of disease and poverty'.[29]

Unlike secularists, however, Ali rejected the idea that religious diversity was a potentially fatal problem or that it even bred unusual conflict: 'Religious differences,' he once noted to Gopal Krishna Gokhale, a distinguished Hindu social reformer and Congress politician, 'have not caused half the bloodshed that territorial nationality is causing every day.'[30] Besides, Ali believed, Indian Muslims were as Indian as Hindus, for they 'have developed local ideals and local altars and local shrines and the literature that appeals to their inmost sympathies is racy of the soil from which they have sprung'.[31]

This urbane and independent-minded journalist soon drew the ire of British officials. Most problematic of all from the British standpoint was that *The Comrade* developed an interest in covering global Islamic politics—particularly with regard to the Ottomans.

India and the Young Turks

As British intellectuals and officials warned of 'Pan-Islamism', Muslims like the Ali brothers and Iqbal denounced the term, insisting that Muslims sympathising with their co-religionists elsewhere in the Islamic world was simply Islam.[32] Their concern with the Ottoman Empire was far from some fanciful obsession with the idea of a powerful Islamic polity—it was the outcome of extensive interaction with Ottoman elites. Maulana Abdul Kalam Azad, the Muslim Congress legend who would play a leading role in the Khilafat Movement and eventually become independent India's first education minister, met a group of Young Turks in Cairo shortly before the 1908 revolution. Later, he visited Istanbul, where he met Young Turk leaders who 'expressed their surprise that Indian Musalmans were either indifferent to or against' the demands of Indian nationalists. This helped convince him that Muslims needed to engage with the Congress.[33]

Before the revolution, Young Turk leaders also met the prominent Indian Shi'a intellectual and Muslim Leaguer Sayyid Amir Ali in London, where he lived, and again when he visited Istanbul in 1907. Ali made a considerable impact on them; Ahmed Riza Bey, the deputy of the Ottoman Chamber after the 1908 revolution, wrote that his scholarship:

> enabled the Turkish reformers to convince the Sheikh-ul-Islam that the grant of a constitution by the head of a Muslim state was not opposed to the precepts of the Koran, and that the Caliphate would not suffer in prestige by admitting non-Moslems to civil equality and rights with Moslems in the Courts of law.

Ali continued corresponding with them in the wake of the revolution, and in 1909 addressed a letter to the Sheikh-ul-Islam expressing support for the new order on behalf of the Indian Muslims.[34]

The Italians and Ottomans went to war in 1911, followed by the Balkan Wars—when Serbia, Bulgaria, Greece and Montenegro fought the Ottomans and took nearly all of their remaining European territory. It was during this period that Indian Muslim pro-Ottoman agitations properly took off. In 1911 the Ali brothers helped establish the Red Crescent Mission in Calcutta, raising money for aid to be sent to Ottoman lands. *The Comrade*'s office was used as a headquarters for the project.[35]

On 7 October, the Muslim League passed a resolution calling for a boycott on Italian goods.[36] The British government, officially neutral in the war, moved to secure assurances regarding the fair treatment of the Ottomans from the Italian government, in response to Indian Muslim discontent.[37] As Jawaharlal Nehru later aptly put it, recalling the importance of the issue for his Muslim comrades: 'The last remaining Muslim Power was threatened with extinction; the sheet-anchor of their faith in the future was being destroyed.'[38]

The Balkan Wars in 1912 and 1913 revolutionised Indian Muslim politics—even at Aligarh, the great bastion of loyalism, Muslim students took to political activism in opposition to the university administration.[39] Protests took on an anti-colonial tenor, motivated by a generalised anger at European power. Aligarh was 'becoming a hot-bed of sedition', the Viceroy of India worried—in no small part due to Mohamed Ali, who was holding secret meetings with students there on the plight of the Ottomans.[40]

In October 1912, Shaukat Ali put out the call for an Indian 'volunteers corps to fight against the filibustering gang of dacoits in the Balkans', and put his money where his mouth was by offering himself up for the cause. The government refused to enrol any such fighting force.[41] Instead, Indian journalists went to Istanbul and photos of Ottoman statesmen were plastered over the pages of Urdu newspapers and the walls of houses. 'People living in far distant villages and obscure places nevertheless went to the nearest town every other day to get the Turkish news,' reported one witness in 1913.[42]

Sayyid Amir Ali and the Aga Khan, the leader of the minority Isma'ili sect who had been president of the early Muslim League, visited the front lines and sent a dramatic message to India calling for help: 'many Turkish wounded lying unattended... Mercy's sake send funds. Appalling destitution. Do not let Muslims starve and die'.[43] Not only were vast sums raised, but Indians also funded and organised a programme to settle Muslim refugees from the Balkans in Adana, in Anatolia.[44] Meanwhile the wars were uniting Indian Muslim institutions and notables like never before. Among Islamic scholars, different groups—including the Deobandis, Barelvis and Firangi Mahalis, each with their own seminaries and teachings—joined hands to support the Ottomans. The great Deobandi seminary Darul Uloom even issued a fatwa, a legal ruling, declaring that supporting the Ottomans was an Islamic obligation.[45]

The view from London

India shaped British foreign policy towards the Ottomans. The Foreign Office adopted an approach designed to ensure the survival of the eastern part of the Ottoman Empire, including Arabia, for 'the effect of the opposite course upon our own Mussulmans in India would be disastrous.' Concern over Indian Muslim sentiment meant that when the Ottomans recaptured Edirne in July 1913, the British were remarkably reticent to pressure them to give it up. When the war was over, the Viceroy told the Imperial Legislative Council that Britain had lobbied the Balkan states on the Indian Muslims' behalf.[46]

Importantly, though, supporting the Ottoman cause didn't mean that Indian figures like the Ali brothers endorsed all Ottoman policies. When one former minister of the autocratic Sultan Abdulhamid told the press that constitutional government was anti-Islamic and that 'we are monotheists and believe in the rule of one', Ali disagreed and declared that 'not one of the three hundred million Mussalmans of the world suspected that monotheism in faith involved autocracy in secular politics.'[47] Indian Muslim thinkers engaged with the Ottomans on their own terms.

In fact, their concern for the Ottoman Empire helped encourage the Young Turks to embrace global Islamic politics, which was a partial counterweight to their increasingly fervent brand of Turkish nationalism.[48] With that came increasing visits by prominent Ottomans to India. Journalist Tevfik Bey arrived in India in May 1913 and stayed for almost a year, reporting on pro-Ottoman sentiment there and arguing strongly that the Ottomans should build close ties with the Indian Muslims. He became friends with the Ali brothers and Azad.[49]

At this time Marmaduke Pickthall, one of the most unusual men of his generation, was rising to prominence in London. He is often thought to be the inspiration for the character of Mr Fielding in E.M. Forster's novel *A Passage to India*, the Englishman who loves India and is in return beloved by Indians.[50] Pickthall was born in 1875 and lived in a Suffolk rectory, until his father died when he was five. The family moved to London and sent Pickthall to Harrow. He found it dreadfully strict and claustrophobic. After leaving school he married a young woman named Muriel Smith, and then—not even eighteen years old—left England to explore the Middle East. This changed his life.

'When I read *The Arabian Nights*,' Pickthall later wrote, 'I see the fault line of Damascus, Jerusalem, Aleppo, Cairo... What struck me, even in its decay and poverty, was the joyousness of that life compared with anything that I had seen in Europe. The people seemed quite independent of our cares of life, our anxious clutching after wealth, our fear of death.' Aged only nineteen, Pickthall declared that he wanted to take the leap and become a Muslim—but was discouraged from it by the Sheikh of the great Ummayad Mosque in Damascus, who told him fortuitously to 'wait until you are older, and have seen again your native land.' He did, and ultimately became a Muslim in England.[51]

Though a keen imperialist and loyal to the British Empire, Pickthall was intensely interested in the Ottomans. He strongly supported the 1908 revolution, and felt that Britain should support the Ottomans in their new era. For if Britain were to oppose the Ottomans, he reasoned, it would damage the British Empire's relationship with its Muslim subjects—meaning a pro-Ottoman stance was the most strategic for Britain. Meanwhile, for Muslims under British rule, it would mean the working of 'their own territorial loyalty and extraterritorial patriotism [...] in the same direction.' Instead, though, Britain went the opposite way.[52] Pickthall admired Prime Minister Benjamin Disraeli's policy in the 1870s of supporting the Ottomans, by which 'England was to become the mentor of the Islamic world, to foster and assist its revival, using Turkey as interpreter and intermediary somewhat in the way that people dealing with live wires use rubber gloves.'[53] But the mood in Westminster was different by the 1910s. In the years leading up to the First World War, Pickthall joined Indian Muslims like Sayyid Amir Ali in London to lobby fervently for the Ottoman cause—speaking in debates, giving lectures and writing incessantly to the government. British intelligence kept him under close watch. This wasn't difficult—Pickthall, surveillance reports noted, never grew 'weary of enlarging in the daily papers on the merits of the Turk'.[54]

By early 1914, the Great War was on the horizon. Its spectre loomed over a visit to India by members of the Ottoman Red Crescent Society, who quietly solicited Indian Muslim help in the event of a war.⁵⁵ Suspiciously, two Ottoman military officers also spent a week in India, although what they did there remains unknown.⁵⁶ The British were rattled and censorship was imposed on the Indian press to silence reporting on the chances that the Ottomans might join the war.⁵⁷ When war between the Allied European powers and Germany broke out, Lord Hardinge, the Viceroy, implored India's premier prince, the Nizam of Hyderabad, to 'stand forth as the spokesman and leader of Mohammadans in India and to declare that England's course is both right and just.' This the Nizam, whose power was dependent on the British, did—albeit reluctantly, since he was aware it might make him unpopular.⁵⁸ As a reward, the Nizam would be declared Britain's 'Faithful Ally' in 1917 and 'His Exalted Highness' the following year.⁵⁹

'Torn between two passions'

The big question throughout India was whether the Ottomans would enter war on Germany's side. *The Comrade* published an editorial expressing hope that the Ottomans would stay neutral, asserting that the Young Turks 'would best serve the interests of the Ottoman Empire by keeping it as far as possible out of the general conflagration in Europe.'⁶⁰ An Ottoman entry on the German side, Indian Muslim notables felt, would be an utter catastrophe; expressions of solidarity with the Ottomans would suddenly equal opposition to the British Empire. Muslims would then have to make a decision on who to support: 'We shall be torn between two passions,' Mohamed Ali predicted sombrely, 'or rather the same passion will be warring with itself within us. When in a household the parents fall out, whichever of them may be at fault, the children are bound to suffer. That will be our plight, and we shall deserve all sympathy that we may secure.'⁶¹ In August 1914, Ali sent a cable to the Ottoman interior minister urging the Empire not to enter the war. It was ignored. The prominent pro-Ottoman Indian jurist Maulana Abdul Bari then cabled the Sultan-Caliph himself, also to no avail.⁶² The Ottomans declared war on 31 October.

The British government went to great lengths to try to appease Indian Muslim sentiment. Pledging—with India in mind—early on in the war that Islam's holy sites wouldn't be wrested from Ottoman control, the liberal prime minister, David Lloyd George, who personally disliked the Ottomans, declared that 'we are the greatest Mahomedan power in the world and one-fourth of the population of the British Empire is Mahomedan. There have been no more loyal adherents to the throne and no more effective and loyal supporters of the Empire in its hour of trial.'[63] The initial response of most Indian Muslim notables to the Ottoman entry was to express loyalty to Britain: as Mohamed Ali wrote, they had 'no difficulty in recognising that this is a mere secular conflict having unfortunately arisen out of the hopeless muddle of the European situation.' But this show of loyalty quickly dissipated as the war progressed and British ministers began making dramatically anti-Ottoman statements.[64]

The Ottomans urged Indians (not just Muslims but Hindus too) to revolt against the British, but to no effect. This war strategy was enthusiastically backed by the Germans, who thought Islam could be used as a weapon against the British and French. It had been a perceived benefit of friendship with the Ottomans for years. As the German adventurer Baron Max von Oppenheim put it in 1906, having travelled widely around the Middle East: 'In the future Islam will play a much larger role… . [T]he striking power and demographic strength of Islamic lands will one day have a great significance for European states.' In August 1914 Oppenheim went so far as to set up a jihad bureau in Berlin, the goal of which was to ferment revolt among Muslims living under British and French rule. An Indian Muslim uprising, he predicted, would 'force England to [agree] to peace terms favourable to us'.[65] German intelligence concurred with this approach.[66]

The chief jurisconsult of the Ottoman Empire, the Sheikh-ul-Islam, declared jihad against the Allied powers, establishing the Ottoman war effort as an Islamic endeavour. The Germans immediately set about putting it into leaflet propaganda targeting 'enemy Moslem soldiers in France'. The British strategy, meanwhile, aimed to counteract 'both within the Turkish Empire and outside the Turkish efforts to set Muslim against Christian by their declaration of a Holy War'.[67]

Even as anti-Ottoman sentiment reached fever pitch in Whitehall, the fear of an Indian Muslim revolt still impacted British war policy. British troops were not deployed to the Hejaz (in Arabia, where the Islamic holy cities were), for example, because they worried it would trigger an Indian insurrection.[68] In fact, as Eugene Rogan writes in his authoritative study of the war: 'Much of the Allied war effort in the Middle East was driven by what proved to be an unwarranted fear of jihad.' Few Muslims in India, or elsewhere in the British and French Empires, rose up against their colonial overlords. Still, the issue weighed so heavily and consistently on the Allies that they were in a sense 'more responsive to the caliph's call than his Muslim target audience'.[69]

One enduring piece of evidence for the prominence of the fear of 'Pan-Islamism' is *Greenmantle*, a novel written in 1916 by John Buchan, the British author most famous for writing *The Thirty-Nine Steps* in 1915, and who is commonly credited with pioneering the spy genre long before James Bond appeared on the scene. *Greenmantle*, a gloriously entertaining spy thriller, was written as a piece of war propaganda and follows a coterie of British spies in their attempt to foil a grand German plot to stir up the forces of Islam in an anti-British jihad. The book both reflected, and helped to stir up, establishment and popular fears about Islamic politics.[70]

Yet in reality the Ottoman appeal failed to trigger an anti-British revolt in India.[71] At the same time, pro-Ottoman sentiment still ran high among Indian Muslims. As Shaukat Ali put it, somewhat hyperbolically: 'There is not a Musalman who in heart does not pray for the victory of the Caliph and the defeat and destruction of his enemies, including Britain'.[72] The truth was that Indian Muslims simply had no ability to launch a successful revolt. They could hardly raise an army and take on the might of the British Empire; the last time that had happened, in 1857, it had gone catastrophically.[73] Moreover, the Hanafi school of law (which was founded by the eighth-century Persian Islamic scholar Imam Abu Hanifa, and later followed not just by most Indian Muslims but also by the Ottoman elite) sanctioned war only on condition that there was a real possibility of victory. In this case there was not.[74]

ANGLICISED RADICALS

Ultimately, India would give Britain more volunteers in the war than every other colony and dominion put together: 1.4 million. Indian soldiers fought on every front, but most were in the Middle East.[75] For some Indian Muslim soldiers, this posed ethical dilemmas. When some were captured by the Ottomans and made prisoners of war, they ended up volunteering for service and fighting for the Sultan.[76] In other cases, Indian Muslims were so unwilling to fight the Ottomans that they deserted the British trenches to join the other side. Those who were caught in the process were invariably shot. On the whole, however, the vast majority of Indian Muslim soldiers remained loyal to Britain.[77]

The Ali brothers fight the law

Marmaduke Pickthall was in Istanbul when the war began. He returned to an England where anti-Turkish sentiment and a zealous Islamophobia were on the rise. Pickthall was immediately marked out as a potential enemy agent. Foreign Office official Sir Maurice de Bunsen wanted him interned as an enemy alien, while Sir Mark Sykes, who would be a joint architect of the Sykes-Picot Agreement that carved up the Middle East for the European powers, denounced him as 'hostile' to Britain. Pickthall wasn't deterred. Ironically, towards the end of the war he was conscripted and became first a private and then a corporal. He was stationed in Suffolk in the East of England.[78]

The Ali brothers would face a different fate. Mohamed Ali had written an article before the Ottoman entry into the war in *The Comrade* which sealed the deal for the brothers. Entitled 'The Choice of the Turks', it heavily criticised the British Empire, while declaring loyalty to it, and concluded that the Ottomans should remain neutral. It was still interpreted as unacceptably troublesome, and the British jumped to take action against the paper after war was officially declared against the Ottomans in November. *The Comrade* was shut down. By May 1915 both the brothers were considered so dangerous that the British government interred them under the draconian Defence of India Act.[79]

It was during this internment that the brothers attracted Gandhi's attention and entered into correspondence with him. They were banned from discussing politics in their letters and could discuss only private and domestic issues—which Mohamed Ali found restricting, since (as he complained to Gandhi) the 'weather is not in India the perennial topic of interest as it is in England', except during the monsoon, during which the weather becomes 'too tragic a subject for writing about lightly'.[80]

Most catastrophic for the brothers was the financial toll their internment took on their families; their children were forced 'to grow up almost in ignorance for want of funds wherewith to educate them'.[81] In response to this ordeal, the brothers underwent a spiritual transformation and sought 'refuge in the Holy Quran'. As Mohamed Ali wrote to Gandhi, 'for the first time, I have to confess it, I read it through and with new eyes.'[82]

In Indian politics, meanwhile, significant changes were occurring. Ali liked rising star Jinnah, although he complained he was 'too spick and span and has never worked with his people with tucked-up shirt sleeves as we poor mortals have to do'. But from prison he watched with approval Jinnah's successful alliance-building between the League and the Congress, culminating in the 1916 Lucknow Pact, which proclaimed Hindu-Muslim unity.[83] And with the brothers out of action, their mother Bi Amma plunged into the fray and started campaigning. She encouraged the throwing off of some traditional cultural restrictions on women by pointing to the time of the Prophet Muhammad—when, she pointed out, 'we, the Women of Islam, also used to shoulder our share of the burden and march along with our men, even to the holy Wars.'[84]

Bi Amma was convinced that the Government of India simply misunderstood the Indian Muslim position on the Ottomans. Her sons, she wrote to the also interned English Congress activist Annie Besant, 'have no particular sympathy with Turkey any more than they have with China'. But Muslims were religiously enjoined to 'show kindliness and compassion' to other Muslims. In fact, 'none could pretend to be a good Mussalman who did not as freely express and promote sympathy with the Mussalmans of Turkey as with those of India or Persia or Arabia.' Bi Amma conceded, though, that the Ottoman Sultan had a special importance—unlike other rulers, he enjoyed 'the power and dignity and status attaching to the Caliphate'.[85]

The tragedy, in her view, was that 'the best of Indian Mussalmans are deprived of their liberty for no other crime than that of freely expressing and promoting sympathy' with the Caliph and his subjects.[86] This she considered an affront to their freedom and dignity; 'Much may and should be done for king and country, but no one is entitled to demand from another the surrender of his soul.'[87] Likewise, the brothers argued that in the name of the British Empire they were being asked to sacrifice nothing less than 'our eternal salvation'.[88]

The war raged on and Muslim discontent grew stronger. As one Anglo-Indian newspaper put it, 'the independent dominion of the Moslem was hemmed in... the future seemed dark for its continuance in any part of the world.' The brothers saw the Allied powers as 'battering and disintegrating the temporal power of Islam', and its 'spiritual influence' as well.[89] Their popularity grew in their absence. In 1917 the Muslim League elected Mohamed Ali as president; that he was interred was apparently no obstacle to this, and his photograph was placed in the empty presidential chair at the Calcutta session in place of the man himself as Bi Amma, veiled, gave a fiery speech to the crowd.[90]

The occupation begins

Towards the end of the war, Britain made a show of having noble intentions towards the Ottomans—mostly to keep Indian Muslims on side. On 5 January 1918, for example, Prime Minister Lloyd George stood up in the House of Commons to assert that 'We are not at war with Turkey to deny its Capital, Constantinople, or detach from her the fertile plains of Asia Minor and Thrace where the Turkish people have an absolute majority of the population.'[91] Lloyd George believed that 'there is nothing which would damage British power in Asia more than the feeling that you could not trust the British word'.[92] But many would soon have that feeling: in 1918 the European powers were secretly plotting to carve up the Ottoman Empire. The plan was that Turkey would constitute only Istanbul, a little area around it and the interior of Anatolia. In October came the armistice. The Ottoman armies laid down their weapons and Allied forces swiftly occupied Istanbul, to the horror of its inhabitants, including the Ottoman imperial family. On 15 May 1919 the Greeks seized Izmir, of great value to the Empire, having secured the British nod of approval.[93]

At this point Abdulmejid was Crown Prince, next in line to the Sultanate and Caliphate. In the late Ottoman Empire, it had been established that the succession would pass to the eldest prince, which Abdulmejid had become when a new Sultan was installed, his cousin Mehmed Vahideddin. Abdulmejid now regretted the war and was furious with the government. The Young Turks had destroyed the Empire, he believed, and he made no secret of it. He told journalists that he held the government 'responsible for everything'. He wished the Ottomans had never entered the war and told journalists that he was ashamed at the massacres he heard had been perpetrated on the Empire's Armenians (the word 'genocide' was not yet in usage).[94] Privately, Abdulmejid wrote bitterly to his son Prince Omer Faruk that 'it is quite obvious that we cannot change things with these narrow-minded people', in reference to the Empire's rulers. 'Our only hope lies in the young ones. If they also come to nothing, then there is no future for the Ottomans, or for Islam. History will curse this generation and us in particular,' he predicted soberly.[95]

In India, the armistice and its aftermath caused a political earthquake. The Ali brothers were finally freed, and—wasting no time—headed straight to the Congress and Muslim League sessions in Amritsar, in Punjab in northern India. They were greeted as heroes by everyone, and gave speech after speech that reduced the crowds to tears. At the Congress session the brothers were cheered upon arrival for a full fifteen minutes. 'Let me be interned for a lifetime if necessary,' Mohamed Ali told the crowd. 'But let Indians be free, let no man say to an Indian, man or woman, that thou art a born slave.' At the Muslim League's session, also in Amritsar, Sir Muhammad Iqbal recited poetry in their honour. 'Their stance during the years of internment and their steadfastness to their faith,' he proclaimed, 'is like the rock on which the structure of Muslim character would be built up'.⁹⁶

Addressing both Congress and Muslim League audiences, the brothers warned that the British wanted to completely destroy the Ottoman Empire—putting the Islamic Caliphate under threat.⁹⁷ The crowds hung onto their every word. The war had ultimately struck a serious blow to the old guard of loyalist Muslims, who were increasingly viewed as hopelessly out of touch. It was radicals like the Ali brothers who now called the shots. And they would set the tone for the politics of the 1920s; the first Indian anti-colonial mass mobilisation was about to begin.

3

'GOD VERSUS MAN'

Mustafa Kemal Pasha was an unlikely candidate to abolish the Caliphate. As late as 1922, the thought likely never crossed his mind, and if it had done, it would have seemed an absurd idea. After all, he was a war hero who fought for the Ottoman Empire. He had nothing against the House of Osman—quite the opposite. Yet Kemal, born in around 1880 in Salonica, a cosmopolitan city now in Greece, would eventually fashion a new nation state from the Empire's ashes.[1] He would be known as Atatürk, Father of the Turks. And he would abolish first the Ottoman Sultanate and then the Caliphate.

As a young man he was an avowedly loyal Ottoman subject. His father was a minor civil servant; his mother, a devout Muslim, initially sent him to an Islamic school, but he later studied in a more modern establishment that introduced him to Western ideas. Kemal ended up at military school in the 1980s, and entered the War Academy in 1899, emerging as a captain.[2] It was his duty to fight for the Empire.

And fight he did. He swiftly rose up the ranks in the military, so that by the time the First World War broke out, he was a lieutenant colonel, as well as a published author of military books.[3] German colonel Hans Kannengiesser described Kemal admiringly as a 'clear thinking, active, quiet man who knew what he wanted… He spoke accordingly but little and was always reserved and retiring without being unfriendly… His stubborn energy gave him apparently complete control, both of his troops and of himself.'[4]

He was a freethinker, too. Kemal was willing to accept the customary importance of Islam in Ottoman societies, but was personally sceptical of much of the Islamic tradition. He respected rationalist and scientific thinkers, and distrusted the ulema.[5] During the Great War, Kemal won praise for winning major battles at Gallipoli, by the Aegean Sea, famously crushing the armies sent by Australia and New Zealand.[6] Award after award came his way—including the prestigious German Iron Cross, given by Kaiser Wilhelm II himself.[7] By the end of the war, which went disastrously for the Ottomans, no one could deny that Kemal was a hero—and this made him perfectly placed to take a leading role in what came next.

'A good deal of grief and vexation'

The Empire was in its death throes, with most of its people suffering from poverty, violence and chaos. With Istanbul under occupation by the victorious European powers, the Dolmabahce Palace itself languished under a claustrophobic atmosphere of repression. Sultan Mehmed Vahideddin relied on his Grand Vizier, Damad Ferid Pasha; he consulted no one else, and most of the princes were too afraid to offer their opinions.[8] Mustafa Kemal, who knew many members of the dynasty, asked Princess Sabiha, the Sultan's daughter, as well as the 'most beautiful of the Imperial Princesses', to marry him. This wasn't an absurd proposal, given the status to which Kemal had risen. But the princess rejected him.[9] Had she accepted, Kemal would have become the Sultan's son-in-law, and the history of the Ottoman dynasty might have taken a monumentally different course. Instead, Sabiha ended up briefly engaged to an obscure diplomat.

In 1919, Crown Prince Abdulmejid's son Prince Omer Faruk was offered marriage to the daughter of the Ottoman ambassador to Berlin. This alarmed him considerably, since he thought she 'had a beautiful figure, but her face did not appeal to me.' He escaped the predicament by pretending he was engaged (he wasn't) to Princess Sabiha (who was already engaged to the diplomat).[10]

Omer Faruk and Sabiha, however, were deeply in love. Abdulmejid was less than pleased about this, given that he saw the Sultan, Sabiha's father, as an enemy. But when Omer Faruk threatened to commit suicide, Abdulmejid reluctantly went to see his cousin to ask for his daughter's hand. 'If you do not allow this marriage to take place,' he bluntly informed the Sultan, 'Faruk will kill himself. My son's life is in your hands. Faruk is my only son and as a father I demand this from you.' He then promptly bowed and left the room.[11] Sabiha gladly broke off her engagement to marry Omer Faruk. Their wedding caused a scandal in the harem, since it was unheard of for princes to marry princesses.[12]

Meanwhile Kemal had thrown himself into the fray in Anatolia, where a resistance movement was forming—the seed of what became known as the National Forces. Kemal tried no fewer than six times to enlist Istanbul's support for a rebellion against the Allied powers between November 1918 and May 1919. But the Sultan, fearful of the Allies, would not budge.[13] The British directed the Grand Vizier, Damad Ferid Pasha, to tell the Sultan to put a stop to it. But Kemal, who struck a highly credible and popular figure in Anatolia, responded by resigning from the Ottoman army, and continued to organise what was becoming an autonomous resistance movement. From then on, the Ottoman Sultanate (and thus the Caliphate) was in direct conflict with the burgeoning nationalist movement.

The Sultan deployed a short-lived and wholly unsuccessful 'Army of the Caliphate' to confront Kemal's forces. It was decisively crushed by the nationalists. And when the Greeks, with British assent, invaded Izmir on the Aegean coast, the nationalist movement became unambiguously the most popular force among Turks everywhere—including in Istanbul itself.[14] In September 1919, the nationalists proclaimed that their goals were the 'independence and integrity of the Ottoman lands with their Islamic majorities, all within the armistice lines of 30 October 1918', as well as the 'integrity of the caliphate and sultanate'.[15] Kemal was elected their leader and from then on directed a provisional government, based in Ankara in central Anatolia.[16]

The imperial family nearly all supported the resistance struggle: 'we all prayed night and day for victory in Anatolia,' recalled Prince Ali Vasib, a descendant of Sultan Murad V who was at that point still a teenager. The Sultan's approach was causing the family, including

Crown Prince Abdulmejid, 'a good deal of grief and vexation'.[17] Resentment towards the Ottoman princes became widespread because they were absent from the nationalist resistance. However, as Ali Vasib lamented, 'it was not generally known that from the very start the Imperial Princes had been prevented from joining the nationalist resistance movement.' The Sultan's decision, made under pressure from the British, cast a spell of doubt over the Ottoman dynasty.[18] Vasib wrote in his memoirs that 'we often met with unpleasant incidents when we went out into the street.'[19] The young members of the family took to staying inside with each other instead, seeking respite in 'dance waltzes, polkas, mazurkas, Scottish dances and quadrilles'.[20]

Prince Abdulmejid, by this point aged fifty, was determined not to be impotent. When Greece occupied Izmir on 15 May 1919, he sent telegrams to everyone from the American president to the King of England and the prime minister of France, urging them to protect Ottoman sovereignty.[21] This was during the Paris Peace Conference, which saw the victorious European powers seek to redraw the map of much of the world. They proposed the dismemberment of the Ottoman Empire. In June a horrified Abdulmejid urged an end to the struggle between the nationalist movement in Anatolia and the Sultanate. Privately, French officials speculated that due to Sultan Mehmed Vahideddin's unpopularity, Abdulmejid could soon become Sultan.[22]

On 16 July Abdulmejid wrote to his cousin again, furiously accusing the government of having 'failed to preserve national unity and solidarity'. He lamented, in particular, that 'the countrywide resistance was not supported' by the palace. In case his letter hadn't made its mark, the Crown Prince went personally to see the Sultan on 29 July, warning him against the Grand Vizier, Damad Ferid.[23] The Grand Vizier hit back by telling the British and French governments that Abdulmejid aimed to seize power. Somerset Arthur Gough-Calthorpe, the British High Commissioner, sent his chief interpreter to warn Abdulmejid that Britain would serve him an injunction if he persisted in his campaign. But Abdulmejid stuck to his guns, saying that the people wanted a 'Turkish government in Turkish lands' and decrying the 'disintegration of Anatolia, and the Izmir disaster'. He pointed to Greek massacres of Anatolian Turks and declared that if people trusted Mustafa Kemal and the nationalist movement, 'it is because their will is not respected by the government in Istanbul.' The Crown Prince was seen by the public as an advocate for the nationalist vision. As though to confirm this, Mustafa Kemal Pasha, by that point president of a new Grand National Assembly in Ankara, invited Abdulmejid to join what was a veritable War of Independence in late 1920.[24]

Abdulmejid declined the invitation, which triggered outrage among the nationalists. It was simply impossible for him to leave—his quarters at the Dolmabahce Palace had been besieged by British soldiers who monitored his every move. The Grand Vizier, told by the British to stop Abdulmejid leaving Istanbul, even restricted his yacht trips. When Kemal's emissary went to hear the Crown Prince's reply to the invitation, he found himself entering a building completely surrounded by British soldiers—only to be kissed on the forehead by a grave Abdulmejid, who explained apologetically that he was unable to leave the palace. 'Please give my best regards to Mustafa Kemal Pasha, and my most sincere wishes for his success,' he said.[25]

Abdulmejid wrote to Vahideddin from his confinement urging him to cast the Grand Vizier (whom he described as 'the imprudent Ferid') aside once and for all, asking him how 'with all of your intelligence' the Sultan could 'allow an unscrupulous treatment that will hurt the honour and dignity of our dynasty in the face of the entire Islamic world and Europe.' Rather dramatically, he asked the Sultan to 'kindly and mercifully issue the decree for my execution', so that he would not have to live to see the Empire so humiliated.[26] The Sultan did not comply.

In 1921, writing to his friend Pierre Loti, Abdulmejid complained that the capital had become unrecognisable: 'The periodic fires cause such devastation, it is almost as though the city is systematically being burned, and wherever a fire breaks out, there is never any water to put out the flames.'[27] He was in abject despair; the following year he told Loti that the 'painful sight to which my uninterrupted stay in Dolmabahce Palace condemned me, the constant presence in front of my eyes of the Greek war ships which have reduced our dear and peaceful Bosphorus to a naval base for their pirate fleet, this unending torment was making me ill'. Hopeless, he spent his time reading, painting and playing music ('I also occasionally give some stern statements to the press').[28]

By contrast, Prince Omer Faruk was a trained soldier and eventually couldn't bear sitting out the battle. In 1920 he left his wife and newborn daughter, Princess Neslishah, to secretly escape Istanbul for Anatolia. Having survived a hair-raising and often arduous journey (which at one point saw the prince hide from British officers inside a cupboard on a ship for over seven hours), when he finally arrived in Inebolu, Mustafa Kemal promptly sent him a telegram saying it was 'preferable for the Ottoman family to remain in Istanbul until the time their services will be required.' This was a significant blow; Kemal was sending a message that the Ottomans had no authority or importance in nationalist circles. Omer Faruk, thoroughly disappointed, headed back to the capital. The Sultan turned a generously blind eye to his son-in-law's adventure and the prince was left with life-long claustrophobia due to the cupboard ordeal.[29]

However, Kemal was privately exploring the possibility of Abdulmejid becoming the Sultan. The two men were in regular communication, and in February 1921, French spies claimed they had intercepted a letter from Kemal offering Abdulmejid the throne (the purported letter has never surfaced).[30] By this point the imperial edifice had been well and truly shattered. In August 1920 the Ottomans signed, under duress, the Treaty of Sèvres with the Allied powers. It surrendered much of the Empire to France, Britain, Greece and Italy, while giving autonomy to various regions, including Armenia. The Arab world, too, was lost.

Apart from destroying the Ottoman Empire, the treaty also took aim at the Caliphate: the Ottomans were forced to renounce 'any rights of sovereignty or jurisdiction of any kind over Muslims who are subject to the sovereignty or protectorate of any other state.'[31] This was a response by Britain to support for the Ottomans among Muslims in their own Empire. Many Muslims in the Arab world, who by now had no time for the Ottoman Caliphate, were quite pleased about it. Further east, however, the response was tremendous.

'GOD VERSUS MAN'

India erupts

It was in December 1918 at the Muslim League's annual session in Delhi that the Khilafat Movement (Khilafat meaning Caliphate) was officially launched.[32] It was the beginning of India's first ever mass protest movement—one that would bring the subcontinent's religious communities together, briefly, in a way that has never happened since. Today the Khilafat Movement is often recalled as a sentimental and bizarre campaign predicated on an eccentric religious interest in the Caliphate. Often it is remembered as being a cynical agreement between Hindus and Muslims: Hindus would help Muslims with the Caliphate issue, and Muslims would join in the Indian nationalist struggle.

Yet these characterisations do little to genuinely explain the movement, which introduced mass civil disobedience into Indian politics for the first time. The movement's aim was far from vague or fantastical: it was to support the Ottomans against the Allied designs, seen as a colonial assault. At the movement's heart was the rise of a new Indian Muslim politics: not only did the Khilafatists present Muslims as a coherent India-wide community with common goals and concerns, they also established an alternative to the older brand of Muslim politics, which was largely the preserve of wealthy landowners and held no mass appeal.

The Khilafat Movement also helped transform the Congress' cause into a mass struggle; it swept away the obscure and elitist private debates about piecemeal political reform that had until then prevailed. Instead, exuberant public processions and large, often ostentatiously emotional rallies ruled the day. The movement adopted an explicitly anti-colonial tenor—it required Indians to protest against British policy and express political commitments that clashed with obedience to the Raj. Mohamed Ali reasoned that success in the Khilafat cause could only be achieved through self-government, which would give Indians their fair say in the running of the Raj, Britain's Indian Empire. This meant the cause of the Caliphate had to be tied to Indian nationalism.[33]

The Khilafat Movement's central claim was that Britain had betrayed its Indian subjects. Muhammad Ali Jinnah, the future founder of Pakistan, sent a message to the British prime minister on 4 September 1919 reminding him that the Government of India had promised during the war not to attack the Caliphate. 'Now that victory has been achieved to which Muslim blood and money have contributed not a little,' he said sternly, 'the Muslims have the right to claim nothing will be done to whittle down or alter the pledges you gave to the world generally and Muslims in particular.' And in what sounded like a threat: 'We need to add that if Great Britain becomes a party in reducing H.I.M [His Imperial Majesty] the Sultan of Turkey and the Khalifa [Caliph] of the Muslim world to the status of a petty sovereign, the reaction in India will be colossal and abiding.'[34]

Colossal and abiding it certainly was. The founding figures of the movement included the Ali brothers, the jurist Maulana Abdul Bari, and future Congress president Maulana Abdul Kalam Azad. The Central Khilafat Committee was formed in Bombay, on 14 November 1919, after which regional committees sprang up across the country. In late November, a Central Khilafat Committee meeting was presided over by Mahatma Gandhi.[35] Sir Theodore Morison, the Government of India's historiographer, warned of a:

> remarkable consolidation of Muslim opinion in Turkey's favour... In India itself the whole of the Muslim community from Peshawar to Argot is seething with passion on this subject. Women inside the zenanes [in seclusion] are weeping over it. Merchants who usually take no interest in public affairs are leaving their shops and counting noses to organise remonstrances and petitions.

He added that 'even the medieval theologians... whose detachment from the modern world is proverbial, are coming from their cloisters to protest against the destruction of Islam. For Muslims this one preoccupation has swallowed up all others; they can think and talk of nothing else.'[36]

Many Hindus also joined in. The Congress Party itself had been a largely high-caste, elite Hindu affair—even as it grandly claimed to represent all Indians. That meant the Caliphate was a cause which could draw Muslims into Congress politics en masse for the first time. The Khilafat Movement aimed for an enthusiastic and romantic ideal of Hindu-Muslim unity, helped by the fact that the movement's core wasn't narrowly spiritual or cultural—it was about supporting the principle of Muslim sovereignty and solidarity in the face of European colonialism. The increasingly mobilised idea of a global Islamic world cut across imperial borders, and the Caliphate served as the ultimate symbol of Islamic power and unity, a sort of global rallying point.

It was further a powerful means of anti-colonial solidarity between different peoples: through global Islamic politics, India was able to play a major role in the worldwide anti-colonial struggle. Faisal Devji has argued convincingly that it was 'natural' for Gandhi to take such an enthusiastic interest in the globally oriented movement because 'no merely Indian movement could have allowed her leaders to play such a role on the world's stage, speaking on behalf of tens of millions beyond the borders of the subcontinent'.[37] As the *New York Times* informed its American readers, Gandhi recognised that 'India's struggle for liberty would benefit by making common cause with other Asiatic countries'.[38]

During the movement's heyday, relations between the Congress and the Muslim League were at their very best, with League chairman Abbas Tyabji even suggesting in December 1921 that the two parties should merge.[39] But there was considerable disagreement within the movement itself about the merits of radical mass politics. Yakub Hasan Sait, a prominent Muslim member of the Congress in the Madras Presidency who had been imprisoned for half a year in 1919 over his participation in Khilafatist agitations, told Mohamed Ali in January 1920 that the cause was being hampered by Muslims too reluctant to take a strong stance against the British.

Sayyid Amir Ali and the Aga Khan were 'were very timid', he lamented; they 'discourage agitation for fear of losing the sympathy of the few Europeans who support the cause of Turkey'.[40] Both men were widely revered in India. Ali, though, was based in London, and was thus at a remove from the public mood in India. Meanwhile Sir Sultan Mohammed Shah, Aga Khan III, was exceedingly popular with upper-class Britons, among whom he was known simply as 'the Aga'. He was sceptical of Gandhi's proposed tactics. Born in 1885 in Karachi in northern India, at age eight he had succeeded his father to become the head of the Nizari Ismaili Shi'as, all fifteen million of whom revered him as their spiritual leader. He claimed descent by blood from the Prophet Muhammad through his daughter Fatima.[41]

The Aga Khan was just as comfortable in the English upper echelons as he was among his Ismaili devotees. Queen Victoria knighted him at the age of twenty and he became a loyalist leader in India, helping to found the Muslim League in 1906; British ministers and royals alike would consult him on Indian affairs.[42] He was also tremendously cosmopolitan, and loved horse racing, golf, theatre and the opera. As a young man the Aga Khan would have made Abdulmejid jealous by mingling with musical geniuses like Stravinsky, Proust and Puccini.[43]

He was also famously generous, investing vast amounts of money into financially supporting his followers, as well as setting up schools and medical facilities in India.[44] Although he was the head of a sect deemed by most Sunni Muslims to be heretical, the Aga Khan was tremendously popular and influential among Indian Muslim notables, and threw himself with gusto into Muslim causes. Ecumenicism and the ideal of Muslim unity in rejection of sectarian conflict was highly important to the Khilafat Movement.

Years later in a letter to Sir Muhammad Iqbal, Jawaharlal Nehru described it as 'remarkable' that the Aga Khan was a 'modern of moderns, highly cultured in Western ways, a prince of the turf, most at home in London and Paris', and yet also involved in 'many public and political activities as well as the leadership of the Indian Muslims'. As a non-Muslim observer, he questioned Iqbal as to how the Aga Khan, a heterodox figure who claimed to have 'almost divine attributes', could fit in with what Iqbal called the 'solidarity of Islam'.[45] Iqbal responded by saying that 'however the theological interpretations of the Isma'ilis may err, they believe in the basic principles of Islam'. He pointed to a saying by the Aga Khan in which he entreated his followers to 'live with Muslims' and treat 'all Muslims as your brothers'. Iqbal suggested wryly that it was up to Nehru 'to decide whether the Aga Khan represents the solidarity of Islam or not'.[46]

No Muslim leader questioned the Isma'ili leader's commitment to the cause of the Ottoman Caliphate, despite his discomfort with civil disobedience. Jinnah was similarly perturbed by mass politics, and was particularly opposed to the role of Gandhi, feeling that the Mahatma had marginalised him in Congress politics. By 1920, Jinnah had largely withdrawn from campaigning for the Caliphate. The movement raged on.

Spectacular mass politics in action

British surveillance reports on the mobilisation provide an invaluable source in painting a picture of what the movement looked like to ordinary people and why it became so powerful. In Bombay on 2 February 1920, according to one such report, the Ali brothers and Maulana Abdul Bari arrived on a train bearing two Ottoman flags on its engine. Thousands of people were there to greet them and the scene immediately descended into chaos: the Khilaftists were almost swept away by the crowd. Two Hindu women garlanded the Ali brothers. Then came flowers—hundreds of flowers, presented by various delegations.[47] Eventually the Khilafatists were able to proceed from the station. The area's mosques were all lit up, and buildings were covered in banners either welcoming the arrivals or displaying the Ottoman emblem.[48]

On the third and last night of the visit, there was a public gathering of around 10,000 people. The atmosphere was electric. Poems written for the occasion were recited; 'Shaukat Ali burst first into tears, and later into song.'[49] This was spectacular mass politics at its peak. Shortly afterwards on 9 February, the Central Khilafat Committee met and elected Shaukat Ali as its secretary, before resolving to have 5,000 blankets sent to poor Muslims in Asia Minor.[50]

The movement succeeded in capturing the imaginations of many students and professors at Aligarh, the Ali brothers' alma mater—to the consternation of the university's loyalist administration.[51] British officials worried that 'people's minds have been unsettled by these visits of Gandhi and the Ali Brothers', since 'Gandhi's doctrines… are largely anti-British and the Ali Brothers are supplying the fanatical flame of Islam.'[52]

Having made their mark at Aligarh, the Ali brothers headed to the northern city of Lucknow, in the United Provinces, to visit the Firangi Mahal, the most traditional of Islamic seminaries. It was traditionally strongly opposed to anything that smacked of either Aligarh modernism or political radicalism, but Maulana Abdul Bari had overseen a dramatic cultural shift within the institution, urging its scholars to embrace the new political mobilisation. So it was that when the Ali brothers arrived in Lucknow, they found nearly a thousand students, the next generation of ulema, waiting to greet them at the station, and the brothers' carriage was 'dragged' to the seminary. There, in an unambiguous gesture of conciliation between the Firangi Mahal and Aligarh modernism, the brothers were each invested with an honorary degree—and thus the title of Maulana, the honorific given to Islamic scholars.[53]

Despite the radicalism of the movement, though, the Khilafatists firmly presented themselves as subjects of the British Empire, not as agitators against it. They were, they insisted, simply asking for what they were due as British subjects. Addressing the assembly at the Firangi Mahal, Mohamed Ali made this clear: He 'bore no personal grudge against the British Government,' according to an official report of the proceedings.[54] The Khilafatists affirmed their loyalty to Britain, and argued that the British Empire 'is as much Mahomedan [Muslim] and Hindu as it is Christian… British ministers are, therefore, bound to protect Mahomedan interests as any other.'[55]

Along with this came an official commitment to non-violence, as promoted by Gandhi, who had become an India-wide hero. At the 1920 Khilafat Conference in Lucknow, Mohamed Ali declared that 'the Indian army is the army of Mahatma Gandhi; the Indian police is the police of Mahatma Gandhi; every man is on the side of Gandhi, nay, on the side of religion and country.' On another occasion he went further still and proclaimed that 'After the Prophet, on whom be peace, I consider it my duty to carry out the commands of Gandhi.' Lord Reading, then the Viceroy, remarked that a fallout between Ali and Gandhi would mean 'the collapse of the bridge over the gulf between Hindu and Muslim.'[56]

'GOD VERSUS MAN'

The Khilafatists travelled all over India. On 9 February the Ali brothers and Abdul Bari arrived in Gujarat, in the west. They toured the city of Surat, which had once briefly been under Ottoman control in the sixteenth century, in a motor car displaying a 'silk-embroidered Caliphate flag'. The brothers campaigned in the nearby town of Rander before visiting Ahmedabad, Gujarat's largest city, which had a Hindu majority. There no fewer than 50,000 people took part in a pro-Khilafat procession. Banners and posters made by local Congress politicians were displayed in the streets calling for Hindu-Muslim unity: 'Hindus and Muhammadans are the eyes of one body. They should work together for Home Rule; if they do so, success will be achieved early', read one. Another exhorted the crowd to 'Prove the Hindu-Moslem Unity'. One banner, specifically addressing Hindus, read: 'The Caliphate question is a matter of the greatest importance. It is the duty of every Hindu to show his sympathy.'[57]

A few days later, Gandhi assured Shaukat Ali that the Hindus of India 'are solidly on your side', for the cause 'is not merely scripturally true but it is morally just'.[58] The Ali brothers had become celebrities. In some places, though, not everyone understood what the movement was about or who the brothers were. In Karachi some people, upon seeing the famously large-bodied Shaukat Ali in a car, 'enquired if he were a famous wrestler'.[59]

Even where the movement was well understood, the leadership's inability to regulate every idea articulated at political rallies often led to inconsistent messaging. At one rally in Larkana, a city in Sindh in the north, Islamic scholar Maulana Shamsudin solemnly told the crowd that Muslims had a duty to be loyal to Britain as long as the Caliphate was maintained. But then, according to a police officer's report, Maulana Haji Ahmed ('who is very old and crazy-looking'), stood up—'though the President and most of the audience told him not to speak'. He wept and urged every Muslim in the crowd to collect weapons in order to fight the British, disregarding Gandhi's orders. The event escalated even further when firebrand writer Abdul Aziz rose to give a speech which, the police officer noted, was 'couched in a most vulgar style and was quite in keeping with the character of the speaker'. Upon seeing the officers taking notes, Aziz began hurling epithets and 'defamatory remarks' in their direction.[60]

Meanwhile, although it was British India where the movement really mattered, it still had something of an impact in some of the princely states, under indirect British rule. In March 1920 the Nizam of Hyderabad, who had urged loyalty to Britain during the First World War, made a significant intervention by telling the Government of India that he believed Khilafatist sentiment, 'which has a strong religious basis', was being provoked by 'what they consider will be a breach of faith on the part of the British government if the pledges given [during] the war were not fulfilled.' He warned ominously that this could result in a 'political situation of the gravest possibilities.'[61]

The Nizam was put in a precarious situation by the Khilafat Movement. On the one hand, he had a reputation to maintain, and needed to preserve his popularity among Indian Muslims. He also genuinely sympathised with the Ottoman plight. Yet as an authoritarian ruler he was thoroughly uncomfortable with mass politics, and wary of angering the Raj. Thus the Nizam swung back and forth between condemning the movement's radical tactics and expressing sympathy for its broader cause. In the end, this proved strategically apposite, allowing him to remain in the good books of the British while retaining his credibility among Indian Muslims, so that the Khilafatists could assure him 'that Muslim India looks up to you even now as the beacon of Islam in India'.[62]

The European tour

In early 1920, the Khilafatists secured a meeting with the Viceroy, who agreed to support a delegation to Britain to speak to the government. A group of Khilafatists headed to Europe. They were Mohamed Ali, prominent newspaper editors Sayyid Husain and Sayyid Sulaiman Nadvi, Abul Kasim, a member of the Bombay Legislative Council, and the politician Mushir Husain Kidwai. The group reached London towards the end of February, by which point the Paris Peace Conference was underway.[63] Ali was deeply impressed by Marmaduke Pickthall and his pro-Ottoman activism, and put him in charge of managing Khilafatist activities in Britain.[64] Pickthall, by this point, was an unpopular figure in British public life, widely seen as an 'enemy of Christendom'. One British intelligence report suggested that Pickthall 'may be regarded as somewhat of a crank, but in all probability, at heart he is a loyal British subject'. This was quite true, and one of Pickthall's arguments in favour of the Ottoman Empire had always been that it would be a bulwark against Russia, which he saw as an 'ever-present danger'—both under Tsarist rule and after the Bolsheviks took control.[65]

The Khilafatists soon found, to their dismay, that virulent anti-Ottoman sentiment was everywhere in England. Leading public intellectuals, like the Oxford historian Arnold Toynbee, as well as the Archbishop of Canterbury and most of the press, furiously condemned the Empire, with their arguments often hinged upon the protection of Christianity in the Balkans.[66] However, the British government was still set on retaining Ottoman sovereignty in Istanbul. This was a direct result of the Khilafat Movement; Lord John Arbuthnot Fisher told the Indian delegation that 'it is not a secret that the decision which has been taken by the Allied and Associated Powers to retain Turkish sovereignty in Constantinople has been to a large extent influenced by the desire of the British Government to meet the religious feelings of its Muslim subjects in India'.[67]

Yet this willingness to listen to the Indian Muslims had its limits. The Khilafatists were eventually given an audience with the prime minister, but it was unhelpfully delayed for months and held only after a treaty had been signed. The meeting finally took place on 22 April and went terribly. Lloyd George was entirely dismissive of the Khilafatists. Mohamed Ali forthrightly informed him that the Caliphate was crucial for the defence of Islam. He tried to appeal to the leader's republican sympathies, explaining that the Caliph was 'Commander of the faithful; he commands them within the law of Islam and on behalf of God. He does not arrogate to himself a kingly function. I think, Sir, that will appeal to you personally—that the doctrine of the Khilafat is the doctrine of a Republic'.[68]

Ali also told the prime minister that the Khilafatists were willing to live with changes in the Ottoman Empire which would give communities much more autonomy. 'Consistently with our desire to have autonomous development ourselves,' he said, 'we could not think of denying it to Arabs, Jews, or Christians within the Turkish Empire.' But Lloyd George was not going to accept it. He pressed Ali on whether he supported Faisal I of Arabia, who had revolted against the Ottomans with British assistance. Ali, of course, did not—he believed Islam's holy cities had to be under the Caliph's control.[69]

They also discussed the plight of the Armenians. 'I do not overlook the fact of the massacres,' said Ali. 'No Muslim would dream of giving his support to those truly guilty of massacres and other equally revolting crimes. The Indian Khilafat delegation must put on record its detestation of such conduct and their full sympathy for the sufferers whether they are Christians or Muslims.' He called for an international commission to investigate what had happened. But the prime minister was still unmoved.

Ali left the meeting furious, telling Shaukat Ali in a letter that he thought the prime minister was a 'little Englander'. He despised little Englanders, who 'are grossly ignorant about their empire and apart from any material advantage it confers, take no interest in it except that an eighteenth century lady of fashion took in her mulatto slave-boy that she could show off in society.'[70] Ali spent considerable time talking to Labour politicians, including the party's leader George Lansbury, who was more sympathetic. He even addressed the Labour conference in Scarborough on 2 July. But the party was ultimately too engrossed in domestic issues to pledge any serious attention to the Khilafat Movement.[71]

Eventually the group, thoroughly disheartened, headed to Paris, where they met a range of journalists and intellectuals. While they were there, the Treaty of Sèvres, spelling the destruction of the Empire, was signed.[72] Before that, they had sent a telegram to Sultan Mehmed Vahideddin from the Hotel Regina in Paris on 11 May explaining that they had 'come to Europe on behalf of the 70 million Mussulmans of India and the 250 millions of our compatriots of other creeds'. They referred to Turkey as a 'noble and brave, but distracted and divided nation'.[73] Seventeen days later they wrote to him again, informing the Sultan frankly that he would be violating Islam if he accepted the treaty.[74]

With remarkable boldness, the delegates informed Vahideddin that many critics of the Ottoman Empire, assessing the various nationalist revolts, especially by Arabs, believed that 'the Turks have themselves to thank for this state of affairs', considering the rise of a chauvinistic Turkish nationalism among the Young Turks. They suggested that 'it would be fatal not to confess even to ourselves such truth as there is in these complaints and criticism'.[75] Finally, they issued a call for Muslim unity, denouncing ethnic divisions between Arabs and Turks, as well as sectarian division, for 'this is the very moment when all sects and sections of Islam can be welded together' (they noted the strong support of Shi'as for the Khilafat Movement).[76]

Unsurprisingly the Sultan, who had ignored his Crown Prince, likewise ignored the Khilafatists. In France they met Jean Longuet, one of Karl Marx's grandsons, who published an interview with Ali in his paper, *Le Populaire*. The French government itself, though, wouldn't budge on its position.[77]

The Khilafatists then went to Rome, where they met Prime Minister Giovanni Giolitti, who expressed his sympathies—to the alarm of British spies monitoring the delegation's activities. Ali also spoke with the Papal Secretary of State, Cardinal Gasparri, who was keen on improving relations between Muslims and Christians. Ali took his chance and asked for a meeting with Pope Benedict XV. What would the British think about such a meeting, the Cardinal asked. Ali replied innocently that his intentions were purely religious and peaceful.[78]

On Wednesday 28 July the delegation was granted the meeting. They prepared to go to the Vatican that morning—but just before the group was supposed to set off were informed they had to dress in special ceremonial clothing. The Khilafatists were aghast. 'It looked horrible,' Ali said later, 'but I managed to look less ridiculous, though, perhaps, not less bizarre, by throwing the Aba [traditional black cloak] over the evening dress.'[79]

The meeting was a roaring success; Ali liked the Pope very much. For his part, the Pope seemed enthusiastic about engaging with the

Islamic world. 'I am told that His Holiness receives people while sitting on the throne,' Mohamed Ali wrote to his brother Shaukat, 'but in this case, the pope came all the way from the throne to receive us at the door, and while the monsignor in attendance knelt, His Holiness said aloud, "Welcome! Welcome! Welcome!" with utmost cordiality and shaking us by the hand, took us to his throne and did not sit until he had made me sit in a chair quite close to him.'[80]

Ali explained to the head of the Catholic Church that the Khilafatists aimed to secure the integrity of Islam through the power of the Caliphate, in the face of the threat posed by the occupation of Ottoman lands. He also said that the Indians were in the middle of a peaceful non-cooperation movement to protest for their goals. The Pope, Ali found, was sympathetic and 'hoped we would succeed in gaining our object peacefully; but he acknowledged that it was not we who desired to war on people of other faiths, and he assured [sic] that the Catholic world desired peace with the Islamic world, and accepted our assurances on this head.'[81] Ali emerged from the Vatican full of praise for the Pope, and was buoyantly optimistic about Muslim-Catholic relations: 'This was no temporal sovereign,' he told Shaukat Ali, 'but he still commands the allegiance of hundreds of millions of people and, at any rate, we do not want any good Christian to be antagonised merely because we stand up for our rights'.[82]

By that point he had apparently given up on the Sultan and was instead closely following the progress of the nationalists in Anatolia. In August, he met leaders of the armed struggle who had gathered in Territet, in Switzerland. British spies found that Ali was in direct correspondence with Mustafa Kemal, whom he greatly admired. Kemal was the man of the hour, and unlike the prisoner-Sultan in Istanbul, cut an attractive and impressive figure to outside observers. Asad Fuad Bey, a senior Turkish diplomat, later said that the Khilafatists' European tour (frustrating though it often felt for the delegation) had been considered by the Turkish nationalists to be 'very useful'. They believed it had helped influence European public opinion against the idea of British, French and Italian troops directly intervening to help the Greeks fight the nationalists—a move that Lloyd George had considered ordering.[83] The Turks asked the Indians to keep the Khilafat Movement going.[84]

'GOD VERSUS MAN'

The perils of populism

Back in India, everything was heating up. A ruling issued by hundreds of ulema forbade cooperation with the British government on Islamic grounds. People with government titles and offices were told to give them up. Students were encouraged to leave government schools. Foreign goods were to be boycotted and enlistment in the army was condemned.[85] At a gathering on 27 March 1921, Mohamed Ali declared that 'I have made it an object of my life to alienate every Muslim from the Government… If it is a crime I am prepared to suffer for it.'[86] It was a crime. The brothers were arrested that September and charged with conspiracy to tamper with the loyalty of the troops.[87]

In their absence from the campaign trail, the Women's Khilafat Committee took centre stage. Bi Amma and Mohamed Ali's wife, as well as the great writer and Congress activist Sarojini Naidu, were especially prominent. Bi Amma addressed gatherings all over the country, encouraging unity between Hindus and Muslims. 'Avoid activities which harm the country,' she urged in Erud in the Madras province. 'Don't allow disunity to ruin your struggle and give victory to your rulers.' Some ulema, scandalised that a woman should be giving speeches, denounced her actions. The Central Khilafat Committee hit back strongly, pointing out in a statement that 'in the early days of Islam women used to accompany men to the battlefields and help them.'[88]

The trial of the brothers and five other leaders of the Khilafat Movement took place in Karachi on 28 September. It was a star-studded event, with prominent politicians racing to the city to watch the proceedings. The trial attracted so much attention that it had to be held in a public auditorium.[89] The brothers didn't miss the opportunity to put on a good show—they refused to stand when the magistrate entered. Their chairs were then removed to force them to stand, at which point the Ali brothers spread their cloaks on the floor and sat down on them.[90] Mohamed Ali then refused to present any conventional defence, and instead used the trial to make various grand political proclamations, to the delight of the Indian spectators and the fury of the judge.

Ali refused to even accept he was a defendant, and declared that the trial was not the Khilafatists against the Crown, but 'God versus man'. He addressed the British fear that Muslims were more loyal to the Ottomans than to the Raj head on by insisting that loyalty to the divine command—and thus the Caliphate—came before anything else, and accused the British of suppressing his religious freedom. By the end of the speech, which grew steadily more emotive throughout, tears were running down his cheeks.[91] The accused were ultimately found guilty of 'making statements conducive to mischief' and sentenced to two years of rigorous imprisonment.[92]

But they had won in the court of public opinion, and their example inspired a younger generation of Indian politicians. Jawaharlal Nehru, for instance, told a court in 1922 that he would go to jail 'most willingly and joyfully', for 'jail has become a heaven for us, a holy place of pilgrimage... Big bodied, great-hearted Shaukat Ali, bravest of the brave, and his gallant brother are there, and so are our thousands of co-workers.'[93]

Amid all the enthusiasm, though, the movement was beginning to fall apart. Even from the very start, in places it had spiralled into chaos, often with catastrophic consequences. In 1919 the movement briefly promoted the idea of *hijrat*—migration out of India on the grounds that British India had become enemy territory for Muslims.[94] The Ali brothers soon realised that *hijrat* was a disastrous idea and denounced it. But that was to no avail; in the end, thousands of Indian Muslims headed to Afghanistan, where they ended up as destitute refugees.[95]

Passions, once unleashed, proved impossible to control. In 1921, not formally connected to the movement, Muslim rebels in south India's Mappila declared their own Caliphate in opposition to British rule. For six months the army struggled to crush what had become an autonomous guerilla movement. Muslim peasants attacked Hindu landlords, and then some turned on other Hindus.[96] The Khilafat Movement's leaders were horrified by reports of the conflagration, and especially by Muslims attacking and forcibly converting Hindus to Islam. For their part, the insurgents denounced the Ali brothers as infidels.[97] Many Hindu leaders, horrified, started to reassess their support for the movement. The beginning of the end came in

February 1922, when a group of rogue activists set fire to a police station and killed twenty-one officers. Gandhi called off the civil disobedience agitation and the Khilafat Movement was plunged into crisis.[98]

But then, later that year, came the event that suddenly took the wind out of the movement's sails altogether: the triumph of Mustafa Kemal Pasha and the Turkish nationalists.

4

THE LAST CALIPHATE

'Under the right circumstances and in a calm and prosperous country,' the French magazine *L'Illustration* informed its readers on 9 December 1922, 'Abdulmejid would have been a Turkish Francois I, and the court of the caliph of Constantinople, like that of the caliphs of Cordoba, would have become a new centre of Islamic art.'[1] In the real world, the Caliphate of Abdulmejid II was fraught with tension from the beginning. He was the first Ottoman Caliph who wasn't also a Sultan; he was also the first Caliph of modern Turkey. This was an unprecedented situation—and it was set to be a brief one.

To begin with, Abdulmejid was well liked by Mustafa Kemal Pasha, and as the Crown Prince he was perfectly placed to step into the role of Caliph. This became possible when the nationalists claimed victory. On 26 August 1922, the Turkish nationalist movement launched a massive offensive against the Greek army— the goal being to drive them out of Anatolia for good.[2] It succeeded, and on 9 September, Turkish units triumphantly entered Izmir. The Greek retreat triggered the evacuation of nearly half a million Greeks from Anatolia. That was the turning point.[3]

Having resigned themselves to the idea of a peace treaty, the Allies asked both Istanbul and Ankara to each send delegations to a peace conference. The new Grand Vizier, a distinguished statesman named Tevfik Pasha, was terrified that the Allies and Ankara might reach a settlement together, with the Ottomans left out in the cold. He sent a message to Ankara on 29 October, declaring that 'If the Sublime Porte [the Ottoman government] does not attend the

Peace Conference, it will mean that the six-century-old historical identity of the Ottoman State has been crushed'. His suggestion was that Istanbul and Ankara should act together, as a unitary force.⁴ The nationalists who had fought the war were unimpressed by this. They had already resolved to crush the 'six-century-old historical identity of the Ottoman State' themselves.

The abolition of the Sultanate

The armistice signed by the Allies and Ankara was a significant win for the nationalist movement, and paved the way for its ultimate victory the following year. Ankara was now independent and in charge, while Istanbul, the Ottoman capital, remained under Allied occupation. The Grand National Assembly in Ankara proclaimed its authority and those who dissented were treated ruthlessly. One such figure was the journalist Ali Kemal (an ancestor of Boris Johnson, who would almost a century later become prime minister of Britain from 2019 until his resignation in disgrace in 2022). Ali Kemal had spent the last few years publishing articles, with the Grand Vizier's approval, attacking the nationalist movement. With the armistice his fate was sealed. In November 1922, he was arrested in Beyoglu; while in Izmit being taken to Ankara, he was lynched by a mob and killed.⁵ There was no room for perceived enemies of the new government. Mustafa Kemal wasted no time in announcing the definitive death of the Ottoman Empire: on 1 November, Ankara declared the Sultanate abolished.⁶

Abdulmejid was primed to step into his cousin Mehmed Vahideddin's shoes. Vahideddin was still the Caliph, but no longer the Sultan. A new question quickly emerged: what would happen to the Caliphate? This was an institution that could not so easily be dispensed with, given its immense Islamic significance. Succession to the Prophet and leadership of the world's Muslims, Ankara was fully aware, could not be abandoned without provoking serious reactions from Muslims around the world. As it stood, Vahideddin was no longer addressed as 'Your Illustrious Highness' or 'Supreme Sultan', but he was still 'Your Excellency the Caliph'. But Vahideddin could not accept this; he insisted that a Caliphate divorced from a

Sultanate 'is unacceptable, even to the most incapable member of our family.'[7] Not everyone in the family agreed.

According to Vahideddin, the abolition of the Sultanate had been a cruel and underhand affair. He later recalled that after the armistice, the Caliphate and Sultanate 'were waiting to know their fate' when Refet Pasha, Ankara's representative in Istanbul,

> contacted the Palace requesting to meet us. We fixed the date and the time and he came. He expressed his opinion. We listened.[8] This tiny little man, hiding behind grand ambitions and concealing his true intentions, told us that if we gave up the constitutional monarchy, which we had sworn to protect, and accepted a restricted caliphate, as if the original one did not exist, we would save both our position and ourselves.[9]

But shortly afterwards, the papers were so full of attacks on him that he realised he would have no easy existence as Caliph in the emerging Turkish nation. There was little point in trying to oppose the powerful and enormously popular Mustafa Kemal, he realised:

> Blindness and ingratitude were everywhere. We were exasperated by the greed and the radical changes surrounding us. We could not see the possibility of either opposing or complying with this kind of caliphate. Thus we decided to leave this treacherous region, until public opinion calmed down and the general situation reached some clarity.[10]

He asked General Harington of the British occupation forces to help him escape, explaining that he believed he was in danger of being assassinated. The general asked for the request to be made in writing ('I naturally did not wish to be accused of kidnapping a Sultan'). The Caliph obliged: 'Considering my life is in danger in Constantinople,' he wrote, 'I take refuge with the British Government, and request my transfer as soon as possible from Constantinople to another place.' He signed off as 'Caliph of the Muslims'.[11]

Vahideddin made his surreptitious departure from Istanbul onboard a British battleship on the morning of Friday 17 November, and headed for Malta.[12] Later, living in San Remo on the Italian Riviera, he insisted to his family members that he had not 'run away from Istanbul', but had in fact followed the example of the Prophet leaving persecution in Mecca to travel to Medina (he ultimately returned to conquer Mecca)—'we left with the intention to return,' he explained.[13] That would never happen.

A new type of Caliphate

Since Mehmed Vahideddin had retained the title Caliph, the government in Ankara set about deciding what should be done about the Caliphate. 'Protecting the Holy Relics,' symbolically important to the Caliphate, 'is paramount,' Mustafa Kemal, in the position of commander-in-chief, told Refet Pasha. 'The British must resort to arms, and shed blood, if they want to take the Relics.' The Holy Relics included the mantle of the Prophet (known as the Sacred Mantle) and his standard. They had always been closely guarded in the Topkapi Palace, and were now doubly secured.

Next, a new Caliph needed to be appointed. By this point, Crown Prince Abdulmejid was willing and ready to step into the role. Even before the Sultanate had been abolished, Abdulmejid had sent his aide Major Remzi Bey to greet Ankara's representative, Refet Pasha, when he arrived in Istanbul on 19 October 1922 and offer Ankara his support. The Pasha's carefully worded response made the new government's intentions crystal clear: he hailed Abdulmejid as 'heir to the holy office of Caliph, which we have always vowed to preserve'.[14]

With Mehmed Vahideddin at sea, Kemal sent Refet to formally ask Abdulmejid to take control of the Caliphate. Abdulmejid instantly said yes, and signed a statement declaring that 'I fully endorse and approve of the decision taken by the Grand National Assembly of Turkey regarding the caliphate and the sultanate.'[15] Many members of the imperial family had strongly advised him not to go along with the process, which would legitimise the abolition of the Sultanate.[16] Abdulmejid disagreed; an Ottoman Caliph in Istanbul would be more convincing to most Muslims than an exiled one who had fled on a British battleship. Accepting Ankara's designs was also the best way to ensure the security of the House of Osman.

The next order of business was to depose Vahideddin from the Caliphate. This was done in absentia—Vehbi Efendi, the minister for religious affairs, declared that Vahideddin—by fleeing to an enemy state—had effectively given up the Caliphate himself.[17] Kemal told the Grand National Assembly that the Caliphate had to be kept within the Ottoman dynasty. He noted that while the Assembly represented the Turkish nation, it 'cannot decide by itself on behalf of the entire Islamic world, my good sirs'—since the 'holy office of Caliph is a sacred position that involves the entire Islamic world.' And so, he declared, the Assembly needed to 'uphold this sacred office until the entire Islamic world comes to a common agreement'. He concluded that 'it is our historical duty to preserve and recognise the House of Osman.'[18] Kemal's recognition that Muslims outside Turkey (in reality, this involved Indian Muslims more than anyone else), had a legitimate concern for the Caliphate was the key factor that determined the role being offered to Crown Prince Abdulmejid—whatever Kemal might personally have wanted.

One potential problem was that Abdulmejid was in Istanbul, which was still under British occupation. Theoretically, the British could act against Abdulmejid—but Kemal calculated correctly that they would not risk rousing the fury of their Muslim subjects. His statements on the issue elicited a clear scepticism about whether Turkey would keep the Caliph around for long. He said that if the Caliph was imprisoned by the British, it would matter to the Islamic world but not to Turkey, 'with its new form of government.' He argued that the Islamic world at large should 'assist us to protect us and preserve the Caliph.'[19]

What followed was unprecedented: for the first time, an Ottoman Caliph was elected into office. The Grand National Assembly, Vehbi Efendi assured everyone, was the legitimate representative of the nation and fully entitled to elect the Caliph. On 18 November, the Department of Religious Affairs officially deposed Mehmed Vahideddin. In an open session, with 163 deputies present, the Assembly then voted on whether to elect Abdulmejid Caliph. There were nine abstentions and 148 votes in favour of Abdulmejid. There were only two dissenting votes, in favour of Sultan Abdulhamid's son, Prince Abdurrahim Efendi.[20]

In India, when the news broke that the Sultanate was abolished, many Muslims thought at first that the story was propaganda with no truth to it. After an initial period of denial, some ulema condemned the new government in Ankara. But most Khilafatists supported the development. They argued that it heralded a return to the type of Caliphate that existed in Islam's early days, when the Caliph was elected. The Khilafat Conference in December publicly endorsed the move and Kemal was heralded as a hero and labelled the 'Sword of Islam'.[21] The victory of Turkish nationalism over the European powers led to widespread and raucous celebrations among Indian Muslims; it was seen as a great anti-colonial triumph, and a victory for Muslims in general. Ankara sent a green flag, meant to represent Islam, to India, which was escorted around and exhibited to great fanfare by the Ali brothers and their mother. Not just Muslims but many Hindus too rallied enthusiastically to the flag 'wherever it appears'.[22] The Khilafatists threw their support wholeheartedly behind the new order in Turkey.

'Like an imperial procession'

Abdulmejid became Caliph on Friday 24 November 1922. Some Muslims in Turkey worried about whether Abdulmejid was suitable for the position considering his unconventional artistic proclivities, but these concerns weren't widespread or strongly held enough to cause a furore.[23] Refet Pasha went to brief him before his Oath of Allegiance ceremony. Immediately the seeds of conflict were sown. Abdulmejid was told in no uncertain terms that he was not to issue any political statement, nor could he wear military uniform for the ceremony—he should don a frock coat or high-necked jacket instead.[24] The message was clear: as Caliph, Abdulmejid had to toe the line and couldn't intervene in politics. The vision of the Caliphate that Ankara was setting forth was an altogether new one, and so a novel conception of Islam's role in the world: the Caliph as a mere puppet, and preferably not too visible. Privately, though, Abdulmejid had a markedly different idea of what the Caliphate should be.

The Caliphal procession made its way to the Topkapi Palace, which was once the administrative heart of the Caliphate. The streets were packed and resounded with the sound of ballads and anthems. Around mid-morning, Abdulmejid arrived at the palace and entered the legendary Chamber of the Sacred Mantle. In this most closely guarded of places, Abdulmejid paid his respects to the Prophet's mantle and standard. In the throne room next door he then gave his oath; 101-gun salutes were fired all around the country and Caliph Abdulmejid II proceeded in a royal carriage to the Fatih Mosque for the Friday prayer.[25]

Deputies sent from Ankara, riding in motor cars as part of the procession, felt disquieted at just how grand the whole event was. In front of them they saw carriages carrying the Ottoman princes, and beyond that the Caliphal carriage accompanied by cavalry, led by aides-de-camp on motorbikes. It was an eclectic mixture of old and new. Behind the deputies were cadets and lancers, and on either side were gigantic, cheering crowds. 'This has turned into an imperial parade,' remarked one worried deputy.[26]

The procession took fifty minutes to reach the mosque, where worshippers who had been there since the morning prayer were waiting, presumably rather fatigued. All the students of the Istanbul madrasas were lined up on one side of the mosque courtyard, as well as the students from Istanbul University. They faced an array of senior civil and military officials on the other side. The Caliph proceeded down the middle to the sound of the national anthem, performed by the imperial orchestra. Entering the mosque, he disappeared briefly into a private imperial box, before emerging to sit among the other worshippers.[27]

Then came another 101-gun salute, followed by the call to prayer. The sermon was delivered, unusually, in Turkish instead of Arabic—a sign of changing times. The sermon exhorted the nation to be ready for hard work ahead, and was followed by prayers for the Caliph, the Grand National Assembly and Turkey. It was a patriotic affair. Afterwards, Abdulmejid visited the tombs of multiple sultans, including Mehmed the Conqueror, who had taken Istanbul in 1453.[28]

The next day, the Caliph issued a statement addressed to the Islamic world at large, stressing the Grand National Assembly's legitimacy as the sole representative of the nation and its intention

THE INDIAN CALIPHATE

to support the Islamic world. This made it clear that he accepted Ankara's authority.[29] That same day he gave another statement to the Turkish people, quietly requested by Ankara, which condemned the deposed Sultan, accusing him of having sown division and given up the Caliphate by cooperating with the British. Abdulmejid urged the Turkish people to 'forget this affair and look ahead to the future. May God bless the future of our country and our religion.' He even launched a personal attack on Mehmed Vahideddin: 'My father was his uncle. He did not even remember it. How painful it is to have to mention it. Now he has been discarded not only from his position, but also from the family.'[30]

For his part, Vahideddin was furious when he read the statement. 'It is easy to sit on [Sultan] Murad's emerald throne,' he proclaimed acidly from his villa in San Remo, 'but [Abdulmejid] is not even worthy to reach this hero's boots. Poor man, they sent him an imam's coat, and pretending still not to notice he strives to drag his robe to the throne.' Even stronger words came from the exiled Mufti Sabri Efendi, formerly the Sheikh-ul-Islam, who suggested that Abdulmejid 'cannot represent our beloved Prophet; he cannot even be the devil's representative, as even the devil would not accept such foolishness.'[31] Sabri's qualms went largely ignored; nearly everyone accepted the new Caliphate and Abdulmejid grew a beard, which made him look more pious.

The Caliphate of Abdulmejid II

Princess Neslishah, daughter of Prince Omer Faruk and Princess Sabiha, recalled visiting the Dolmabahce Palace for the first time—when she was only two years old—to see her grandfather, the Caliph. She remembered wearing a dress with a white tulle top and light pink skirt. 'The palace mesmerised me,' she recalled. The Dolmabahce, built from an eclectic mix of baroque, rococo and neoclassical architecture synthesised with traditional Ottoman design, had 285 rooms and six bathhouses. Its forty-six halls were large, grand and airy, with high and ornately decorated ceilings. Neslishah recalled that 'everything was glittering, and the crystals, the enormous chandelier above my head, the furniture, the dimensions of the room, all filled me with admiration.' Abdulmejid sat on his throne 'like an armchair' to receive his family members. He hugged and kissed Neslishah.[32]

For the imperial family, Abdulmejid's time as Caliph was their last hurrah. The Caliph threw two big dinners for them at the Dolmabahce, 'sumptuous' in Prince Ali Vasib's recollection. The first, on 29 November 1922, was for the princes and princesses; the second was for the princes (and the princes by marriage) only.[33] True to form, Abdulmejid also established a 'Caliphate Orchestra', which performed in the palace and was conducted by Osman Zeki Bey, a violin virtuoso who composed Turkey's national anthem that year and would later become the first conductor of the Presidential Symphony Orchestra of Turkey.[34]

One of the House of Osman's most well-liked personalities was Prince Osman Fuad, a military commander who had fought at various points in the First World War on Europe's western and eastern fronts, and in Palestine and Tripolitania. In 1918 when the Armistice of Mudros was signed, Fuad, then in Tunisia, was so unwilling to comply with the agreement and surrender to the Italians he had been fighting that he instead handed himself over to the French—who promptly gave him to the Italians anyway. By late 1919, he was back in Istanbul, but in less than a year became so furious with the Sultan's policies that he left with his Egyptian wife, Princess Kerime Halim, ironically on an Italian steamboat.

The couple lived in Rome for around two years, before returning to Istanbul after Abdulmejid became Caliph. They lived in the Ciragan Palace, where Osman Fuad took to riding in his cavalry officer's uniform and jumping over obstacles in the palace gardens. The prince played the flute, violin and banjo with great skill despite being unable to read music, and enjoyed 'gypsy and Viennese music', as well as jazz. He was extremely popular in Ottoman high society, and threw light-hearted parties at the Ciragan where he would entertain his guests by playing jazz on the violin, and sometimes the banjo, with Prince Ali Vasib as his piano accompaniment. Although some people 'condemned him for being too Western in his ways', Ali Vasib later recalled, the prince was 'liked and admired by nearly everyone.'[35]

Meanwhile the poet Abdulhak Hamid, 'dignified in bearing and elegant in appearance', fell into economic hardship—at which point Osman Fuad invited him to stay in the Ciragan Palace. Hamid loved parties and adored alcohol even more, so he was eager to move there. But then the Caliph himself generously extended an invitation for him to live in the Dolmabahce's out-buildings. With no choice but to accept, the poet was forced to live under the palace's relatively austere regime, unable to drink (the Caliph was teetotal in compliance with the Shari'a) and expected to return home early every night before the palace gates closed. He was, however, able to engage in extensive poetic repartee with the Caliph. It is unclear whether he found that to be any consolation.[36]

At the same time, though, political tensions were rising. Let Abdulmejid sit quietly in his palace and paint, was the consensus in Ankara; a Caliphate that was visible and assertive in Istanbul would be a risk to the government, since it would rival the latter in prestige. Ankara and Istanbul ended up facing each other in mutual distrust. In effect, competition between the two was a contest between a globally oriented Islamic politics on the one hand, and European-style nationalism on the other. It was an ironic touch that much of Istanbul was in Europe, and Ankara was in Asia.

As Princess Neslishah put it, Abdulmejid 'had no intention of abiding by the given guidelines.'[37] He made it his goal not just to preserve but to enhance the prestige of the Caliph. This, he thought, was entirely justified. He was a devout Muslim and a proud Ottoman. The Caliphate had existed since the Prophet's death, and the Ottomans had ruled a vast empire for centuries—it was a rich legacy. By contrast, the Grand National Assembly was a recent construct with no such grandeur. And so Abdulmejid resolved to establish a very clearly living and breathing Caliphate.

In a stunning failure to read the room, the *New York Times* assured its readers in April 1923 that the Caliph, 'a monogamous landscape painter, doesn't seem likely to cause anybody discomfort by his political pretensions.'[38] In reality, Abdulmejid's spectacular weekly processions to the mosque (he went to a different one each time) for the Friday prayer were increasingly perturbing Ankara. Ali Vasib, who rode as part of the Caliphal retinue, thought the processions were 'even more ostentatious' than in the days of the Sultanate.[39] 'Obviously,' he reflected in hindsight, 'such behaviour was bound to invite criticism.' For him, the processions could be perilous. During one the prince's horse 'slipped and fell on the paving stones', and he narrowly avoided falling head over heels by using his spurs to get the horse back up ('Had I not been able to save myself, of course, it would have been highly embarrassing').[40]

Foreigners, especially Americans, were entranced by the processions and always turned up to watch them.[41] On one occasion, Abdulmejid went to a mosque by crossing the Bosphorus in spectacular style, on a fourteen-oared barge exuberantly decorated with paintings of flowers. The helmsman and oarsmen wore white breeches and black waistcoats, and Abdulmejid flew the Caliphal standard, which had a green flag with a crescent and star against a red background, encircled by white rays.[42]

Ankara formally requested that the Caliph dress humbly in a frock coat, which they judged would distinguish him appropriately from his forebears. In response, Abdulmejid swiftly became fond of wearing a turban on his Friday processions (which he had also been forbidden from doing). This proved so popular that before long, photographs of the turbaned Caliph were being produced and sold on the market.[43] His secretary, Salih Keramet Nigar, later reckoned it was that dress choice which sounded the death knell for the Caliphate.[44]

Abdulmejid also took to hosting political meetings in the palace. Once, when his horse bit his hand, the princes went to the Dolmabahce to see how he was—only to find the Caliph there engaged in free-flowing conversation with Istanbul's important political and military leaders.[45] All this sent alarm bells ringing in Ankara. Increasingly it appeared that Ottoman Istanbul, far from having been reduced to a pretty museum, continued to radiate authority and Islamic prestige.

The Republic of Turkey

On 24 July 1923, Turkey signed a peace treaty at a hotel in Switzerland's Lausanne. This secured Turkey's independence, with the treaty's terms overwhelmingly favouring the Turks. Most significantly, the Allied occupation ended. Turkey had entered negotiations from a place of strength, and legend has it that Ankara's representative Ismet Pasha's negotiating tactic was to exaggerate his (real) hearing impediment; when any Allied representative demanded something that went against Turkey's interests, he simply pretended he was unable to hear. Through the sheer frustration this caused, the strategy helped secure favourable terms for Turkey.[46] After the liberation of Istanbul, the nation was declared a Republic on 29 October 1923 and Kemal was elected president by a thumping majority in the Assembly.

This was a great leap forward in Ankara's quest to make Turkey a progressive, Western-style nation. It plunged the status of the Caliph into great ambiguity: was he to be treated as a head of state, even a symbolic one, now there was a president? No one knew. Abdulmejid must have recognised the threat to his position, even as he sent the president a telegram conveying his congratulations and praying that his appointment would be good for the country.[47]

In the West, the dawn of the Republic was greeted with immense enthusiasm. Dr John Finley, an American traveller who spoke at length with Kemal in Ankara, was practically glowing as he recounted his time in the country. He was delighted during a train journey to be seated in a coach with 'red plush cushions in the company of Turkish deputies' who were almost identical in manners and dress to English admirals. He was even happier to arrive at the station in Askeshir (which he had previously visited in 1919, finding 'nothing readable but an old copy of *The Cornhill Magazine*') and find multiple different daily papers available. This was real modernity, he felt, and was even more confident about it after he observed the Grand National Assembly in session.

Finley declared enthusiastically that Turkey was no 'sick man' but rather a 'young woman who has just thrown aside her veil and is taking her first hopeful face-to-face view of the world.' The 'interested and hopeful—and I think I may add, the beautiful—face of Latife Hanim [Kemal's wife]', he thought, could not be more different to the 'stooped Caliph, whose grey hair was covered by a tassled fez'. They seemed to him to embody contrasting aspects of

Turkey: the future and the past. The Assembly he thought looked like a 'remodeled clubhouse'.[48]

On the day the Republic was established, Mustafa Kemal Atatürk made it clear where his project drew inspiration from. 'We drink from the culture of France,' he told a French reporter, which could hardly have been more explicit.[49] For the Ali brothers in India, Kemal was still a hero. Maulana Mohamed Ali expressed his delight that Turkey had become a Republic, noting that the first three Caliphs, close companions of the Prophet, 'were the chief servants of the commonwealth'. In those days 'Muslims had themselves appointed their ruler and would depose him just as readily if he acted against the Laws of God.'[50] But this enthusiasm dissipated as Ankara made abundantly clear its intention for the House of Osman to be left out in the cold. In November, Prince Omer Faruk received a letter from the Ministry of Defence informing him that his position in the army had been terminated, leaving him so devastated that he retreated into his bedroom to cry.[51]

The Istanbul press began speculating that the Caliph would abdicate. In response, Abdulmejid issued a statement asserting that he was recognised as Caliph by the Islamic world and would only stand down if that Islamic world turned against him. This was an extraordinary proclamation; without a sultanate or empire and in the face of increasing opposition to the Caliphate from the Turkish government, Abdulmejid was explicitly drawing his legitimacy from the world's Muslims. He was articulating his own vision of the Caliphate, and by extension of Islam in the modern world—a vision distinct from that imagined by Ankara. He went so far as to suggest that in the future a 'Caliphate Congress' could be convened in Istanbul, drawing representatives from across the Islamic world. This foreshadowed what was to come after the Caliphate's abolition.[52]

Meanwhile, Abdulmejid doubled down on asserting the Caliphate's autonomy. When US President Woodrow Wilson died in February 1924, Ankara refused to lower the flags on government buildings, since at that time it had no diplomatic relations with Washington. But in Istanbul, the Caliph ordered the Turkish flags on his palace and yacht to be lowered.[53] Increasingly, government officials saw the spectre of the Caliphate as a serious threat. As outside observers saw it, the Caliph, far from acting as Ankara's puppet, appeared to be 'pitting his enormous religious prestige and power' against the republican government.[54]

The Indian intervention

By late 1923 rumours were swirling around Khilafatist circles in India that conflict between Kemal and Abdulmejid was growing to the extent that Ankara could plausibly abolish the Caliphate. The Central Khilafat Committee decided to send a delegation to Istanbul. The Government of India, though, refused to give them passports and the plan didn't materialise.[55] The Aga Khan and Sayyid Amir Ali thus took it upon themselves to make an intervention. They sent a letter to the Turkish prime minister, Ismet Pasha, on 5 December 1923, sending it also to the pro-Caliphate press in Istanbul. In an unhappy mistake, two newspapers, *Tanin* and *Ikdam*, published the letter before the prime minister had even received it. The letter then appeared the following day in another paper, the *Tevhid-i Efkar*.

In the letter, the Aga Khan and Ali—neither of whom were Sunni—decried 'the very disturbing effects the present uncertain position of the Caliph-Islam is exercising among the vast populations who belong to the Sunni communion… owing to the diminution in the Caliph's dignity and prestige'. They reminded Ismet Pasha of the support the Indian Muslims had shown to Turkey and informed him sternly that the fate of Islam itself was at stake:

> What we respectfully urge is that the religious headship of the Sunni world should be maintained intact in accordance with the Sheriat [Shari'a]. In our opinion any diminution in the prestige of the Caliph or the elimination of the Caliphate as a religious factor from the Turkish body politic would mean the disintegration of Islam and its practical disappearance as a moral force in the world… The Caliph's position and dignity should not, in any event, be less than that of the Pontiff of the Church of Rome.[56]

The letter gave the Turkish government considerable leeway in how to deal with the Caliphate; far from calling for the restoration of the Sultanate, it conceded that the Caliph could be a figure removed from temporal power. But it urged that the Caliphate itself should not be threatened.

The Turkish government exploded. The three newspaper editors who published the letter were swiftly arrested and tried with high treason before one of the dreaded Tribunals of Independence, set up by Ankara to root out dissidents. The unfortunate Lutfi Fikri Bey, a pro-Ottoman politician and member of the Liberal Union, was tried alongside them for having coincidentally written a letter at the same time, also calling on the government to safeguard the Shari'a and expressing support for the Caliphate. He was sentenced to five years' penal servitude. The editors were eventually released, but their papers were suppressed.[57]

The official line from Ankara was that Britain was behind discontent at Turkey's approach to the Caliphate—because, the government claimed, Britain aimed to install the Aga Khan, who had recently been made Grand Commander of the Victorian Order, as Caliph. This was certainly news to the Aga Khan, and the claim was rather undermined by his public endorsement of the Ottoman Caliphate. But Ankara made the most of his being leader of the Isma'ilis, something which the Khilafat Movement had embraced in a spirit of ecumenicism. One Turkish government spokesman attacked the Aga Khan as being merely the head of a small sect. A Kemalist commentator, meanwhile, likened him to the head of a minor Protestant church standing against the Vatican.[58] Jawaharlal Nehru later wrote that Mustafa Kemal 'was not very polite to the Aga Khan', painting him as a heretic and 'an accomplice of British foreign policy'. He added that Kemal abolished the Caliphate by 'making the Aga Khan's move a pretext'.[59]

Most of the Khilafatists, who had publicly supported the formation of the Turkish Republic, were furious at the Aga Khan and Sayyid Amir Ali for having jeopardised relations between the Indian Muslims and Ankara. On 18 December the Ali brothers and other Khilafatists signed a telegram addressed to Kemal assuring him they were devoted to the Turkish cause and fully supportive of the establishment of the Republic. Kemal duly thanked them for their good wishes. In his public pronouncements, Shaukat Ali avoided attacking the Aga Khan and Sayyid Amir Ali. 'These two men had great love for Islam', he said, 'and were serving it in their own way.' He noted delicately that the Aga Khan, not being in India, had perhaps grown somewhat out of touch.[60]

The upshot was that as Mustafa Kemal saw it, there were multiple actors challenging the Turkish government. There was the turbaned Abdulmejid on his grand Caliphal barge; there were pro-Caliphate politicians in Istanbul; there were also in Istanbul dangerous opinion-formers, including journalists and the president of the bar, sympathetic to the Ottomans; and there were the dogged Khilaftists in India. 'No matter what happens,' Kemal vowed on 4 December 1923, 'the country will become modern, civilized, and innovative.'[61]

Global Islamic politics, which the president had previously welcomed as valuable and which had convinced him to keep the Caliphate after the Sultanate was thrown out, now seemed to be a fundamental threat to his own political agenda. The Caliph himself, meanwhile, was also threatening the coherence of the Republic—there simply could not be a Presidency and a Caliphate together, Kemal resolved. Ultimately, he became convinced that in order to complete Turkey's transition into a modern, Western state, the Caliphate needed to go.

The *New York Times*, which monitored the situation more closely than any other Western paper and which was sympathetic to the anti-Ottoman viewpoint, reflected that Ankara's 'republican program could not afford to suffer in political prestige from the hampering medieval dogmatism of the world's most dogmatic creed [Islam].'[62] Kemal was an ardent moderniser and had no qualms about destroying Islam's most distinctive and long-lasting institution.

Abolishing the Caliphate, the government also reasoned, would help Turkey in its dealings with the European powers. During the Lausanne negotiations Ismet Pasha had thought that getting rid of the Caliphate would encourage the British to acquiesce to Turkey. In late February 1924, the British High Commissioner in Istanbul wrote to London that he had 'heard from a very secret source' that Ismet Pasha 'hoped that the banishment of the caliphal family and the nationalisation of the eximperial property (which is also said to be part of the plan) would allay British suspicion of Pan-Islamism, and would tend to make His Majesty's Government less intractable on outstanding disputes.'[63]

By early 1924, the Turkish government had decided: the Caliphate would go.

The writing on the wall

In the first three months of the year, there were a series of high-profile attacks on the House of Osman in the Ankara press. One paper published a piece attacking not just the Caliph but his family; another predicted that Abdulmejid would imminently abdicate, and called for an Islamic congress in Istanbul to elect a new Caliph.[64] A journalist who was an old classmate of Prince Ali Vasib asked him for an interview. According to Vasib, after he declined, the aggrieved journalist's newspaper 'printed an entirely imaginary interview with me, again intended to present me in an unfavourable light, that occupied several columns.'[65]

Members of the House of Osman were generally oblivious as to what Ankara had privately decided, until relatively late in the day. Most thought it highly unlikely that they would be forced to leave Istanbul. Princess Sabiha was unusual in suspecting that exile was imminent and would be permanent. She tried to plan ahead, writing in late February to her father, Sultan Mehmed Vahideddin in San Remo, explaining that:

> I, of course, together with the children, will follow [her husband] Faruk. My sister is trying to rent her house and will live off that. My mother, if the women of the family are to be allowed to stay on, will stay with my sister. If not, I shall find another solution. There is not much time left to think.[66]

By this point, the Caliph was beginning to see the writing on the wall. Yet he continued behaving publicly as if all was well. If, on Friday 29 February, Abdulmejid was dismayed when his weekly procession was attended by more American tourists than Muslim faithful, he did not show it. Instead, he kept up appearances, greeting the crowd with dignity. Privately, however, he knew his position was untenable.[67]

THE INDIAN CALIPHATE

With rumours of the Caliphate's impending abolition plastered all over the papers, Vasib, only a young man, went to see the Caliph at the Dolmabahce to ask him how he planned to save the dynasty. Abdulmejid received him in one of the palace's 'magnificent rooms' on a sofa by a seafront window. Vasib sat on an armchair opposite the Caliph. 'His face looked pale and unhealthy and he appeared to be very much on edge,' he recalled; Abdulmejid was speaking hesitantly and with long gaps between his words (although, Vasib noted, 'he always talked rather like this').

The young prince expected the Caliph to provide some insight into what Ankara intended, and a plan for resolving the situation or perhaps for the imperial family to act in concert to safeguard their interests. Instead, he sat there with his heart sinking as he listened to the Caliph slowly explain that he had absolutely no idea what was going to happen, but hoped the rumour circulating in the press that Ankara would give each member of the imperial family money equivalent to a ten years' stipend was true. 'He then began to work out how much this would come to in my case.' For Vasib, it was a crushing moment. He realised the family was doomed, and left the palace 'absorbed in my thoughts'.[68]

The end was nigh; now everyone knew it. A few days later, Vasib was in a room with the Lord High Chamberlain, Hikmet Bey, and the poet Abdulhak Hamid when the Caliph walked in and announced: 'I rather think our family are going to be sent into exile soon. If they send me official notification that this is going to happen, what do you think I should do?' Hamid replied that there was no other option but to comply and leave, before noting rather unhelpfully that the Caliph's revered ancestor, Sultan Selim, would not have done so. Abdulmejid made no reply.

Finally, on 1 March, the Caliph made one final, last-ditch effort to save the Caliphate. He cabled the Grand National Assembly warning that to abolish it would mean divorcing Turkey from the rest of the Islamic world, and that it would be terrible for the global Muslim consciousness.[69] It was a futile attempt. The Caliphate's fate was sealed. Abdulmejid's daughter Princess Durrushehvar was only ten years old but even she realised what was going on. 'I was walking slowly in the garden of Dolmabahçe Palace, engrossed in my thoughts,' she later wrote of her last night in Istanbul, the city she loved.

> The blue waters of the Bosphorus slapped the shores unceasingly, singing their sorrowful song, while the sun above spilled rays of gold on the waves. The islands, like a silver cloud from afar, announced the beginning of the Sea of Marmara. In front of me majestic mosques and gracious minarets, reminders of the glorious past, watched their reflection in the translucent waters, while the palace, hiding centuries of secrets in its forbidding heart, appeared among the dark cypresses.[70]

The princess asked her father if she could read the evening news. The Caliph said no, not wanting his daughter to 'read sentences that would break tender hearts like mine.'[71]

5

SLINGS AND ARROWS

On the evening of Monday 3 March 1924, in one swift blow, 1,300 years of Islamic history were brought to an end. Three bills were put before the Grand National Assembly. The first abolished the Caliphate, stripped every member of the imperial family of Turkish citizenship, exiled them, confiscated their palaces and ordered them to liquidate their private properties within a year.[1] There were no half measures taken. The second bill suppressed the Ministry of Pious Foundations, a pillar of the old Ottoman order. The third bill destroyed the entire infrastructure of Islamic schools across the country.[2]

There was dissent—quite a bit of it. Debate raged in the Assembly for over seven hours, to the chagrin of the twenty-three-year-old clerk tasked with transcribing everything that was said.[3] Some politicians suggested keeping the Caliphate as an institution, while expelling the House of Osman. But the abolitionists had their way. Their star speakers were Vassif Bey, member of one of the Tribunals of Independence, and Prime Minister Ismet Pasha. 'If Constantinople is today in our hands,' Ismet declared in the Assembly to widespread approval, 'it is because we have fought to death the Greeks and the Caliphate… If other Moslems have shown sympathy for us, this was not because we had the Caliph, but because we have been strong.' This sentiment won out and the Assembly passed the bills; six members of the dubiously named Popular Party were so horrified that they promptly resigned.[4]

It fell on Haydar Bey, the governor of Istanbul, accompanied by Istanbul's Chief of Police, Sadeddin Bey, to deliver the news to Caliph

Abdulmejid.⁵ By then it was nearly midnight. The Dolmabahce Palace had its telephones disconnected and police officers and soldiers encircled the complex.⁶ As they stood outside the palace, the enormity of what they were doing must have weighed upon the emissaries. They were there to depose the leader of the Islamic world.

They entered the Dolmabahce and were directed to the library. Abdulmejid was there with his brother-in-law, Damad Sherif Pasha, reading the Qur'an.⁷ The emissaries, not keen to waste any time, read the expulsion order. The Caliph looked stunned. 'I am not a traitor,' he said gravely. 'Under no circumstance will I go.' He turned to his companion: 'Pasha, Pasha, we have to do something! You do something too!'

But at that cataclysmic moment, Damad Sherif had nothing to offer his Caliph. 'My ship is leaving, sir,' he replied, before bowing and promptly leaving the room (he later became a close ally of Abdulmejid in exile).⁸ The Caliph had known that the abolition was coming, but at that moment he was in a state of disbelief. This couldn't happen, he argued. He tried to explain to the emissaries that he wasn't involved in politics. He even showed them his books, insisting that he was simply interested in intellectual pursuits. The emissaries, unimpressed, informed him that he would be forcibly removed from the palace if he resisted the eviction.⁹ Abdulmejid returned to reciting the Qur'an.

The palace quickly became full of activity, as one by one its inhabitants were awoken and told to prepare to leave. Ten-year-old Princess Durrushehvar walked into the main hall and saw her family standing around, all of them in tears. She went and hid in a dark corner.¹⁰ Her recollections of the night, written decades later, convey a sense of betrayal not primarily by the government but by Turkey's people: 'My father, whose family had been ruling for the past seven centuries, had sacrificed his life and his happiness for the people who no longer appreciated him.'¹¹ Her housemistress found Durrushehvar and fell upon her, sobbing. 'Don't forget me, please,' she said.

The princess decided to say her goodbyes. Her English teacher, Seniha Sami Morali, found herself awoken in her quarters by a knock on the door. It was Durrushehvar, who threw her arms around her teacher's neck and cried, 'We are leaving, farewell!' The teacher quickly dressed and went upstairs, where she saw the deposed Caliph. He was still reading the Qur'an.[12]

The women and eunuchs who were to be left behind would soon be rendered penniless, relying on charity donations of food.[13] That night, they wept. Around five o'clock in the morning, the family departed from the palace. Abdulmejid performed the morning prayer for the last time,[14] before walking out with his three wives, his son, his daughter and the senior housemaids.[15]

Standing outside, Abdulmejid told the Chief of Police he would continue praying for the happiness of his people: 'And be sure, even dead in my grave, my bones will carry on praying.'[16] He was solemnly saluted by the soldiers and police who were there, then entered a car bound for Catalca, to the west of Istanbul, where the family was to be bundled onto the Orient Express.[17]

A long convoy of cars set off. On the way out of the city, Durrushehvar found herself staring out of the window at Istanbul's darkened but still magisterial skyline. 'At least do not forget us,' she said quietly, as a sort of farewell.[18] Once Istanbul was left behind the journey took a turn for the dramatic. The cars plunged frequently into pools of mud and stopped multiple times in front of large pits, which had to be filled up with stones so the cars could drive across.[19]

At one point in the journey the convoy passed a school where children were playing in the garden. Recognising Abdulmejid, they began cheering and applauding, understandably oblivious to recent political developments. It was the closest the Caliph got to a send-off.[20] When the family arrived in Catalca they were accommodated while waiting for the train by a kindly Jewish stationmaster. He told them the House of Osman was 'the benefactor' of Ottoman Jews: 'When our ancestors were banished from Spain and were looking for a safe place to live, the Ottomans… reunited them with the safety of their lives, honour and possessions, as well as the freedom of their religion and language,' he proclaimed. 'We are indebted to serve them as well as we can in these dark days.' This brought tears to Abdulmejid's eyes.[21] The Orient Express arrived around midnight. Abdulmejid's secretary Salih Keramet later recalled that many of the passengers 'stuck their heads out of their windows, looking at us with curiosity'.[22]

Back in Istanbul, the princes were given two days to leave and a thousand Turkish lira each; the princesses had just over a week to arrange their departure.[23] Prince Ali Vasib's father was so sure that the family would never be exiled that throughout the previous month he had continually dismissed all such fears. Even as Abdulmejid was being deposed, he was relaxing in an armchair. It was only when policemen arrived at the house and formally announced the expulsion order that the family began preparing to leave. When the princes left Istanbul, a crowd 'looking downcast and subdued' gathered to see them off.[24]

In total, 155 members of the Ottoman family ended up in exile.[25] Many of them assumed their departure would be temporary, and that Turkey would shortly invite them back with open arms. They were wrong. The women of the family were eventually allowed to enter Turkey again after 1952; the men, not until 1974.

Neutral territory

The biggest practical issue the House of Osman faced was a depressing lack of money. They weren't wealthy; successive sultans had fastidiously prevented princes from accumulating wealth, fearing intrigue and rebellion. Princes conventionally received a monthly allowance from the treasury, which was never particularly generous. The richest members of the House of Osman were usually the Sultan's daughters, although even they were relatively poor.[26] Ankara gave each prince and princess 1,000 pounds sterling and a passport valid for a year, as a sort of parting gift.[27] They would have to make the money last.

As the train passed into Bulgaria the next morning, Abdulmejid sat with his doctor and secretary to discuss the future. He had been given an envelope of passports (with visas hastily stamped by the Swiss consulate), and another with 2,000 British pounds inside, enough to last a few weeks at most.[28]

By the second evening of what Durrushehvar called 'our sorrowful journey', the train passed through the woods of Serbia. It was a bright day, and colourful flowers and birds abounded. The princess felt the whole region 'laughed at our misfortune.' Even the clouds in the sky, she thought resentfully, 'moved on unperturbed with stealthy delight, as if they were all exulted'.[29] For some members of the family, the train journey was spent in sober reflection. Perhaps, they thought, the republican government would serve the Turks well and be good for them. 'But would they be able to love them as much as we did?' Durrushehvar wondered.[30]

The idea of returning to Istanbul and resurrecting the glory of the old sultans was alluring. Durrushehvar took to wondering hopefully whether some 'worthy descendant' would come along and 'follow the noble path of their illustrious ancestors,' in which case 'perhaps the glorious ancient times would not be just a memory, but would come back.' This was just a 'vague consolation'.[31] Her father, meanwhile, was already nursing ambitions to stage a grand comeback, and wanted to set up camp in Switzerland because of its much vaunted political neutrality. There, he calculated, he would be able to mobilise politically and work towards restoring the Caliphate.[32]

The Orient Express reached the Swiss frontier on 7 March. Immediately, problems arose when the officer in charge of passport control at the border station of Brig, who hadn't been forewarned of the House of Osman's arrival and was rather shocked, decided it was much too risky to allow a train full of Ottoman princes and princesses, the deposed Caliph of Islam among them, into the country without asking serious questions. Famously, the King of Greece and Emperor of Austria had both come to Switzerland in exile after the Great War—and their politicking there had caused problems for the Swiss. The passport control officer wondered aloud why the federal government, if it had agreed to the Caliph's entry, hadn't seen fit to inform him. The train was kept at a halt (most of it was inside a tunnel, with the passengers confused and increasingly alarmed) as the officer went to make some calls.[33] The Caliph's entourage, outraged, started shouting at the Swiss officers and hurling insults at them in Turkish.[34]

A few hours and several exchanges between the federal government and passport control later, the Caliph was officially granted permission to enter Swiss territory. But he was presented, as a condition of entry, with a letter to sign that promised he would neither engage in political activity nor even make any political statements. Abdulmejid signed the letter with absolutely no intention of sticking to the promise, and the Orient Express was allowed to proceed.[35] The Ottomans disembarked at Territet, a picturesque suburb on the beautiful Lake Geneva. 'The other passengers were chatting and laughing,' Durrushehvar recalled, 'while we were all utterly disheartened.' Abdulmejid gave the train guard, whose eyes filled with tears, his watch as a gesture of gratitude.[36]

The staff at the Grand Hotel des Alpes de Territet must have been awed when the deposed Ottoman Caliph marched in with his immediate family. Durrushehvar was struck that the lights were on in every room and corridor, 'just as in a fairy tale'.[37] Turkish and Swiss flags were raised on the hotel's flagpoles.[38]

Over the next few days, Abdulmejid and his men began to go through messages that had been sent from around the Islamic world—including India, Egypt and Indonesia—expressing sorrow over the Caliphate's abolition.[39] His presence in Territet caused quite a stir among the local Swiss, and an endless stream of photographers flowed in and out of the hotel to photograph the Caliph and his family. Abdulmejid gave an interview to a journalist from *L'Illustration*, the French paper which had covered him during his time as Caliph.[40]

A week later, more members of the family arrived in Territet, including Princess Sabiha, with her daughters Neslishah and Hanzade.[41] The Grand Hotel became a base for the Ottoman exiles. More significant was the political activity that quickly commenced, with the hotel serving as a headquarters—in flagrant violation of Abdulmejid's pledge to be apolitical—for scheming about a revival of the Caliphate. Delegations from various Muslim countries visited, many of them likely aiming to gather information about Abdulmejid's state of mind and what, if anything, he was planning. At that point, Abdulmejid still clung to the hope that Mustafa Kemal would see the error of his ways and invite the Ottomans back with open arms. Most of the exiles were optimistic that they would at some point return to Istanbul.[42]

As a result, they didn't worry about saving what little money they had. The Grand Hotel was hardly cheap, and Abdulmejid made no attempt to introduce any money-saving efforts, doling out generous handouts to family members.[43] As usual, only Princess Sabiha saw the situation clearly. She wrote a despairing letter to her husband's aide-de-camp in Istanbul, complaining about the way the family were behaving: 'All those that are here with us live as always with high hopes. They do nothing all day. There is no possibility of getting out of this outstanding and critical situation, with such pathetic and inefficient attempts.'

Sabiha was painfully aware that the Russian royals, thrown out of their country after the communist revolution in 1917, hadn't made the triumphant return to their country that they had once hoped for. She feared that the fate of the Ottomans would be the same. The hotel, she realised, was 'highway robbery', with all its attendant luxury quite unnecessary. Most of the money the family had was being spent on room and board.[44] As money became tighter, Abdulmejid set to work painting and composing music, hoping he could raise money by selling his paintings and compositions.[45]

Young Durrushehvar found Switzerland to be quite the culture shock. It was pleasant, certainly; Territet looked like a 'beautiful garden'. Abdulmejid took her on a walk around the local area, and she marvelled at the clean streets, flowered walls and beautiful buildings, which all compared favourably to poverty-ridden, tumultuous Istanbul. 'My father looked sad,' Durrushehvar noticed; 'perhaps he was having the same thoughts as I was.' The two of them walked 'slowly and sadly' through the streets.

On another occasion, to cheer their spirits, her father took her on a rowing boat on the lake. But the beauty on display just made them both more upset.[46] Back in Istanbul, Abdulmejid had once remarked that there were two things in the world he wished to see above all others, but probably never could: the mountains of Switzerland and the paintings in the Louvre in Paris. He hadn't known that both those wishes were to come true—at a devastatingly high price.[47]

THE INDIAN CALIPHATE

The political fallout

'Of all vast changes wrought by the war', opined *The London Times* in an editorial after the abolition of the Caliphate,

> the downfall of Hapsburgs, Romanoffs and Hohenzollerns, the resurrection of ancient States and the rise of States unknown before, the evolution of novel forms of government and the emergence of new ideas and new feelings among mankind, no single change is more striking to the imagination than this: and few, perhaps, may prove so important in their ultimate results.[48]

In Turkey, the government hailed the end of the Caliphate as the dawn of a glorious new era.[49] All things Ottoman were quickly designated relics; by 8 March it had already been decided that the Topkapi Palace would become a museum.[50] Meanwhile, the Republic declared war on everyone who sympathised with the Ottomans. Several Tribunals of Independence across the country began rooting out dissidents who opposed the Caliphate's abolition. The programme to reform and modernise Turkey didn't prize subtlety or the consent of the population; even discussing the Caliphate was declared an act of treason.[51]

On 9 March, Imams were banned from praying in their Friday sermons for the Caliph, as had always been the norm. The newspapers, fearing the consequences of doing otherwise, uniformly praised the reforms. Over the next few months the government put the ulema under intense surveillance. In Ramadan, preachers required government licences to give sermons in mosques.[52] Meanwhile, it was all justified in Islamic terms by Ankara. Kemal, aiming to assuage Indian Muslim opinion, issued a statement announcing that the Turkish government hadn't in fact destroyed the Caliphate. In an ambitious intellectual manoeuvre, he argued that the authority of the Caliphate was to be found in the Assembly, and so if Indian Muslims wanted to be loyal to the Caliphate they should support Turkey.

Western newspapers expressed 'incredulity' at the idea that 'the Angora [Ankara] Assembly possesses spiritual sovereignty over 300,000,000 Mohammedans scattered throughout the world', and that those Muslims would 'subscribe to its attempt to exercise the powers of Allah's vicegerent on earth.' Meanwhile some British officials, misreading the situation entirely, suspected that Kemal intended to take matters further and proclaim himself Sultan-Caliph.[53]

In fact, the abolition had launched a high-stakes contest by different Muslim rulers to claim the Caliphate. It was open season on the institution. The difficulty for each of them was that they couldn't simply demand the allegiance of their own subjects; to be the Caliph of Islam, they had to win recognition from the Islamic world at large. Whitehall was quietly fixated on the various Arab contenders to the institution, although Britain was officially strictly neutral. 'Our policy has been, and will remain, one of complete disinterestedness,' the new prime minister, Ramsay MacDonald, insisted dubiously in the House of Commons.[54]

The *New York Times* noted that the abolition put Britain in rather a difficult position. The possible establishment of a new Caliphate in Mecca, with Emir Hussein bin Ali (formerly the Sharif of Mecca, and a descendant of the Prophet) at the helm, or in Egypt, with King Fuad adopting the title, would put Britain at loggerheads with Turkey—which was opposed to any Caliphate emerging anywhere in the world. It was, of course, uncomfortable for the Turkish government that few Muslims outside of the country accepted its claim to the authority of the Caliphate.

But Britain had another problem too: the existence of a Caliphate anywhere at all in the Middle East meant that Indian Muslims would continue to focus their attention on the region's politics. The government's concern about this is a significant testament to how seriously Indian Muslim lobbying power was taken. 'In respect to the Near East as in respect to Russia,' an American reporter noted dryly, 'there is always India looming up in British calculations'.[55]

Meanwhile, the French press speculated that the British aimed to:

> dominate the countries lying between the Mediterranean and India and also are anxious to free the Indian Moslems from the influence of independent Turkey. They desire to constitute an Arab Caliphate which would consolidate the British domination from Maifa and Jidda to Bassora, and which, by ordering the Indian Moslems no longer to look to Angora, would again make it possible to use

them as a means of checking the Hindoos in their struggle for independence.⁵⁶

The French government strongly opposed the ascension of Hussein to the Caliphate, a fear soon dispelled when he abdicated from the throne in October 1924 in the face of defeat by Ibn Saud, the founder of the Saudi dynasty that came to rule the Hejaz.

Prominent French writer Claude Farrère, sympathetic to the Ottomans, wrote in favour of Abdulmejid and his family being invited to France. On this point many in the country agreed with him, although fewer agreed when an emboldened Farrère called on the French government to grant Abdulmejid a French colonial possession from which he could run a revived Caliphate. This particularly idiosyncratic idea garnered no support.⁵⁷

As time went on, more candidates for the Caliphate emerged. In 1925 Abd el-Karim, the enormously popular Moroccan leader who had recently won a breathtaking victory against Spain, was put forward for the role of Caliph by a group of Egyptians who argued that Karim's record of fighting European imperialists made him the only man who could win the confidence of the world's Muslims. Egypt's King Fuad was unhappy about this, and many felt he himself struck a plausible candidate, being the ruler of the Islamic world's largest nominally independent nation.⁵⁸

Ultimately, though, none of these figures could amass the international support they needed to credibly claim the Caliphate. In Switzerland, meanwhile, Abdulmejid hadn't waited long to throw down the gauntlet. After his exile, authorities and notables across the Islamic world waited with baited breath to see what he would do. Many might have wondered if he would quietly accept a life in Europe. Instead, Abdulmejid made it clear that he still considered himself the rightful Caliph.

On 11 March from the Grand Hotel, he made his first public statement on the issue. 'The decision to abolish the Caliphate by the National Assembly of Turkey is inappropriate and illegitimate,' he declared. 'The Caliphate is the religious and historical institution of not just Turks but all of the Muslim world collectively', he added, deploying the same logic which had seen him made Caliph.⁵⁹

Abdulmejid added that the Assembly had elected him, 'with the united votes of the legislative deputies, even after abolishing the Sultanate', and accused the government of later violating 'the principles of national sovereignty'.[60]

Abdulmejid then proposed that a council of Muslims from across the Islamic world be convened, adding that he expected 'the willing and continuous help of all our Muslim brothers in hopes to stand up for our collective and sacred cause'.[61] His thinking was strategic. Most (though not all) of the Islamic world had accepted Istanbul as the seat of the Caliphate because the Ottomans had a powerful Empire that controlled the three holy cities of Islam—as well as Baghdad, the former capital of the Abbasid Caliphate. Functionally, then, it was Ottoman power that mattered. Now, though, the Ottomans were in an unprecedented situation. Abdulmejid could claim the abolition was invalid all he liked, but he had no polity. His idea was to use the prestige of the House of Osman to be recognised as Caliph by a critical mass of Muslim leaders, scholars and thinkers from across the world, arguing that 'it is now for the Mussulman world alone, which has the exclusive right, to pass with full authority and in complete liberty upon this vital question.'[62] Abdulmejid's vision was for a radical modern reconstitution of the Ottoman Caliphate—without any Ottoman Empire—as an institution deriving its legitimacy from the support of the world's Muslims.

In France, Abdulmejid—well-known and liked as a Francophile artist—attracted considerable sympathy, with *L'Illustration* publishing a puff piece on the Caliph entitled 'The End of the Caliphate'.[63] But the Turkish government asked the Swiss Foreign Office to clamp down on Abdulmejid's political activities. The Swiss government conveyed this to Abdulmejid, who refused to back down and declared that he had a sense of duty to the Islamic world. He added innocently that he was quite sure the honourable Swiss government wouldn't force him to violate his religious convictions.[64]

'Moslems in India Perturbed'

The Khilaftists in India were thunderstruck when the news came that the Caliphate had been abolished. A *New York Times* headline simply read: 'Moslems in India Perturbed'. This was quite true.⁶⁵ From London, Sayyid Amir Ali—who had written the letter with the Aga Khan that had so infuriated Ankara—predicted that the abolition 'will prove a disaster both to Islam and to civilisation. Suppression of a time-honoured institution,' he believed, 'which was throughout the Moslem world regarded as a symbol of Islamic unity, will cause the disintegration of Islam as a moral force.'⁶⁶

This was a dramatic and sombre prediction. Others agreed. Maulana Mohamed Ali was in Aligarh when he heard the news; one of his daughters was sick and dying. He was stunned and lost all respect for Mustafa Kemal. 'I have no sympathy with those who want to break the ties of Islam for the sake of winning the plaudits of Europe for their so called progressiveness,' he declared to a crowd at Aligarh.⁶⁷

Most of the Khilafatists supported Abdulmejid's proclamation. The idea of a new democratic Caliphate, with an elected Caliph, started doing the rounds. Many argued that this was the best idea, given that the Caliph was originally elected by the Prophet's esteemed companions. For Maulana Shaukat Ali, the idea of Abdulmejid—who naturally commanded legitimacy, having been the Ottoman Caliph—being elected back into the role seemed like the natural way forward.⁶⁸ Not everyone agreed. Maulana Abdul Kalam Azad was sympathetic to Kemal's proclamation that the Caliphate's authority had passed to the Grand National Assembly.⁶⁹ Sir Muhammad Iqbal, who had grown uninterested in the Khilafat Movement because he was unimpressed by the late Ottoman Empire, was particularly enthused by the idea, eloquently explaining and rationalising Ankara's assertion for an Indian audience.

Iqbal believed that modern Muslims needed to 'rebuild the laws of Shari'ah in the light of modern thought and experience'.⁷⁰ This, he argued, was what Turkey had done: 'Turkey's Ijtihad [independent reasoning] is that according to the spirit of Islam the Caliphate or Imamate can be vested in a body of persons, or an elected Assembly.' He thought this was 'perfectly sound', and that republicanism was a 'necessity' in the modern age. In Turkey he saw vigour and vitality.⁷¹ In fact, Iqbal declared, among Muslim nations 'Turkey alone has shaken off its dogmatic slumber... She alone has claimed her right of intellectual freedom; she alone has passed from the ideal to the real—a transition which entails keen intellectual and moral struggle'.[72] Forget about the Caliphate for now, he suggested—Muslim countries must focus on becoming independent and reforming themselves. Each Muslim nation 'must sink into her own deeper self, temporarily focus her vision on herself alone, until all are strong and powerful to form a living family of republics'.[73]

But the Republic of Turkey didn't quite share Iqbal's vision of Islamic reform. Instead, it pursued a campaign of militant secularisation.

Forging a secular state

'Our national ideal,' proclaimed President Mustafa Kemal Pasha in 1933, 'is to develop continuously, by every means and measure, our nation's high character, relentless diligence, innate intelligence, commitment to knowledge/science, love of the fine arts, and the feeling of national unity… How happy is he who says I am a Turk.'[74] A new constitution in 1925 gave all Turkish citizens equality before the law and a raft of rights, including freedom of thought and speech.[75] The government also granted universal male suffrage.[76] But although democracy was held up as an ideal it was never truly enacted, and Turkey was functionally a one-party state until 1950. For the government in Ankara, developing Turkey required a firm hand and iron grip, and the country simply couldn't afford the free and fair elections that existed in older and established states like France and Britain.[77]

Dissent certainly existed and occasionally turned into open revolt. In February 1925, a major rebellion erupted in Kurdish districts in the south east. Thousands of Kurds, led by the dervish and tribal leader Sheikh Said, took up arms against the government. They demanded the restoration of the Caliphate, an end to what they saw as anti-Islamic reforms and more autonomy for the country's Kurds instead of imposed Turkish nationalism. The rebellion was put down by Ankara's military might—including aerial bombardment.

The Sheikh himself was then executed along with thousands of his comrades and supporters.[78]

The nation had to adopt a new identity. In 1925 a law was passed banning non-European headgear for men, including the fez and the turban. Instead, everyone was expected to wear European brimmed hats.[79] In 1928, in a particularly radical Westernising move, the government announced the introduction of a Latin alphabet and the Ottoman script was thrown out of the window.[80] Remarkably, Kemal gave officials a two-hour lesson on the Latin alphabet in the Dolmabahce Palace, formerly Abdulmejid's residence.[81] Westernisation, treated as a necessary component of modernisation, also meant secularisation. The government's logic was simple: Islam was backward; secularism was progressive.

Thus in 1928 the Grand National Assembly passed a bill removing all references to Islam in Turkey's constitution. Henceforth deputies were to swear 'on honour' and not 'before God'.[82] Article 2 of the constitution, 'The Moslem religion is the religion of the Turkish State', was done away with, as was Article 27, 'The application of religious dispositions depends on the Grand National Assembly'. Dr Stephen Panaretoff, a respected Bulgarian diplomat, mused that the abolition of Islam as Turkey's state religion had the potential to secure nothing less than the 'genuine emancipation of the Turk' and 'genuine freedom of conscience'. Westernisation and modernisation was now possible, he thought, in a way that it had never been during the days of the Ottomans; the 1908 project to create a constitutional monarchy had been impossible because the 'glamour of the Sultan's power had a dazzling effect upon the mass of the Turkish population', while the Caliphate meant that 'sweeping liberal reforms' would have failed to pass. 'If the Turks can succeed in all the radical reforms they have undertaken,' Panaretoff concluded delightedly, 'they will have written an entirely new page in their history and in the history of Mohammedanism.'[83]

Islam had been completely redefined as a strictly private affair— if even that, since the government aimed to engineer Turkish citizens who would be more modern and Western at heart than Westerners themselves. People went suddenly from living under a government that justified itself in Islamic terms to being told it was treasonous even to try to bring Islam into the political realm. Many, unsurprisingly, suffered from psychological whiplash.

Ramadan that year felt palpably different from the old days. What used to be a great spiritual event for which all ordinary life would ground to a halt was now no such thing; the government placed limited emphasis on the month of fasting, and no time off was given to government employees. The mosques were emptier at night than they used to be. Most radically different of all was the month's twenty-seventh night, on which the Caliph used to appear in public for the prayer. Now there was no Caliph and the night seemed 'an echo from the past; the ranks of worshippers not so crowded, the fervor and volume of the prayers not so thrilling.'

By contrast Eid, when everyone was allowed to eat again, was widely and enthusiastically celebrated. Yet after the festival finished, guns boomed across the Marmara and the Bosphorus, as if to signal 'the urgent need to catch up once more with that utilitarian hustling West with which republican Turkey has cast her destinies.'[84]

By August 1928 the government was actively encouraging Turks to drink alcohol and listen to fashionable jazz music. President Kemal himself decided to set an example: at one public function the zeibek, a traditional Turkish dance, was announced in his honour. Kemal swiftly rose and condemned 'Oriental music and dances', before declaring that 'Turkey is gay and must express this national gayety in the music and dances of the vitalised Western world.' He condemned the Ottoman past as having been fundamentally hypocritical. 'Ten years ago Turkey's leaders were hypocrites under the shadow of the Caliph's mantle,' he informed the crowd, 'drinking alcohol but denying alcohol to the people on orthodox grounds. They were unwilling to drink publicly but consumed more copiously in private than myself, who drink publicly to the health of the Turkish people.' Kemal then proceeded to dance the foxtrot with several women.[85]

On Turkey's making a 'dash' at creating a new order, Marmaduke Pickthall put his thoughts bluntly: 'I rather wish they hadn't'. Yet he thought it was good in the sense that it 'has forced the Muslims of other countries to think seriously what are, and what are not, essentials of religion.'[86] He criticised the ban on imams reciting the

Qur'an in Arabic: 'The ritual Arabic is a bond between Muslims as Latin is a bond between Roman Catholics, and it is the more needed in our case, for we have no hierarchy.'[87]

Pickthall was also particularly disturbed by the attacks on the traditional Islamic education system, and was perplexed to meet Turks who 'proclaim themselves good Muslims and break all rules', eating pork and drinking alcohol—'not in the manner of the naughty young Egyptian of a former day—*moi, j'adore le jambon*—but earnestly and with an almost missionary ardour. But they vow they would shed the last drop of their blood in defence of Islam. And I believe it.'[88] If many Turks were confused by the reforms, most people in the wider Islamic world were utterly baffled.

'A clear conscience, a strong faith'

Life in Switzerland, meanwhile, was difficult. Finances were a constant source of worry. Unable to procure a piano, Caliph Abdulmejid resorted to using his violin to compose an orchestral symphony. He also composed a piece entitled *Hymne* (French for 'anthem'), the first lines of which were published on 15 June 1924.[89]

In July, Abdulmejid sent a letter to the poet Abdulhak Hamid. 'Your old friend', he wrote, 'who loves you and reveres your eternal greatness, could once again not prevent himself from sending you his affectionate greetings from his place of exile.' Quoting Shakespeare's *Hamlet*, Abdulmejid described himself as having been subjected to the 'slings and arrows of outrageous fortune'—but unlike the Prince of Denmark he was still 'hearty, with a clear conscience, a strong faith', and at ease with himself. Abdulmejid described his separation from his 'most beloved homeland' as painful to his heart.[90] He quoted a couplet (here in an English translation), which he likely composed himself:

> Wail not, though you be like a moth on fire
> For this is, o poor lover, the etiquette of love.

(The beloved here would appear to be Istanbul.) Another couplet he quoted showed he hadn't given in to despair:

> What else can we hope for, as long as the Moon and the
> Sun keep making their ways across the Heavens,
> So may our cup keep going around this gathering of love.[91]

Shortly after the letter was sent, the Caliph's fortunes changed. Since March, his secretary Salih Keramet Nigar had been saddled with the unenviable task of seeking support from Muslim leaders—mostly to no avail. The Iranian ambassador, for one, expressed his sorrow at the events but explained that Iran's Qajar dynasty was facing the same predicament as the Ottomans, and in no position to help. The Afghan ambassador, meanwhile, told Keramet straightforwardly that his government admired and supported the Republic of Turkey. There was to be no help from those quarters.[92]

On 14 April, Keramet brought Abdulmejid an article written by Maulana Mohamed Ali, which declared that the Muslims of India would use all means possible to revive the Caliphate.[93] It cheered the Caliph, but the intervention he found most electrifying came from Sayyid Amir Ali. The scholar argued from London that the Caliphate represented the unity of over 250 million Sunni Muslims, so 'no Muslim country can justify the attempt to change, or abolish a collective Muslim institution, disregarding the beliefs and opinions of other Muslim communities around the world'.[94] Only a council of ulema could depose the Caliph, Ali maintained, rendering Ankara's move invalid. In fact, Turkey had 'lost its primacy among other Muslim governments while trying to get closer to the level of advanced democracies'.[95] The Caliph's secretary observed that reading the article seemed to set Abdulmejid's 'mind at rest'.[96] After sending a message of thanks to Ali, Abdulmejid directed Keramet to go and meet him in person.[97]

In May, Keramet managed to travel to London with a visa. There he found Ali so severely ill and frail that he was forced to remain lying down while talking to the secretary. Ali, speaking very quietly, suggested that if 'the Islamic council envisioned by His Highness [Abdulmejid] can meet, a plausible solution that could put an end to this current crisis could be found'. He noted that this was a 'remote possibility', since 'some harmful political ambitions have already started exploiting this crisis'.[98] Keramet, clearly a fan, handed Ali a copy of one of the latter's books, *The Spirit of Islam*, and asked him to sign it.[99]

But the frail and elderly scholar also informed the secretary of a new development. There was in fact, he revealed, one Muslim notable who was concerned about the Caliph's plight—and willing to financially support Abdulmejid and his family.[100] This could save them from destitution. He was, moreover, no ordinary Muslim notable. In fact, since the fall of the Ottomans, the Nizam of Hyderabad had become the premier Muslim ruler in the world.

PART TWO

Sultans of old, O Osman, have all died
By your rule are Muslims now identified.
　　　　　　　　　　　　– Nizam VII, Mir Osman Ali Khan

Ancient, romantic customs are constantly fostered and are still dominant;
modern progress merely improves, but does not kill them.
　　　　　　　　　　　　　　　　　　　– Princess Durrushehvar

6

AN ORIENTAL DREAM

British civil servant Philip Mason, working in Hyderabad in the 1940s shortly before the state's fall to the Indian Union, was once invited to tea with the Nizam. He was picked up in a Rolls-Royce and driven over to a palace a little outside of the capital, on top of a steep hill. Having left the car, Mason and his companions were greeted by two rows of courtiers in silken sherwanis lining a steep staircase leading up to the palace.

Making their way towards the staircase, the party was surprised to notice at its foot an 'ill-dressed little man in an old nondescript sherwani' and a 'dingy cap'. He seemed to be aimlessly hanging around. Mason thought he 'seemed uncertain of his role and indeed to have no place in the proceedings; we thought it tactful to ignore him and addressed ourselves to the stairs.' At that point, multiple aides-de-camp stepped forward to hiss urgently 'like geese or samovars' that the man in front of the steps was in fact His Exalted Highness—the Nizam of Hyderabad. This was India's premier prince, a billionaire and the richest man in the world.[1]

The party swiftly turned towards him and 'presented our humble duty.'[2]

The largest of the princely states

Today, Hyderabad is one of India's largest cities and the capital of the southern state of Telangana. One side of the city, which the locals call 'Cyberabad', boasts wide roads, flashy restaurants and an endless stretch of high-rises displaying the logos of nearly every major international technology company. But until the mid-twentieth century, it was the capital of the lineage of the Nizam. Six of these princes lie buried, side by side, in the Mecca Masjid, the largest mosque of the Old City, packed every day with people praying, socialising, and sleeping among the tombstones.

Under the British Raj, around half of the Indian subcontinent's landmass was governed only indirectly by the Empire. These were the princely states, which contained a quarter of India's population.[3] They varied wildly in size; some were glorified estates, while others were the size of countries. The princes paid tribute to the Raj but enjoyed a large measure of autonomy within their own borders. The largest state was Hyderabad, governing vast swathes of southern and western India. Including the province of Berar, administered by the British but formally under the Nizam's sovereignty, Hyderabad was 100,000 square miles large, roughly the size of Italy, with a population of sixteen million.[4] If Hyderabad had become a member state of the United Nations, it would have been among the top thirty in size and top forty in income. It had no seaport but boasted copious amounts of coal, iron ore and cotton.[5]

The polity was governed from Hyderabad city. In the first half of the twentieth century, the capital was one of India's most stunningly beautiful cities, and was certainly safer, cleaner and richer than most under direct British rule. The roads were smooth, the streets were well lit and there were many green and well-vegetated spaces.[6] Journalist Dosabhai Framji Karaka marvelled at the sight of 'the picturesque minarets of the old city silhouetted against the grey dusky sky', describing the place as 'a Moslem city mounted against an Oriental blue heaven.'[7]

He toured the streets of the city: 'The tradespeople sit, pictures of patience, upon the floor in their long verandah-like shops, just as their forefathers sat centuries ago'. These humble-looking, underfed-seeming men 'sitting behind heaps of grains and pulses in their dingy little shops may appear to be hovering on the brink of bankruptcy, yet they may be transacting a business amounting to thousands of rupees a day.'[8] To Western visitors, Hyderabad seemed almost unreal. Writer Elizabeth Cooper thought the city had 'dropped to the earth from an Oriental dream'. She wrote wondrously of 'pretty, dark-eyed women', of men on street corners 'with their great wreaths of white flowers and the elephant swaying slowly down the street, looking with keen, twinkling eyes at the people who make way for him'.[9]

The state had been overseen since the early eighteenth century by a succession of Nizams, short for Nizam al-Mulk, which means 'administrator of the kingdom' in Persian, for centuries one of India's courtly and literary languages. Asaf Jah I, who served the Mughal Emperor Aurangzeb Alamgir, became effectively independent in 1724 and began Asaf Jahi rule over what would become known as Hyderabad State.[10] In today's India, the princes are largely remembered as venal, decadent and ineffectual British pawns. In the twentieth century Jawaharlal Nehru, leading the Indian struggle for independence, condemned the states as 'sinks of reaction and incompetence and unrestrained autocratic power,' power which, to make matters worse, was 'sometimes exercised by vicious and degraded individuals'.[11]

But Hyderabad's elite proudly thought their state to be better governed than British India.[12] Most of the population were peasants, but Hyderabad was also fast modernising. Officials enacted policies that varied wildly from the norm in British India, and the Nizam's government often had to work against British policy to construct mosques and temples. British officials likewise agitated against workers' housing and urban agriculture near the British military cantonment in the capital.[13] Although the late nineteenth century had seen considerable reform, the turning point was 1908, when devastating floods destroyed much of the city and paved the way for a grand project of urbanisation and modernisation under the new Nizam, the seventh of his dynasty, Mir Osman Ali Khan.[14] Over the next few decades, major reservoirs were built to provide drinking water for the city. A High Court was constructed in vivid red and white stone in 1919, and in 1927 a modern hospital was built.[15]

Osman Ali Khan declared war on the city's major problems of congestion, slums and poor sanitation. The slums were removed and their dwellers were housed in model colonies, drains were put in place and new transport infrastructure was built. Housing plots sprang up and playgrounds and parks were established.[16] As British civil servant Sir Arthur Lothian noted, Hyderabad had the 'finest thoroughfares of any Eastern city.'[17]

Elsewhere in the state, peasants were relatively better off than most of their counterparts in British India—although no peasants anywhere were well treated.[18] In the late nineteenth and early twentieth centuries, however, Hyderabad's famine relief policies set it far apart from British India. Devastating famines that caused mass die-offs were a recurring and almost defining feature of direct British rule. Colonial policy—agrarian capitalism and a simple lack of concern with alleviating suffering—was responsible.

In stark contrast, during the Deccan famines of 1876–8, Hyderabadi policy involved not just material relief programmes but also a suspension of revenue demands.[19] Refugees poured en masse out of neighbouring British India into Hyderabad State, where they were put up in relief houses.[20] Some localities in the Bombay Presidency in British India, such as the Sholapur and Ahmednagar districts, were left nearly empty.[21]

This approach continued into the reign of the seventh Nizam; the 1938 Hyderabad State Manual recorded that an increase in industrial employment and irrigation improvement had contributed to a relatively prosperous agrarian scene, and a significantly lower risk of scarcity.[22] The Public Works Department specifically employed Dalits (demonised as the 'untouchables' or outcastes) as a form of affirmative action, and the Hyderabad Forest Department introduced initiatives to employ Advisasis, tribal people.[23]

During the seventh Nizam's early reign, the state also modernised politically, although this didn't stretch as far as democratisation. In 1922 Hyderabad separated the judiciary from the executive, the first princely state to do so—and that same year the Nizam abolished the death penalty and banned bonded labour.[24] This policy was the direct result of the government's deep-rooted but constantly evolving ruling ideology.

A Muslim capital

Hyderabad was culturally Deccani, of the south. But the state had started as part of the Mughal Empire, and the Asaf Jahi dynasty presented itself as the successor to the grand Mughal legacy, with all its associated prestige and splendour. Hyderabad's elite drew simultaneously from both Mughal and Deccani identities.

State institutions were transformed in the late nineteenth century. Increasingly, officials were educated abroad, usually in Britain, returning with cosmopolitan and modern outlooks.[25] Meanwhile in British India, Urdu and Persian scribes and former Mughal officials were dismissed en masse and turned up at the Nizam's court, where they competed for influence with native Hyderabadi elites.[26] Modern, Western ideas fused with a Mughlai (Mughal-style) ideology of paternalistic, benevolent governance.

Islam was of the utmost importance to all this, although most of the population were Hindus. The ruling Asaf Jahis were Sunni Muslims, of the Hanafi legal school, like the Ottomans.[27] The seventh Nizam was, by all accounts, a pious Muslim. In 1935 when he visited the shrine of a saint, Khwaja Banda Nawaz Gaisu Daraz, in Gulbarga, a guard of honour had been set up by its entrance for him. The Nizam promptly dismissed it, saying he had come to pay and not receive respects. On another occasion that year, he went to a mosque and was spotted by a poet, who approached him and began reciting an ode in his praise. The Nizam quickly stopped him, saying: 'In the house of God, king and beggar are both equal. Nobody is small or great.'[28]

Asaf Jahi rule was Islamic in the sense that it drew heavily from the Indo-Islamic, particularly Mughal, political tradition. Central to this was the Islamic concept of *maslahat* (public interest), which had been crucial to the Mughals and provided the justification for government policy.[29] Hyderabad presented itself as the heir to Indo-Islamic civilisation. While the Nizam played no active role in political life in British India, most Indian Muslim politicians looked to Hyderabad as a centre of Islamic power and prestige, of great cultural importance. Sir William Barton, the British Resident (a representative and adviser) in Hyderabad from 1925 to 1930, thought the Nizam showed 'in his temperament traces of the imperiousness inspired by the once unchallenged supremacy of the old Delhi emperors.' 'Hyderabad,' he declared, 'is still redolent of Mogul [Mughal] tradition.'[30]

The Nizam was also a Muslim ruler of importance beyond India. In the late nineteenth century, Hyderabad had become a hub for modernist Muslim intellectuals from across the Islamic world. For example Jamal al-Din al-Afghani, the famous anti-colonial modernist thinker, lived there in the early 1880s—with the Raj keeping a close eye on his activities.[31] Hyderabad was also a centre of migration for people from all over the Islamic and Arab world, who typically came to work as soldiers and scholars within the state apparatus. Many of the most high-status soldiers and armed guards in the state were Habshis, from East African countries like Somalia, Ethiopia and Kenya. And Habshi nobles from Sachin and Janjira, states on India's west coast, married into Hyderabad's nobility.[32]

Osman Ali Khan had his own special Arab irregular forces, called the Nazm-i Jamiat, which performed watch and ward duties in the palaces.[33] Many of the Arab and Afghan migrants married locally, so that their descendants were mixed.[34]

Arabs from the region of Hadhramaut in modern-day Yemen were particularly prominent within the state's governing structures, often marrying Habshis (who by the 1920s were identified as simultaneously Somali, Arab, Yemeni, Indian and African).[35] Modern-day Yemen, Qatar, the United Arab Emirates, Oman, Bahrain and Kuwait were legally part of Britain's Indian Empire in the early twentieth century, as Sam Dalrymple has shown in his recent book *Shattered Lands*. Abu Dhabi (now one of the wealthiest cities in the Middle East) was first on the standard alphabetical list of Indian princely states—something almost entirely forgotten today.[36] Arab rulers often wore sherwanis and adopted Indo-Islamic high culture. Even today the Sultan of Oman often dons formal subcontinental attire.[37]

It was in this context that some sultanates in a large region in the southern Arabian peninsula, now South Yemen, were effectively founded with funds from Hyderabad. Most prominent of these was the Qu'aiti Sultanate, an Arab dynasty which entered into a marital union with the Asaf Jahis. The last Sultan, Ghalib al-Qu'aiti, now dispossessed of his dominion, is still alive; the seventh Nizam was his great-uncle.[38] This close connection with the southern Arabian

AN ORIENTAL DREAM

Peninsula helped establish Hyderabad as an important polity within the wider Islamic world.

Recognising its status, Marmaduke Pickthall headed to Hyderabad after the end of the Khilafat Movement, where he fell in love with the capital. The Nizam set up a journal called *Islamic Culture* in 1927 to influence British discourse about Islam; Pickthall was made editor. He was also commissioned to produce an English translation of the Qur'an for the first time. The resulting Pickthall translation was almost universally considered a monumental achievement, and is still widely printed and used by English-speaking Muslims to this day.[39] When Pickthall left Hyderabad in 1935, he handed *Islamic Culture* over to Muhammad Asad, a convert to Islam of Jewish heritage who would later be remembered as one of the greatest Muslim thinkers of the century.[40]

For Pickthall, Hyderabad was a 'sort of capital city for all Muslims', for people 'come there from afar, attracted by the fabled wealth of His Exalted Highness.' In 1936 Pickthall declared his hopes for Hyderabad publicly:

> I have sometimes thought that if England were ever again minded to adopt a benevolent Islamic policy, Hyderabad might well be made the centre of that policy, because, though the majority of the subjects are Hindus, the State has the prestige of the old Mughal Empire, and is itself no bad example of Islamic government; because it is dear to the hearts of all the Indian Muslims, and because it is unreservedly pro-British.[41]

Hyderabad was indeed an Islamic capital—and the Ottomans having fallen, the Nizam was in many ways the foremost Muslim ruler in the world. To top it off, his polity was in India, home to the world's largest Muslim population—and it was part of the mighty British Empire. It was no wonder that many thought Hyderabad could be the seat of a revived Caliphate.

Hindu-Muslim relations in Hyderabad

That the vast majority of Hyderabad's population was Hindu didn't discourage the Nizam from promoting the state's Islamic importance. Similarly, the Ottoman Caliphate itself had a mostly non-Muslim population for most of its lifespan. But what did this mean to Hyderabad's Hindus? As Partition drew closer, the fraught religious politics of British India seeped into Hyderabad. Traditionally, however, Asaf Jahi rule was self-consciously pluralistic; as the great scholar of Hyderabadi history Narendra Luther put it, the juxtaposition between minority-Muslim rule and a majority-Hindu population 'necessitated a discreet accommodation on both sides and gave rise to a rare synthesis.'[42]

The Nizams didn't levy the *jizya*, a poll tax that was often paid by non-Muslims throughout Islam's history but which was rarely enforced by Muslim rulers in India.[43] Osman Ali Khan, like his predecessors, patronised temples and churches as well as mosques and Muslim shrines.[44] And the dynasty depended on Hindu landed elites for 'military, fiscal and symbolic support', with the bureaucracy including Parsis, Christians and Hindu Kayasthas.[45] While the civil service, military and police were largely staffed with Muslims, Hindu groups had a significant presence in commerce, banking, law and agriculture.[46]

At the same time, Muslims and Hindus were far from two homogenous and hostile groups. Maharaja Kishen Pershad, the prime minister in the 1920s, was a Hindu but was not considered a Hindu representative—he was simply the prime minister. In general, Hindus and Muslims dressed alike and ate the same food. They celebrated each other's religious festivals. Within the Muslim fold, the Sunni–Shi'a divide was not particularly accentuated, and Sunni notables, following the Nizam's lead, organised events during the Shi'a commemoration of Muharram.[47]

Once, at a birthday party, Philip Mason was shocked to see a young boy with a Hindu name wearing a Turkish fez, which he took to be a Muslim hat. 'Oh, here in Hyderabad we do not care for things like that!' his neighbour replied. 'It is one of the nice things here that we are so delightfully cosmopolitan.'[48]

The world's richest man

Osman Ali Khan, who succeeded his father to become Nizam in 1911, was one of the most unusual and multifaceted figures of the twentieth century. After his support for the British effort in the First World War, he was promoted from His Highness to His Exalted Highness. The British threw in an honorary title of Lieutenant General, and he was knighted for good measure. The Osmania University, named creatively after Osman Ali Khan himself, gave him another title: Sultan-ul-Uloom (king of learning).[49]

In the West, he was most famous for his wealth—in the 1930s, *TIME* magazine proclaimed him the world's richest man.[50] The great American industrialist Henry Ford and his son had a combined fortune of less than half the value of the Nizam's jewels alone. It was believed that he had two billion dollars' worth of precious stones, mostly diamonds and rubies, stashed in underground vaults—along with 250 million dollars' worth of gold bars.[51] Ruth St. Denis and Ted Shawn, two American modern dance pioneers, were stunned by their visit to Hyderabad in 1926 and returned to New York gushing that the Nizam could 'buy and sell Henry Ford, Rockefeller, Mellon and others' multiple times—and still afford to live on Park Avenue. But the Nizam, St. Denis marvelled, dressed like a 'Greenwich Villager of ten years ago'.

The Nizam was indeed avowedly austere. He 'might have stepped out of the Old Testament', the *New York Times* reported.[52] While as a young man he enjoyed wearing expensive clothes, he eventually gave them up.[53] Later he wore a sherwani and pyjamas, like nearly every man in Hyderabad. He also wore a Turkish hat with a tassel, which had become a trend even as it was banned in Ataturk's Turkey.[54]

The ruler rode in a coach of gold on state occasions, and a 'shabby, rattling vehicle of 1926 vintage' on normal days. 'He lives in almost Spartan simplicity,' Sir Akbar Hydari, the minister for finance, said admiringly. 'Money has no meaning for him, although he knows how to manage it well.' The Nizam refused to get rid of any clothing until it had been rendered completely beyond saving, and even then he would personally inspect it before it could be thrown away. Famously, he gave people dinner invitations on bits of paper taken from old envelopes, and once, at a race track, the Nizam stopped at a stall to buy some ice cream, only to storm away furiously when he heard the price.[55]

This austerity didn't just come with age. When he got married as a young prince in 1906, the Hyderabad army was called to attention at the wedding, awaiting his arrival. Twenty-one guns were fired in spectacular fashion, in accordance with Asaf Jahi tradition. At that point, the guests all looked expectantly to his coming—probably, they assumed, on a giant elephant, as was customary. Instead, the prince arrived in a 'battered old car'.[56]

As Nizam, he lived in the King Kothi Palace, an unassuming building, with his wives, concubines and daughters.[57] The British who met him often mocked his austerity. Civil servant Sir Conrad Corfield wrote that his friend had visited the Nizam in his palace, and upon arriving was shown into a room which was empty but for 'someone dressed like a table servant'. He made to sit down to wait for the billionaire prince's arrival—until the supposed table servant 'greeted him politely and he realised it was His Exalted Highness!'[58] But in truth, the Nizam was an impressive operator. Corfield himself found him to be shrewd and 'completely well-informed' about Hyderabad's affairs.[59] Sir Arthur Lothian, Resident in the 1940s, recorded that the Nizam had his ear 'very close to the ground and very little escaped his knowledge.'[60]

In autumn 2024 I interviewed Sultan Ghalib al-Qu'aiti, who was born in 1948—the year that his dynasty, the rulers of the Qu'aiti Sultanate in the southern Arabian peninsula, ceased to be associated formally with Hyderabad, which fell that September. The charming and scholarly dispossessed Sultan, now in his seventies, looks very much like an Arab ruler but speaks perfect Urdu and has a deep knowledge of Indian cultures and history. His Sultanate in what is now southern Yemen had a significant population of Indians, both because of the Raj and the state's Hyderabadi links. But in 1967 the young ruler, still under British protection, was overthrown in a coup by the National Liberation Front, an Arab nationalist militia which later declared the socialist republic of South Yemen. After he was deposed, he went to Oxford and Cambridge, and became a respected historian of Islam, Hyderabad and his own lost state.

Sultan Ghalib knew an older Nizam, stripped of his power. When I spoke to him, he was disdainful of contemporary accounts that painted the ruler—the Sultan's great uncle—as a comical figure. He recalled that the Nizam's family so revered him that they wouldn't dare to look him in the eye. 'Such was the Nizam's piercing gaze that it would penetrate right through you. You stood with your gaze down, hands folded like in prayer. You never looked at him,' he said. 'You only answered in monosyllables.'

The Sultan told me that as a child he was treated fondly by the Nizam, who had particular affection for his niece—the Sultan's mother. The Nizam 'always liked the Arabs because they were not afraid of the British', the Sultan said. The British, he noted, were hardly pleased about that—which made the Nizam like the Arabs all the more. 'The Nizam was very clued up. He was a workaholic and operated strictly by the clock. He could be very, very kind, but he could also be very tough.' He was a devout Muslim, with 'slightly Shi'a leanings', the Sultan remembered, since his mother was a Shi'a. The Nizam, who styled himself after the pious Mughal Emperor Aurangzeb, 'saw himself as a saintly figure, and would be genuinely pleased, if supplicated, to place his hand on one's head and recite a prayer. I include myself on several occasions as an example.' He had alcohol served at official banquets for British and other foreign guests but never drank himself. He did, however, take opium—just a 'small amount, on his doctors' orders, to keep him calm. He had a fiery temper'.[61]

Journalist Dosabhai Framji Karaka went to interview the Nizam after the fall of Hyderabad, once he had lost his power. He wrote that Osman Ali Khan was wearing a red fez and an ordinary-looking, 'biscuit-coloured' sherwani. By that point he had grey hair and a trimmed moustache. His eyes though, were 'Deep, rich, piercing' and belonged to a man 'possessed of some spiritual force'.[62] Karaka wondered: 'was this an unrecognized Caliph?'

During the interview, Karaka (whose book was glowing about the Nizam and scathing towards India's Congress Party) found the Nizam polite, attentive and quick-witted. At the end, he bowed and shook his visitor's hand. 'Glad to have met you,' he said. Karaka recounted that the Nizam 'stood there before me for just a few moments more, a Mogul to the tips of his fingers. As I closely watched the venerable expression on his face and those deep, piercing eyes of his, I came closer to the belief which I now hold, that he is on his way to a Caliphate.'

The Nizam's palace

Today, Hyderabad's Old City—away from the swanky hotels and flashy high-rises—is a historical treasure chest, if you know where to look. Throughout the neighbourhood, amid a mass of perfume shops, biryani restaurants and tea vendors, historical artefacts are hidden in plain sight. Some of the stately residences are crumbling, such as the King Kothi Palace, where the Nizam lived. Others have fared better: the Chowmahalla Palace, which hosted ceremonies of state, is now a museum.

The Chowmahalla is really not one but four palaces in a quadrangle, with a pool of water in the middle. The Nizam would enter through the front gates, while everyone else used a side entrance in the wall: 'the car would swing into a short circular driveway which leads to a portico almost medievally Spanish in appearance'. Then came another door and a long, narrow, twisting corridor which eventually opened into the courtyard at the heart of the palace complex.[63] Each of the four palaces had its own reception room, and each was coloured differently (though always with an element of gold): ruby red and gold, purple and gold, green and gold and pink and gold. The chandeliers were Turkish and Venetian; the furniture pre-revolution French and occasionally English, from the Victorian period.[64]

The Nizam gave audiences to his noblemen and courtiers on Eid, Nowruz (the Persian New Year) and his birthday in the Chowmahalla's Durbar Hall, a spectacle of late Indo-Islamic architecture with all the usual vaulted arches, towers and turrets. Around nine o'clock in the evening on these occasions, the Nizam sat cross-legged on a white marble throne, surrounded by his sons, as his noblemen and courtiers (all 'especially overdressed for the occasion... in rich silks and brocades') paid homage and offered gifts to exhibit their loyalty.

Arab guards bearing swords and daggers stood around the hall, and musicians would play pieces written especially for the occasion.

AN ORIENTAL DREAM

The women of the court watched from the gallery. One side of the hall opened onto a traditional Mughal garden, flanked by beautiful cypresses and palms, and dotted with fountains.[65] Today, the fountains no longer run. The whole palace, usually full of tourists (mostly Indian Muslims), feels like a giant relic.

Not so the Falaknuma Palace, which was once in disrepair but was fabulously restored in the early part of this century and made into a luxury hotel, a pilgrimage destination for India's wealthy elites. One afternoon I turned up at the palace with James Wrathall, a good friend of mine from Cambridge. We had intended just to take a look at the palace from the outside, but that plan failed and we ended up accidentally staying for afternoon tea—an elaborate affair involving Earl Grey and unusual paan (betel-leaf) sandwiches, which we enjoyed as European classical music played in the background. This was an expensive paragraph to write.

The Falaknuma is very much alive and bustling. Architecturally it is extraordinary, melding a European Palladian style with Indo-Islamic twists. The complex was built by Vikhar-ul-Omara, a wealthy nobleman, in the 1880s. He gave it to the sixth Nizam when he was facing bankruptcy in exchange for financial help. The palace was where the Nizam then hosted the Viceroy and visiting British royals; sometimes he stayed there himself.[66] Its grand marble staircase was built in an Italian style, and at its foot is a statue of Calliope—the Greek goddess of epic poetry. Along the wall are portraits of British imperial heroes like Clive of India, the Marquis of Hastings and Lord Metcalfe. At the top of the stairs there is a portrait of Salar Jung I, the 'builder of Hyderabad'.[67] To the left of the landing is the throne room, in which the Nizam and Viceroy would sit side by side on gold chairs on formal occasions. The room was more often used for ballroom dancing. In the old days, two tiger skins lay on the wooden floor and bibelots of naked Greek goddesses stood behind the chairs.[68]

Beyond lies the banquet hall, home to a 101-foot-long dining table that could seat more than a hundred guests. There is a room for playing cards, too, and billiard and smoking suites with oak-panelled walls, wooden ceilings and leather chairs studded with brass. In the palace's glory days an elaborate hookah with four tubes would sit by the chairs, and smokers could gaze upon a picture on the wall depicting 'a buxom Indian damsel reclining on a chair in a thinking position, her right hand resting under her head.'[69] The Falaknuma perfectly exemplifies the dizzyingly cosmopolitan and paradoxical world of elite Hyderabad in the late nineteenth and early twentieth centuries.

The King Kothi Palace, meanwhile, hosted the zenana, the term used in India for the harem.[70] The Nizam, though generally austere, still had four wives, each with their own luxurious quarters. His first wife, Dulhan Pasha Begum, was the daughter of a nobleman, and looked 'more lovely than any bird of paradise', thought one visitor who saw her 'as the amber dusk of India was stealing in through the latticed window'.[71] She and the Nizam had three children—a daughter and two sons. Another of the Nizam's wives was Gowher Begum, a niece of Aga Khan III.

The Nizam's unmarried daughters weren't kept in seclusion—they attended parties and went to races.[72] In the zenana, there were forty-two women. The Nizam's favourite concubine was a Hindu woman, Leila Begum, who bore him no fewer than eight children. Most concubines, tasked with spending nights with the Nizam, were from poor families. Many mothers would send word that they had a beautiful daughter, often through the maidservants of courtiers' wives, to the Nizam's courtiers. If the plan worked and the Nizam became aware of the young woman's existence, he would either direct a senior woman of the palace to go and look at her and decide if she should be admitted, or would summon her to the palace to decide for himself.

From time to time, an attendant of the Nizam's mother was admitted to the zenana: on the ruler's birthday, the chosen girl would be 'bathed in sandalwood oil, perfumed with attar, dressed in new clothes of silks and gold and sent to the Nizam with his mother's blessing.'[73] To have a daughter in the zenana was considered a superlative honour, and for this reason, it wasn't unusual for a nobleman to present his daughter to the Nizam. She would end up in the zenana, paid an income according to her status and the children she had borne the Nizam.[74]

Whereas the Ottoman harem was guarded by eunuchs, the Nizam, unusually, had an all-female guard protecting his zenana, tasked with ensuring that none of the concubines had any secret communication with men visiting the palace.[75] The air within was perfumed with mimosa and jasmine. On a normal day, the women would lie 'on couches of brocade and silk', drinking perfumed coffee and talking. Some of them played musical instruments, while others sang or read poetry, 'their eyes holding longing or resignation'.[76]

Arabian Nights

The extravagance of Hyderabad's courtly culture, drenched with opulence, was legendary. Hyderabadi Congress politician Sarojini Naidu proclaimed the court to be the 'only true eastern court left in India', with 'all the barbaric splendour that recalls the stories of the Arabian Nights'.[77] The *New York Times* described it simply as 'weird'.[78] It published an account in 1926 of life at court that emphasised its most exotic elements:

> A strange pageant passes through his marble halls—magistrates, philosophers, rich marawis of India who come to display their gorgeous fabrics and jewels, debauchees who fan themselves with peacock feathers, gourmands fattened by high living, the dreamy-eyed users of hashish, the effete, the supercilious, the curious, the coarse, the delicate, the pleasure-loving and the effeminate result of old culture with his highly pitched voice.[79]

These elites attended buffet suppers at which:

> the men were elegant in black sherwanis or gorgeous in gold brocade, the ladies wore saris of sapphire or flame-colour or starlit blue; they moved here and there between flowering bushes, enjoying the scented dusk, just cool enough after the heat of the day, clustering like bees round their queen in the flood-lighted centre of the gathering, or stepping for a moment away from the bright centre to rest the eyes or to look up at the brilliance of the stars. Everyone seemed to be happy and witty and amused; the tables were covered with Persian pilaos, Mughal kebabs, Indian curries, French salads—dishes to suit every taste.[80]

Sultan Ghalib told me that the Nizam 'did not like the display of excess in any form by any member of his family'. The Sultan recalled that his mother, the Nizam's niece, attended official dinners and would say that 'should any family member appear to take a second helping, the Nizam would swiftly cast a disapproving glance in that person's direction'.[81]

In the early years of his reign, the Nizam had taken to ballroom dancing and held regular parties attended by everyone from the British Resident and his wife to 'local jazz fiends', at which orchestras would play such fashionable pieces as 'Whispering' and 'I'm Forever Blowing Bubbles'.[82] According to Sultan Ghalib, however, the Nizam wasn't personally fond of any form of Western music, 'which he would tolerate when the occasion demanded', usually for the entertainment of British guests. Hyderabad was, after all, the Sultan said, the 'last repository of Mughal culture'. Thus the Nizam 'was well versed in Indian classical genres to an expert level, and would invite and listen to the renditions of great Indian classical performers of his day, to which selected members of his court would be invited and his family would listen from behind screens'. One such musician was Ustad Bade Ghulam Ali, one of the most renowned classical singers of the century—who moved to Pakistan after the fall of Hyderabad.[83]

Often, the Nizam's guests would gather on couches and cushions to watch a 'graceful dancing-girl, slim as a golden lily', whose 'body sways from the waist to the strains of the wailing sitar, played by a boy who sits on the floor beside her.' American readers of the *Times* were treated to a vivid description of a courtesan's performance:

> She sweeps downward like a bird alighting from a tree. She is up again, her gleaming back glistening for a moment before the next plunge… Light as a soap bubble, she floats over the velvet carpet, her curved thumbs thrust out in invitation to the watching men. Suddenly her long lashes droop and ambush the dreamy eyes. She sinks to the floor and is still. Poor golden lily! Her appeal must ever be to the animal appetite.[84]

In reality courtesans, common in Indo-Islamic courts throughout their history, were often highly educated property owners who wielded immense power.[85] Often they lived in luxury apartments; wealthy courtiers would bid for a courtesan, and her patron would shower her with money and gifts in return for the pleasure of her company. The British criminalised them and categorised courtesans as prostitutes. In Hyderabad, by contrast, they preserved their prestigious status and enjoyed significant patronage.

Hyderabad's courtly culture—with all its dinners, classical music performances, patronage of Islamic art and scholarship, courtesans and concubines—was quite typical of Indo-Islamic courts. There were some British influences, certainly, but the Nizam's court represented the last significant flowering of Indo-Islamic high culture, in all its famous sophistication, beauty and (as many saw it) decadence. This elevated Hyderabad's position in the consciousness of Indian Muslim thinkers, and cemented its status as heir to the Mughal legacy.

And the most significant aspect of this culture was poetry, of central cultural importance in India. The development of Urdu literature began in early modern Gujarat and reached its apotheosis in late Mughal Delhi.[86] In Hyderabad, it replaced Persian as the official language of the state in 1884.[87] Many of the greatest Urdu poets of the age, who would previously have flocked to the Mughal court, gravitated towards Hyderabad. Foremost among these in the late nineteenth century was Nawab Mirza Khan 'Dagh' Dehlvi. He was raised in Mughal Delhi but after its fall made Hyderabad his adopted home; one of the greatest Urdu poets ever, Dagh's verse was known for being intricate, sophisticated and intensely erotic.[88]

Under the seventh Nizam, Prime Minister Maharaja Kishen Pershad oversaw the poetic life of the capital.[89] He produced no fewer than sixty books, despite his busy day job. His literary salon was famous, and frequented by poets from across India, including Iqbal.[90] The great Hindu Bengali poet Rabindranath Tagore visited Hyderabad in 1933, on the Nizam's invitation. Tagore was particularly impressed with Osmania University, which was the first Indian university to teach in an Indian language (Urdu), telling the Nizam that 'I have long been waiting for the day when freed from the shackles of a foreign language, our education becomes naturally accessible to all our people.' Tagore was greeted as a celebrity and hosted at countless mushairas (gatherings where poetry was recited).[91]

From 1911 to 1938, at least 61 Urdu poets in the Deccan were women. Many in Hyderabad were from the aristocracy, but some were middle-class too.[92] This had a long precedent: Mah Laqa Bai Chanda, the second Nizam's favourite courtesan, was the first-ever published female Urdu poet.[93] As in much of the Islamic world, poetry was recited and enjoyed across society—from princes and nobles to street urchins.[94]

The Nizam's court was frequented by Qawwali masters, who performed renditions of mystical poetry to the beat of the drum and the gurgle of the hookah. Osman Ali Khan himself was a dedicated poet, and composed his verse with a pencil on small scraps of paper. His tutor, the accomplished poet Jaleel Manikpuri, would mark his work with red ink, providing tentative corrections and enthusiastic praise. The poems would then be recited in Maharaja Pershad's mushairas—invariably to ecstatic exclamations of appreciation and wonder all round.[95]

At one point the Nizam was given the idea by some of his courtiers that his poetry should be made a set text for students at the Osmania University. He proposed it to the Urdu professor, Moulvi Abdul Haq. Horrified, the professor replied that the Nizam's verse was so stunningly accomplished that the professor himself couldn't hope to properly teach it. The Nizam agreed to abandon the idea.[96]

Given that a major trope in Urdu poetry is the benighted lover pining after a cruel or otherwise inaccessible beloved, the Nizam—with his zenana of concubines—was forced to compose often extremely imaginatively. He was unlikely to have been talking from experience when he wrote the following (here in an English translation):

> She would not hear the story.
> Of yearning love and pain.
> No word she let me utter
> All efforts were in vain.[97]

Nor this:

> Nay, ask me not the reason
> Why tears of blood must flow.

> Ask blood-stained lids and lashes;
> They must the reason know.⁹⁸

But the Nizam also used poetry to express his vision of Islamic rulership, and his view of himself as a Muslim leader:

> Sultans of old, O Osman, have all died
> By your rule are Muslims now identified.⁹⁹

It was likely with this in mind that he agreed to financially support the deposed Ottoman Caliph.

7

'I WILL NOT GO BACK TO A SLAVE COUNTRY'

Syed Ali Imam, who had been Hyderabad's prime minister from 1919 to 1922, visited Sayyid Amir Ali in London shortly before Caliph Abdulmejid's secretary, Salih Keramet Nigar, had arrived there. The latter informed the prime minister of the scale of Abdulmejid's financial struggles, and asked him to tell the Nizam.[1] Ali Imam duly returned to Hyderabad and suggested to Osman Ali Khan that he would greatly enhance his standing in the Islamic world by financially supporting the deposed Caliph.

The Nizam, who felt guilty for not having supported the Ottomans in the First World War, readily agreed to the plan.[2] 'I consider it a religious duty to help [Abdulmejid] as much as I can,' the Nizam said, 'in accordance with the religious principle that one Muslim is the sibling to another Muslim'. Abdulmejid was overjoyed, and his letter of thanks expressed 'heartfelt gratitude and appreciation to you for supporting the Muslims.'[3] The British sought assurances from the Nizam that he was not seeking to revive the Caliphate, which he gave before they allowed him to pay the deposed Caliph a pension.[4]

A Caliph on the French Riviera

The Caliph now had some breathing room, and wanted to settle down. France, where some other Ottoman exiles had settled, seemed the obvious option. The French Riviera was fast becoming the stomping ground of Europe's aristocracy.[5] The French were widely seen as having achieved the pinnacle of fine living and high culture; Paris, not London, was the most fashionable capital in Europe. And the south of France, which was warm and bright and terribly romantic, was alluring to anyone artistic—like writers, painters, actors and musicians—or simply rich.[6] For a Francophile like Caliph Abdulmejid, the Riviera was a dream.

Its coastline was famously dazzling, with intimate bays, olive trees and pines, and fresh air perfumed with rosemary and thyme. The sea was nearly always blue. When the American Jane de Glehn arrived on the Riviera after the war, having witnessed devastation in eastern France, she was stunned by its 'innumerable villas perched on the hills and clouded with flowers', its 'glowing white walls and basking blue bays'. It was like stepping into another, glorious world.[7] Prince Omer Faruk and Princess Sabiha ended up there; so did some of Sultan Abdulhamid's descendants.[8] Prince Ali Vasib, a young man in the prime of his life, found Nice to be marvellously beautiful and cosmopolitan. He was delighted to be woken up on his first and 'gloriously sunny' morning there by a band of Italian musicians playing Neapolitan melodies on the street below.[9]

Vasib made the official inquiries with the French government to secure Abdulmejid a visa to come to France.[10] In October 1924, the Caliphal family settled in a villa in Cimiez, a glamorous high-society district.[11] But the rent was exorbitant, and the family soon moved out and set up house in a nineteenth-century seafront villa in Nice, called the Palais Carabacel. It was owned by an Italian Catholic, who had placed two marble angels in front of the villa. Abdulmejid thought this unseemly for the residence of a Caliph, so he planted magnolia trees in front of them, until eventually the angels were hidden from sight.

Inside the villa, a grand marble stairway opened up in two wings. On the landing was a stained-glass portrait of St George—also placed there by the Catholic owner. Abdulmejid found another creative solution, ordering two statues of boys with objects on their heads (commonly found in Venice) to be placed in front of the portrait. But St George was still slightly visible, so the Caliph had a full-length mirror put in front of the statues to completely block the portrait from view.[12]

'I WILL NOT GO BACK TO A SLAVE COUNTRY'

Abdulmejid tried to keep up many of the customs observed in the Dolmabahce at home, but in public, his granddaughter Princess Neslishah later recalled, 'he was a real European. If it hadn't been for the fez he wore, he would have looked like an accomplished European intellectual.' Abdulmejid dressed smartly but simply—in the winter, he wore a scarf and coat, and was driven around in a large Fiat by a uniformed Austrian named Adolf.[13]

In the villa, he read prolifically and never missed his five daily prayers. He also hosted many of Nice's artists and writers for tea; breaking with Ottoman convention, the women of the house would attend these gatherings.[14] For leisure, the Caliph painted in the attic, which he had converted into a sort of studio. Evenings were for music: often he would hold concerts, with his daughter-in-law Princess Sabiha on the violin, Princess Durrushehvar's mother Lady Atiye Mehisti playing the cello and Abdulmejid himself on the piano.[15]

Most of the food served was French. At one point, Abdulmejid employed a cook who had worked in the palace in Vienna, but the Caliph offered him so much unsolicited advice on how to prepare the meals that the cook finally barged into the dining room one day, exclaimed 'Your Majesty, I cannot work in a house where people don't understand anything about food!' and promptly resigned.[16] By contrast, in Prince Omer Faruk's house the food was always Turkish: usually meatballs and pilaf rice. The Armenian cook was also fond of making salads, which the women of the household liked, but Faruk hated ('Am I a goat to eat weeds?').[17]

Princess Durrushehvar spent her teenage years on the Riviera, and it shaped her just as much as her childhood in Istanbul had done. She studied Turkish, English, French, Persian and Arabic, played music, rode, swam and went on daily walks with her father. From the age of eleven the princess began submitting short stories and essays in French to children's magazines, winning 'a good many prizes' for her writing and pictures.[18] The British Resident in Hyderabad, Sir Terence Keyes, would in 1932 be terribly impressed by Durrushehvar, then a young adult, judging her to be 'extraordinarily well-educated' with an 'excellent style in English and French'. Her magazine contributions showed 'real poetic feeling', although her music skill 'is hardly up to her critical standard', Keyes judged, conceding that she at least had 'temperament and enthusiasm'. Overall, he thought, Durrushehvar 'is beautiful; has great dignity and *savoir faire* and a very strong character.'[19]

Durrushehvar's English teacher, Julia Gertrude (who had a room in the villa) was an English spy—or so everyone believed. It didn't help that every Tuesday on her day off she would put on a special hat, announce 'I am going to my lawyer', and vanish until late in the evening. The Ottomans were convinced she was doing one of two things: reporting to the British Consulate in Nice, or meeting a fellow spy to file a report on goings-on in the villa. But since there was more music than intrigue afoot, no one was particularly bothered.[20]

The exiles also witnessed France's dark side, which it owed to its expansive Empire. Abdulmejid once took his grandchildren on a day out to the local zoo and was stunned to see an exhibition set up as an African village, replete with straw and grass—and men, women and children from Africa. 'The men and women were wandering around practically naked, and the French people were staring at them as if they were seeing wild animals, but enjoying it,' Princess Neslishah later recalled. The children were disturbed; the Caliph was horrified. 'Look what these civilised French people are doing, exhibiting humans like animals,' he said, disgusted, and they left the zoo. Abdulmejid's Francophilia wasn't boundless.[21]

The Caliph took to visiting the beach in the summer, though not in Nice, since he 'thought that Muslims living in Nice might get strange ideas if they saw the caliph swimming'. Instead he had Adolf drive him to Cagnes-sur-Mer and could be seen roaming around in his swimming shorts.[22] Meanwhile, Ali Vasib spent so much time sunbathing he received a painful sunburn, but since 'the beaches were full of good-looking girls of every kind', he decided to endure it.[23]

High society in the south of France

Celebrities were so common in the south of France that unlike in Switzerland, no one batted an eyelid at the House of Osman's presence. Far more prominent was legendary dress designer Coco Chanel, who lived on the Riviera with the Duke of Westminster.[24] Famous Irish director Rex Ingram, whose wife Alice Terry was one of the most glamorous film stars of the day, was living in Nice at that time. Vasib danced with Terry at the Negresco, while her husband, who had recently won accolades for directing the smash hit *The Four Horsemen of the Apocalypse* (1921), made the Caliph's acquaintance. The two became good friends, and Abdulmejid introduced him to Islam. The movie director soon became a Muslim, and the Caliph produced an oil painting of him.[25] Abdulmejid's influence was clear in Ingram's later artistic output: he went on to direct *The Garden of Allah* (1927), a romantic drama set in Algeria based on a 1904 novel and starring his wife as the heroine.[26]

Finances were tight, however. The Nizam's money only went so far; the family was large and life in Nice was expensive. In late 1925 Sultan Mehmed Vahideddin (still in San Remo) asked the family to give him power of attorney so he could try to re-establish the House of Osman's rights over property in formerly Ottoman land in the Arab world. Abdulmejid strongly opposed this: after all, he reasoned, he was the Caliph—and Vahideddin's escape from Istanbul had been less than glorious. Most of the family, though, were keen on putting on a united front to launch a lawsuit. A deputation from San Remo presented Abdulmejid with a document to sign, giving his cousin power of attorney. The Caliph caused a stir by signing the document as 'Abdulmejid Han, Caliph of the World, Successor to the Prophet of the Lord of the Universe' (the Sultan, by contrast, had signed simply as 'Mehmed Vahideddin'). This made the document unusable, since it cast doubt on whether Vahideddin was indeed head of the family.[27] The Sultan then died of a heart attack in 1926, after which Abdulmejid was given full power of attorney.[28]

The Caliph ultimately resolved to divide his money by giving everyone (male or female) equal shares, apart from people whose fathers were still alive—including Vasib.[29] He was devastated that he had to sell some tie pins and cufflinks.[30] But others cut more tragic figures, like Princess Seniha—the sister of the late Sultan Abdulhamid II, who in Istanbul 'wore a crown', looked 'very imperial and had a beautiful face'.[31] Living in Nice in her seventies, however, her condition had dramatically changed and she was utterly depressed. Seniha once went for a walk and rested on a bench in her old black clothes. A kindly Frenchman passing by thought she was a beggar and gave her some money—which she accepted.[32]

The paradox of life on the Riviera was that while the Ottomans were far from rich, they were welcomed into high society and had to keep up appearances. The provincial governor, Count Benedetti, regularly invited the exiles to dances.[33] Meanwhile Prince Osman Fuad, ever the entertainer, hosted guests at his villa to play billiards and bought an open-topped Italian car.[34] His sister Princess Adile was a single mother to Princess Niloufer, described by Vasib as a 'good-looking, dark-haired girl with a good deal of charm'— but rather spoilt.[35] She would often join Vasib and the others on shopping expeditions in Nice, and on nights out.[36]

The nightclub was invented in the 1920s. The tumult of the war had triggered massive liberalising social change, and wealthy young French women in the 1920s often cut their hair short (which would have previously been scandalous), drove fancy cars, danced the night away in nightclubs and smoked opium and tobacco. It became fashionable to wear 'loose drop-waisted gowns, which grew shorter as the decade wore on', 'worn with silver hose and, against the chill of a Riviera winter evening, cloak-coats edged with fur.'[37] In the winter the Cote D'Azur was at its most vibrant, and the halls of its hotels were constantly full of people drinking and dancing. The younger Ottoman exiles made regular trips into Cannes, with its fashionable music hall where the women wore formal dresses, the men wore dinner jackets or tailcoats and Billy Arnold's famous jazz orchestra played.[38]

In Nice the Ottomans favoured the Negresco hotel, where at a dance one might see, as Prince Ali Vasib put it, 'four or five kings and any number of princes, dukes and counts... the women would put on their finest evening dresses and adorn themselves with jewellery, so that one might have mistaken these paragons of beauty and elegance for the houris [maidens] that are said to inhabit the Muslim Paradise.'[39] In 1926 the dispossessed Shah of Persia, Ahmad Shah Qajar, stayed at the Negresco, and his brother, Crown Prince

Hassan, went out with Omer Faruk, Sabiha and Ali Vasib to a cabaret bar.[40]

Often the local opera house would host nightlong costume balls, at which the guests (including Nice's provincial governor and his family) all donned masks and gowns.[41] This was European high society in all its glittering glory, ultimately to come crashing down with the onset of the Second World War. 'Never again did the world witness such a time of stylish elegance,' Vasib reflected wistfully years later.[42] But still all the exiles longed for Istanbul, which was their home. The Riviera could never make up for it.

The rise of Hindu nationalism

While the Ottoman exiles adjusted to their new lives, in India political conflict was on the rise. As the Ali brothers turned away from the Congress, they explored alternative political ideas for India's future and increased their engagement with the broader Islamic world. This formed the backdrop to Maulana Shaukat Ali's eventual great scheme to tie the Asaf Jahi dynasty to the House of Osman.

The Congress and the Muslim League had only been briefly in alliance, during the Khilafat Movement. What came next was permanent antagonism. A significant turning point was the outbreak of Hindu-Muslim riots in 1924. In Kohat in the north west, a Hindu author published an anti-Islam poem, leading to Muslim mobs attacking Hindus. Gandhi and the Ali brothers fell out over this incident, as both sides blamed each other for the conflagration.[43]

By this point, a Hindu nationalism with a strong anti-Muslim tenor was in the ascendancy. It emerged from the annals of British colonial discourse, which presented India as a fundamentally Hindu land which had enjoyed an ancient golden age, disrupted by a medieval tragedy in which the natives were crushed by Muslim invaders, who governed as foreigners and oppressed them. It was a narrative that conveniently presented British rule as a glorious respite from Muslim depravity.[44] Meanwhile, among Hindu thinkers, the idea of a united India-wide Hindu community had developed and by the late nineteenth century embraced the idea of Muslims being a separate nation.[45]

This strengthened a similar sense among Indian Muslims that they were a single community united by Islam. All these ideas gained new significance with the onset of electoral politics, when politicians seeking votes began thinking in terms of demographic blocs and interest groups.[46] In the early 1920s Muhammad Ali Jinnah, sceptical of how democratic politics would work in India, argued that Indian democracy would produce a permanent Hindu majority, which he argued would mean the majoritarian domination of Muslims.[47] The various political visions that Indian Muslim elites (used to being in charge, or at least at an advantage over Hindus) developed were attempts to grapple with this reality.

In the early 1900s, after Muslims were awarded a separate electorate (reserved seats for Muslims to guarantee that they would enjoy proportional representation), Hindu urban elites began organising Hindu sabhas (associations). These led to the establishment of the Hindu Mahasabha, a faction within the Congress Party that promoted Hindu nationalism, in 1915.[48] It was in the 1920s, against the backdrop of the Khilafat Movement, that Hindu nationalists began to see Muslims (whose true loyalties, apparently, were with Istanbul and Mecca) as their main enemy.[49]

During the Khilafat Movement, some Hindu nationalists supported the cause and advocated for pluralism: the thinker Lala Lajpat Rai, for example, supported the idea of a Hindu nation and saw Islam as a foreign intrusion, but also believed that Muslims and Christians should be allowed to flourish alongside Hindus. He firmly supported the Khilafat Movement in its heyday, and saw it not just as a legitimate struggle for Muslims but also as good for Hindus because of its anti-colonial tenor. That changed by 1924 once the movement had faltered—he came to see Islamic politics as unhelpful to the cause of Indian independence and even as a potential threat to Hindus, making him increasingly sympathetic to the Hindu Mahasabha.[50]

The real watershed moment was the publication of *Essentials of Hindutva* in 1923. Its author, Vinayak Savarkar, is today one of India's most revered and notorious figures. An atheist, he was uninterested in matters of faith and wrote that a 'Hindu is primarily a citizen either in himself or through his forebears'.[51] Of Muslims and

Christians, he asserted that 'their names and their outlook smack of a foreign origin. Their love is divided.'[52] And it was in the 'prolonged furious conflict' between India's natives and Muslim invaders (here he relied on the orientalist historical narrative) that Hindus became 'Hindutva'.[53] Savarkar's teachings defined what came to be the dominant form of Hindu nationalism.

He saw the Khilafat Movement as evidence that Indian Muslims were disloyal to India and fundamentally alien.[54] On 25 February 1925, Savarkar met Maulana Shaukat Ali in Bombay, and the two clashed ferociously. Savarkar asked Ali whether he would abandon the Khilafat Movement, saying he would give up his Hindutva mobilisation—aimed at consolidating a united Hindu community—in return. Ali retorted that Savarkar's movement was 'blatantly anti-Muslim', which the latter fervently denied. Ali then accused Savarkar of hindering the fight against the British; 'a foreign force has occupied us and is hell-bent on ruining both our communities.'[55]

Savarkar demanded that Muslims give up proselytising Islam to Hindus; Ali insisted that conversions weren't based on coercion, and that 'people are taking up the truth faith out of their own enlightenment.' In response, Savarkar recalled centuries of Islamic rule as the explanation for his viewpoint. 'Thieves from across the world came in and looted our possessions,' he declared. 'Today we [Hindus] have gathered some sense, become alert and have decided to keep our doors locked.' What is clear from this debate—which ended without any resolution being reached—is that Hindu nationalists saw Muslim political movements and claims as fundamentally threatening, and this spurred on their own mobilisation.[56]

Shaukat Ali's brother, Maulana Mohamed Ali, blamed the British colonial historical narrative for anti-Muslim Hindu nationalist sentiment. In British history, he complained, the Muslim was painted as 'an unmitigated barbarian whom a cruel fate turned into a missionary.' Ali also criticised Muslim modernist reformers and puritans who demonised the history of Islam in India by portraying it as inauthentic and the 'least splendid portion of the story of Islam'. This, he maintained, weakened for many Muslims their love of India and comfort in their own identity.

Such a Muslim reformist 'dreamt dreams,' Ali complained,

> but they were not those of restored Delhi, or a revived Agra, but of a new Cordova, a reincarnation of Baghdad. There has grown up in his manner a false conception, on the one hand of India as the land of a new Hindu nationality, and on the other, a mischievous isolation and dangerous detachment from the land which has been the home of Mussalmans for so many centuries.[57]

Muslims themselves had to feel Indian to be accepted as such, he argued.

At the same time, though, Ali had no patience for Hindu nationalist demands that Muslims clarify whether they were more loyal to Islam or India; he mocked those demands as being 'the inanities of the young mother who asks the baby, "Will Popsy-Wopsy tell mummy if Popsy Wopsy loves its biggy wiggy daddy more or its teeny-weeny Mummy".' Muslims did not seek separation from Hindus, he maintained, but simply 'freedom to live and fit themselves for an honourable place in Indian unity'.[58]

The Hindu Mahasabha, the Hindu nationalist faction within the Congress, objected to the Delhi Proposals of 1927, which were brought forward by an all-Muslim parties meeting and asked for a guaranteed one-third representation for Muslims in the central government, as well as reserved representation for Muslim politicians in Punjab and Bengal in proportion to their Muslim populations. The Congress leadership caved in to the Mahasabha and the proposals were rejected.[59]

The next year, the Nehru Report (named after Jawaharlal's father, the Congress stalwart Motilal Nehru) took away separate electorates for Muslims without promising them one-third representation at the centre.[60] Secular Indian nationalists, claiming to represent all Indians, thus consistently opposed the Muslim League's proposals for constitutional safeguards for Muslims. In large part, this was due to their ideological conviction that religion was unimportant and backward, and that religious differences would dissolve with India's freedom and the establishment of socialism. They believed the political safeguards the League demanded would only perpetuate harmful religious differences and had to be opposed for the sake of

Indian unity. All the while, though, Hindu nationalists were wielding influence within their own party.

This was a turning point for the Ali brothers and marked their almost total disenchantment with the Congress and turn towards the Muslim League. For Mohamed Ali, India needed to become a federation 'so that the central unitary Government with a permanent Hindu majority should not override [Muslims] every where'. Like many other politicians, the federal principle became his proposed resolution to the prospect of majoritarian domination.

Ali argued for giving 'full power to Muslims in such provinces as those in which they are in a majority, whether small or large, and protection to them in such provinces as those in which they are in a minority, and in order to be absolutely fair to the Hindu community also, precisely the same thing must be done with the Hindus.'[61] In response to the Nehru Report, an All-India Muslim Parties Conference met in Delhi in January 1929 and produced a 'Delhi Manifesto'. Spearheaded by Jinnah, it recommended one-third Muslim representation at the centre and a federal system; the Congress duly rejected it.[62]

And so Muslim thinkers increasingly began to develop myriad political imaginations—alternatives to the mainstream Congress vision for what India after British rule could look like. A revived global Caliphate centred in an Indian federation would be one of them.

The quest for an Islamic modernity

The concept of religion first emerged after what are now called the Wars of Religion (1530–1630) in Europe, as Enlightenment thinkers attempted to carve out a space free from what they saw as the all-encompassing dominance of the Church. Increasingly over the next few centuries, Christianity became marginalised in society, pushed into a distinct 'religious' sphere.[63] Since the process of secularisation in the European context defined what religion was and how Christianity came to be understood, Islam could only wear the religious label uncomfortably.[64]

Sir Muhammad Iqbal argued that Islam did indeed have a 'division of the religious and political functions of the state', but it was just that—

'a division of functions'.⁶⁵ This meant, he argued, that the secular sphere as understood in Europe, which was to be non-religious, made no sense from an Islamic perspective: 'All that is secular is, therefore, sacred in the roots of its being,' he maintained. 'There is no such thing as a profane world… All is holy ground.'⁶⁶ Much like Gandhi, Iqbal was a strident critic of secularism, arguing that 'if politics is separated from religion, it degenerates into gangsterism'.⁶⁷

But the British Empire, along with other colonial powers, had tried to secularise Islam in the eighteenth and nineteenth centuries by strictly defining the Shari'a, Islamic law, as relevant to family or personal status law. This meant that the Shari'a's jurisdiction couldn't stretch beyond private family affairs and Islam was 'effectively reduced to formal religious doctrine'.⁶⁸ One significant Muslim response to secularisation was Islamism, a political tradition that emerged in the late Ottoman Empire.⁶⁹ In the 1920s many prominent Islamist thinkers fled Turkey to escape Kemalist reforms, with some going to Egypt, including former Ottoman Grand Mufti Mustafa Sabri. These figures had a deep influence on the development of Islamism through the Egyptian Muslim Brotherhood.⁷⁰ Many Islamists sought to counter secularisation by adopting a maximalist approach to the Shari'a that in some cases treated Islam itself as a law rather than religion, although this approach wasn't universal.⁷¹

By contrast, Maulana Mohamed Ali didn't see Islam solely as law, instead arguing that 'I have a culture, a polity, an outlook on life—a complete synthesis which is Islam.'⁷² Prizing free thought and speech, he saw 'narrow orthodoxy', obsessed with identifying and attacking heretics, as one of the world's great evils.⁷³ On modernisation he favoured a nuanced approach, taking a famous quote by the Prophet as his guide: 'Take the good, leave out the evil'. Reform was necessary, but that didn't mean embracing everything that came out of Europe and rejecting Islam, since 'to leave Islam from the program of Muslim regeneration,' he asserted, 'would be like acting the play of Hamlet without the Prince of Denmark.'⁷⁴ Similarly, Marmaduke Pickthall—who edited Hyderabad's *Islamic Culture* and thought the Nizam's rapidly modernising polity was a good model of Islamic government—supported reform but criticised the idea of 'mere progress for the sake of progress'.⁷⁵

Their approaches had much in common with that of Caliph Abdulmejid. He was committed to the idea of an Islamic modernity, and didn't see Islam solely through the prism of law or devotional activity. Other spheres of human endeavour were also important— he supported mastering new technology while remaining Islamic in motivation and outlook. Cultural production, he believed, was also key to revival and success: 'Religion, sound morality, science, and culture will ensure the peace and hopeful future of our nation', Abdulmejid had declared during the final days of the Ottoman Empire.[76]

In sensibility, too, Mohamed Ali had a lot in common with the Caliph, being an art connoisseur and a music lover. On a visit to Egypt, Ali was delighted to find musical instruments and paintings in the house of a leading jurist, Sheikh Shawesh. Ali displayed paintings in his own drawing room and opposed what he called attempts to 'imprison women in the home'. Later, after the collapse of the Ottomans, Ali maintained that radical secularisation in Turkey, which he opposed, was nonetheless 'to some extent a reaction against the narrowmindedness of the ulema' there.[77]

These were reformers with radical and innovative visions for Islam in the modern world—not tired restorationists calling for the anachronistic resurrection of an old order. Shaukat Ali and Pickthall both believed that Hyderabad, heir to the Mughal legacy and culture, a modernising and wealthy state, should become the new seat of the Caliphate. At this point, many Muslims suggested to the Nizam that he should seek to promote himself from a prince to a king—and Caliph along with it, so that the wealthiest Muslim family could claim the most vaunted political title in Islam. But the Nizam was perfectly aware that the British would never tolerate this and rejected the idea out of hand.[78] Ali and Pickthall would take a different, and more convincing, approach.

British betrayal and the Palestinian struggle

As Indian politics grew more challenging for the Ali brothers, they sought to deepen their connections with politicians elsewhere in the Islamic world. In January 1926 Ibn Saud proclaimed himself King of

Saudi Arabia in the Hejaz. That summer, a World Muslim Congress was held there, drawing Muslim leaders and notables from across the world to discuss the future of Islam.[79] The Ali brothers, who had been invited, met the King. It went badly—Mohamed Ali implored Ibn Saud to establish a republic and make Saudi Arabia a democratic country. The King, being a king, was unimpressed.[80]

During the same period, the brothers entered into correspondence with Mufti Haj Amin al-Hussaini, then Mufti of Jerusalem and a major opponent of Zionist settlement in the British Mandate of Palestine. Famous today for his stridently anti-British politics in the late 1930s and 1940s, a period in which he sought alliances with fascist Germany and Italy against the British, Hussaini had previously been a radically different figure who worked pragmatically under the British Mandate.[81]

In the 1920s, the Palestinian cause was amassing attention. During the First World War Sir Henry McMahon, British High Commissioner in Cairo, had privately promised the then Sharif of Mecca that if he led a revolt against the Ottomans, Britain would grant him an independent Arab state. The Sharif upheld his end of the bargain, but as historian Peter Shambrook has recently shown, the British didn't uphold theirs—they later falsely denied that the region of Palestine had been included in the offer, refusing no fewer than twenty-four times to publish the correspondence over the next few decades.[82]

The Sharif had been double-crossed, which became clear when in 1917, British Foreign Secretary Lord Arthur Balfour made his infamous declaration that Britain would support the 'establishment in Palestine of a national home for the Jewish people'. This appeared to be a statement of support for the Zionist movement, which campaigned for the creation of a state for the heavily persecuted Jews of Europe. In reality, though, Britain intended to exploit the Zionists by using Jewish settlers in Palestine to help manage resistance to the colonial presence from native Palestinians. The British ultimately wanted Palestine for their Empire, not a Jewish state.[83]

In the 1920s, Mufti Hussaini collaborated with the British Mandate in Palestine, and in 1929 he even agreed to the creation of a parliament with proportional representation for Jews and

Palestinian Arabs, under British authority. The idea was blocked by Zionist leaders, including future Israeli Prime Minister David Ben-Gurion.[84] By 1930, most Palestinians feared that they faced the loss of their homeland. The Mufti, intent on raising the profile of the cause, established extensive connections with Muslim leaders elsewhere. The Ali brothers were particularly sympathetic.

Mohamed Ali had told Prime Minister David Lloyd George during the Khilafat Movement that 'there was every likelihood of all reasonable claims of Jews in search of a home being accepted' by Palestinian Muslims, adding that Muslims 'are not ashamed of their dealings with their Jewish neighbours, and can challenge a comparison with others in this respect' (this was a pointed dig at Europe's long history of antisemitic persecution). However, he argued, the idea of Jewish 'dominance' over the Palestinians was unacceptable.[85] Ali's death in December 1930 and the events it triggered would have far-reaching consequences not just for Hussaini, but for the Palestinian cause itself.

The Maulana's final address

As the Palestinian struggle was escalating, so was Indian political conflict. In London the Round Table Conference took place between November 1930 and January 1931 in the Royal Gallery, in the House of Lords. The event was intended to bring Indian politicians together under British auspices to thrash out a new constitutional arrangement for India. It was a response to the previous decade of agitation and turmoil and aimed to grant India dominion status, which meant self-rule under British auspices—as had been conceded to white settler dominions like Australia and Canada. Labour Prime Minister Ramsay MacDonald chaired the conference, which was attended throughout by government ministers and MPs from other parties.

But there was a spanner in the works: the largest Indian party, the Congress, boycotted the proceedings as part of a campaign of civil disobedience. Many of its leaders, Gandhi included, were in prison during the conference, which set it up to fail. That didn't stop the Muslim League attending, including Jinnah, Iqbal and the Ali brothers, as well as representatives of the princely states. Representing not just Hyderabad but the entire Indian [princely] states' delegation was Sir Akbar Hydari, then the Nizam's finance minister. Born in 1869 to a businessman in Bombay, Hydari had served the Nizam since 1905 in a range of different roles, including home secretary—and it was he who had established the Osmania University in 1918.

Hydari, enormously popular among those who knew him, was the sort of easy-going but sharp man that people liked to talk to, and collected miniature paintings in his spare time.[86] Pickthall served as secretary to the Hyderabadi delegation. Their agenda was to push for autonomy for the princely states within any potential Indian federation.[87] Hydari advocated for a weak central government with maximal autonomy for the princely states.[88]

Mohamed Ali, despite being dreadfully ill, was one of the conference's most prominent personalities. Early on he braved his illness to attend an official dinner, and then stayed after the food to smoke when cherrywood pipes were brought out, telling former prime minister and Tory Party leader Stanley Baldwin warmly that although 'a Conservative belonging to a party of the so-called idle rich, you have at least been human enough to establish this rule, that where only Coronas could be smoked after dinner an honest man could now bring out his shag, put it into a cherrywood pipe, as I used to do at Oxford, and smoke it.'[89]

Ali gave the final major speech of his life on 19 November. Despite being so frail that he had to speak while seated, his address was a tour de force of his characteristic wit and passion. He began by reading a list of his ailments to the assembled politicians:

> my dilated heart; with my approaching and recurrent blindness through retinitis; with my once-gangrened foot, with neuritis—this huge bulking foot through oedema; with albuminaria; with diabetes, and the whole long list that I could give you if Colonel Gidney [in the audience] would not think I was becoming his rival as a medical man.[90]

He followed this up with a poetry recitation, and then got on to business. British domination 'must be killed here', he declared, but not British friendship: 'We have a soft corner in our hearts for Great Britain. Let us retain it, I beseech you.' Tackling the issue of religious division, he said that whereas America was the United States, India would be the 'United Faiths', and quoted Tennyson:

> Not like to like, but like in difference;
> Self-reverent each and reverencing each;
> Distinct in individualities,
> But like each other, e'en as those who love.[91]

Ali told the British MPs that the Hindu-Muslim 'difficulty' was of 'your own creation', a result of 'divide and rule'—although, he added, 'there is a division of labour here. We divide and you rule. The moment we decide not to divide you will not be able to rule as you are doing today.' For the first time ever with democratisation, Ali noted, 'majority rule is to be introduced into India'. The solution to this was a federation, which also allowed for the princes and their order to survive.[92] Although a republican, Ali like his brother was sympathetic to the princely states, having worked in them and believing that they were worth preserving. 'No, Your Highness,' he declared, addressing an imaginary archetypal prince, 'we Our Lownesses, will do nothing without your consent.'

Ali then addressed the pressing question of Muslim loyalty to India, which so troubled the Hindu nationalists. He proclaimed that when it came to the divine command, 'I am a Muslim first, a Muslim second, and a Muslim last, and nothing but a Muslim.' However, he added, 'where India is concerned, where India's freedom is concerned, I am an Indian first, an Indian second, an Indian last, and nothing but an Indian. I belong to two circles of equal size, but which are not concentric. One is India, and the other is the Muslim world... We as Indian Muslims came in both circles. We belong to these two circles, each of more than 300 millions, and we can leave neither.'[93]

He also condemned European nationalism and rubbished the idea that Islam was a source of conflict, telling the British listeners: 'No religious wars, no crusades, have seen such holocausts and have been so cruel as your last war, and that was a war of your nationalism, and not my Jehad.' Ali declared he would accept no compromises and demanded complete Indian independence from Britain. He proclaimed that 'I want to go back to my country if I can go back with the substance of freedom in my hand. Otherwise,' he resolved, 'I will not go back to a slave country. I would even prefer to die in a foreign country, so long as it is a free country; and if you do not give us freedom in India you will have to give me a grave here.'[94]

Later on during the conference, on 4 January 1931, Ali breathed his last.[95]

'Rousing the fanaticism of Moslems'

Tributes poured in from all quarters. Lord Reading, a former Viceroy of India, noted Ali's 'vivid and forceful personality'. While he acknowledged (in an understated way) that the Maulana had 'occasionally caused us trouble', nonetheless,

> our thoughts are filled with admiration for the courage of the man, who insisted, notwithstanding the very serious state of his health, on coming to this country, in order that he might take part in the struggle for the constitutional advance of his motherland, and who has, at any rate, had the consolation of dying in the struggle for a great cause, in which he had implicit faith.

Meanwhile Lord Sankey, president of the conference's Federation Sub-Committee, honoured Ali as a 'fellow member of the University of Oxford, who lived and suffered for his ideals.'[96]

Gandhi (still in prison) was devastated: 'We had differences of opinion between us, but love that cannot stand the strain of differences is like a sounding brass and tinkling cymbal.' Jinnah, meanwhile, implored the Muslim League to 'carry the torch forward, gain strength by his noble and inspiring example of self-sacrifice, and serve Islam and India to the best of our ability.'[97]

News of the Maulana's death reverberated across the Islamic world, reaching Palestine—where Mufti Hussaini saw an opportunity. He moved fast and—before a burial had been arranged in London—sent Shaukat Ali a telegram requesting that he bring his brother's body to Jerusalem to be buried in al-Aqsa Mosque, the

Islamic world's third holiest place, 'in accordance with his honor and his name in the Muslim world.'[98] Ali was pleased to accept the prestigious invitation. For the Mufti, it was an opportunity to raise Jerusalem's political profile by associating it with one of the world's most prominent Muslim politicians. This, he calculated, would help increase the prominence of the Palestinian cause.[99] At that time it was generally viewed as simply one of many anti-colonial struggles, not as anything unique. Hussaini aimed to make Palestine the ultimate Islamic political cause.

And so it was that Shaukat Ali arrived with his brother's coffin in Jerusalem on Friday 23 January 1931. Thousands of Palestinians awaited him by the station, and the coffin was carried as part of a grand funeral procession to al-Aqsa. Prominent Palestinian Christian leaders walked immediately behind it, alongside a group of polite representatives from the British government. The Mufti delivered a eulogy at the funeral, followed by speeches by notables from elsewhere in the Arab world, including renowned Egyptian thinker Ahmed Zaki Pasha (who hailed Mohamed Ali as a martyr) and exiled Tunisian nationalist Abdelaziz Thaalbi. A Christian poet even recited a poem he had composed in Ali's honour. The event was highly politicised and the speeches abounded with strong messages of Islamic solidarity, Arab unity and opposition to Zionist settlement.[100]

The whole affair triggered considerable controversy, with Zionist leaders warning that Ali's tomb would become 'a shrine which would be used as an instrument for rousing the fanaticism of Moslems'.[101] On 8 February, Shaukat Ali had an amicable meeting with Frederick Kisch, the head of the Zionist Commission in Jerusalem, although they discussed nothing of consequence. By the end of his trip Ali firmly opposed the Zionist movement, concluding that it aimed to dispossess Palestinians of their homes.[102]

The most significant upshot was a suggestion that Ali made to Hussaini after the funeral. He proposed that a conference of Muslim notables from across the Islamic world, like the one in the Hejaz, should be held in Jerusalem. No previous conference held since the fall of the Caliphate had seen the Ottomans wield any influence, despite Abdulmejid's wishes. But since Shaukat Ali was an avowed supporter of the Ottoman claim to the Caliphate, this conference was different. Hussaini for his part was delighted by the idea, which presented him with the chance to bring unprecedented prominence to the Palestinian cause. A World Islamic Congress was scheduled for December that year. Almost immediately, it triggered rumours of a plot to restore the Ottoman Caliphate.[103]

These were well founded. Ali's plan was for Caliph Abdulmejid to appear in Jerusalem for the congress—with the goal of securing support for a revived Caliphate. And this scheme soon became twinned with another—one that revolved around a wedding. Sometime in early 1931, Ali turned up in Nice to meet Caliph Abdulmejid. The exact circumstances of the meeting are shrouded in mystery, but they are certain to have discussed the congress. What also came out of it was monumental: Abdulmejid agreed in principle to the idea of his daughter, Princess Durrushehvar, marrying the heir apparent of the Nizam of Hyderabad. This wasn't set in stone—he would have to meet the Nizam's son, and so would Durrushehvar. It is also unclear which of the two came up with the idea, although it was probably Ali. Having secured Abdulmejid's support, the Maulana had to take the idea to the Nizam. He headed to Hyderabad.[104]

8

'A DISTINGUISHED SON OF ISLAM'

In December 2023, I was a few months into researching what had happened to Caliph Abdulmejid once he was exiled from Turkey. I was keen for any detail, however small, about his life in Nice. And then I saw, in the Hyderabadi press, a report about Imam ul-Mulk IV, Nawab Syed Ahmed Khan ('Nawab' being an honorific used by aristocrats), who said he possessed a deed signed by the last Caliph.

Intrigued, I contacted Syed Ahmed Khan and explained my research. Did I want to come to India, at the invitation of his family, to see the documents they had? I agreed, on the understanding that I could write whatever I wanted as an impartial researcher. With me would travel James, an expert in old Arabic and Urdu texts.

We stayed as guests at the charming Old City residence of the aristocratic Imam ul-Mulk family, which still publishes *The Rahnuma Daily*, India's longest-running Urdu daily, formerly patronised by the Nizam under a different name, the *Rahbar-e-Deccan*. The head of the household, born in 1942, is Nawab Akram Abbas Syed, father to Syed Ahmed Khan who arranged my stay: his father in turn was Colonel Syed Mohammed Amiruddin Khan, who served the seventh Nizam for decades and became his military secretary in the 1950s, after Hyderabad's fall.

And it was among the papers of the colonel, who died in 2012 at ninety-nine, that Nawab Syed Ahmed Khan told us he found an extraordinary (and now hotly contested) Arabic deed. The papers included a collection of unpublished handwritten poems by Osman Ali Khan, as well as a volume of handwritten poetry by his son Prince Azam Jah—and letters from Islamic scholars in Mecca and Medina commending the Nizam as a Muslim leader.

THE INDIAN CALIPHATE

One of the documents found by Khan—an exceedingly hospitable and friendly man, with impeccably styled hair and a carefully trimmed beard, who dressed in shirts and suit jackets—was the deed. Khan, who doesn't understand Arabic, told us he had no idea of what the deed, discovered in December 2021, declared—until in early 2023 he showed his grandfather's papers to prominent academic Dr Syed Abdul Mohaimin Quadri. 'I was looking for help to better understand them, and it was during that visit that I learned of their historical importance,' he said.[1]

The deed is addressed to the Nizam and purportedly signed by Caliph Abdulmejid II in Nice on 19 November 1931—a week after his daughter's wedding to the Nizam's eldest son. Through the document, which my friend James translated into English, Abdulmejid transfers the title of Caliph to the Nizam to hold in trust on his death, before it is claimed by the first-born son from the dynastic union. 'I trust that the firstborn son of this new kinship after you [the Nizam] be suitable to the position of the Caliphate and the rulership of Hyderabad Deccan,' the deed concludes.[2]

I held the document at the Rahnuma residence. It was made of thick wheat paper, worn but intact. The ornately formed Arabic words were inscribed in carbon black ink—apart from the Caliph's elaborate signature, which was a bold red. Khan told me the find had filled him with wonder: 'I realised I had uncovered the greatest mystery of a much coveted and cultural treasure.'[3] Proclaiming the deed authentic has proved impossible—at least for me. After I published an article reporting on the deed in August 2024, experts clashed over whether it is real.

But the deed fascinated me because even back in November 1931, it was widely suspected that a transfer of the Ottoman Caliphate to the Asaf Jahi dynasty in Hyderabad was in the works.

'The proposal was an excellent one'

The Nizam had two sons from his wife Dulhan Pasha (along with others from his concubines). The first was Mir Himayat Ali Khan, born in 1907 and known as Prince Azam Jah. He was the heir apparent, due to succeed his father as Nizam upon the latter's death.

'A DISTINGUISHED SON OF ISLAM'

The second son, Mir Shujaat Ali Khan, was born ten months later and known as Prince Moazzam Jah.[4] By 1931 they were young men, and neither was remotely interested in politics.

Sultan Ghalib al-Qu'aiti knew Azam Jah when the latter was much older. 'He was a surprisingly humble man who spoke English better than me and appeared well informed on global affairs although he was simple in his thinking process,' he told me. He recalled, though, that Jah 'had a naughty sense of humour and loved practical tricks.'[5] As a young man, the prince was a devoted big game hunter and a polo player, the sport being fashionable among India's potentates as a result of British influence. Jah put what he valued in life into a very particular order: 'Firstly, polo; after that, my duty; and thirdly, women.'[6] In March 1925 he was so furious at the meagre allowance his austere father allowed him (just 500 rupees a month) that he asked the then British Resident, Charles Russell, to depose the Nizam. Russell instead advised Jah to learn some 'self-control and self-reliance'. Within the next few years, the princes had their allowances raised and in 1928 they were sent to Europe—ostensibly for training in administrative work (in reality this meant shopping, gambling and partying).[7]

The elder brother spent most of his time in Europe playing polo and driving sports cars, while Moazzam Jah spent his days with tailors and haberdashers—and his nights in fashionable nightclubs. Berlin and Paris were his favourite cities. He had an 'unerring flair' for selecting women: he would enter a restaurant, choose a woman to approach within a minute and invariably succeed in his amorous ambitions.[8] Jah was a dandy; many considered him the best-dressed man in Europe. And no wonder, since he had 250 suits brought with him on all his trips.[9]

Every Eid, the Nizam would send the two princes a suit of clothes each as a gift. One year Moazzam Jah returned the gift, complaining that the cloth was of low quality. The Nizam duly summoned the prince and informed him that the suit was made of the exact same cloth he himself used. 'It may be alright for Your Exalted Highness, but not for me,' said Jah. 'Why?' asked an exasperated Nizam. 'Because,' came the reply, 'Your Exalted Highness is an orphan. But my father is alive!' The Nizam, always one to appreciate a good display of wit, slapped his thigh in approval and ordered a new suit to be sent to the prince.[10]

Once they were in their early twenties, the Nizam planned to marry his sons to two of Dulhan Pasha's relations, but the British Resident at the time, Sir Terence Keyes, warned against it on the grounds that the girls were 'uneducated'. In early 1931 the ruler was still mulling it over when, alarmingly, in Europe one of Moazzam Jah's dancing partners contacted Keyes and revealed to him that Jah was talking about escaping from his British minders with his brother to 'marry anyone they took a fancy to in Egypt or Europe'. Coincidentally, it was at that point that Maulana Shaukat Ali arrived in Hyderabad.[11]

Keyes initially took no interest in Ali's presence, assuming he had come 'to cadge money and try to commit the Nizam politically'. It was only later that he realised Ali had come as a marriage broker 'on behalf of the ex-Sultan of Turkey'. British officials, generally possessing limited knowledge of Ottoman convention and history, mistook the deposed Caliph, Abdulmejid, for the last Ottoman Sultan, which he had never been. British intelligence gathering thus yielded that the 'Sultan'—not Caliph—'has a daughter aged about 17' whom Shaukat Ali had met and thought was 'attractive and very well educated'. This was Princess Durrushehvar, although the British hadn't identified her. Abdulmejid, Ali conveyed to the Nizam, 'wants to marry her to Azam Jah'.[12]

Speaking about the meeting publicly later on, Shaukat Ali claimed the Nizam had brought up the idea himself: 'In the course of the conversation when I referred to the Turkish Princess, the Khalifa's daughter; the Nizam himself asked me how I liked the idea of his son marrying the Khalifa's daughter: this enquiry was as I had contemplated. I assured the Nizam that the proposal was an excellent one.'[13] The Nizam recognised the huge prestige such a marriage would bring to his dynasty throughout the Islamic world, although he was concerned that an alliance with a family as distinguished as the House of Osman could also be a burden. It was certainly a break with Asaf Jahi tradition—no heir apparent had ever married an outsider.

'A DISTINGUISHED SON OF ISLAM'

Osman Ali Khan decided, on balance, that the two princes should go to Nice so Azam Jah could meet the princess. 'He says that he would not think of forcing the match if Azam Jah doesn't take a fancy to her,' Keyes reported.[14] Ali later recalled that the Nizam 'directed me to try my best to bring about this relationship... He also issued similar instructions to Mr. Marmaduke Pickthall and Sir Akbar Hydari.'[15] They left India together on a ship bound for Europe.[16]

The Treaty of Hyderabad prevented the British government from intervening in the Nizam's family affairs, a restriction that had previously been ignored when the Nizam tried to marry his sons to 'uneducated girls'.[17] Sir Charles Watson, political secretary in New Delhi's Foreign and Political Department, was concerned—although the full picture was unclear to him. He suspected, correctly, that Shaukat Ali aimed to 'resurrect in India a rallying point for the Caliphate issue'. Indeed, there were 'obvious inconveniences,' he noted, 'in the existence at the Hyderabad court of a princess of the former Imperial Ottoman Family, whose own father was a Reigning Monarch till his death—inconvenience certainly social and possibly political.' Yet Watson concluded that with Azam Jah already set to visit France in September, it was too late to 'intervene to prevent a meeting between him and the princess in question, even if that were possible.'[18]

This was also Keyes' assessment in Hyderabad, although he opposed the scheme. He warned the Nizam that although a marital union with the House of Osman would help his position in the Islamic world, 'it may draw upon Hyderabad increased hostility of certain Hindu elements.' But Keyes ultimately wrote to his colleagues in Delhi that he thought Britain should avoid opposing the marriage, since 'this would antagonise [the] whole Muslim world.'[19]

But Watson in Delhi faced another predicament: the Government of India had asked him to 'find out about the lady's personal qualities'. This was made difficult by the fact that Watson had no idea who the relevant princess was. And since he wanted to avoid taking either Akbar Hydari or Azam Jah 'into confidence', he couldn't simply ask them either. Watson ruefully resolved to tell the government this.

THE INDIAN CALIPHATE

Hyderabadis on the Riviera

The Caliph was now seventy, Azam Jah was twenty-four and Durrushehvar was eighteen. American journalists described the princess as 'slim, brunette and the epitome of Oriental beauty.' She was also 'thoroughly modern', but 'has no use for such Western items as lipstick and short hair'.[20] Unsurprisingly, the princess was sought as a bride by an array of Muslim dynasties. Egypt's King Fuad, Iraq's King Faisal and Persia's Shah Reza each offered immense dowries for Durrushehvar's hand in marriage to various male members of their dynasties.

But ultimately Abdulmejid looked to Hyderabad, likely because of the Asaf Jahi dynasty's unmatched wealth and the fact that the Nizam had come to his aid in 1924.[21] Still, though, the marriage was far from a done deal—the Caliph insisted that his daughter should have the final word. 'I am perfectly happy to give my daughter to the son of His Majesty the Nizam,' he said, 'who is a religious monarch and a distinguished son of Islam. However, the most important condition is that they should like each other, be in harmony with one another, and decide for themselves.'[22]

The princes arrived in France in September and stayed in Cannes, visiting Nice to meet some of the young Ottoman exiles.[23] Durrushehvar was no doubt aware that the marriage would transform her family's fortunes, and was seriously considering the match. Over lunch at the Palais Carabacel, she asked Prince Ali Vasib, with her father present, what he thought of Azam Jah. Vasib felt he didn't know him well enough to comment, and replied 'in a non-committal way.'[24]

But after meeting the prince, Durrushehvar was charmed; Jah, for his part, was smitten. After that, a formal proposal came by way of a deputation from Hyderabad. In a clear sign of how seriously the Nizam took the issue, the deputation included Hydari (Hyderabad's finance minister) and Foreign Minister Nawab Jeng Bahadur.[25] Fortunately, Hyderabad experienced no major financial or diplomatic crises while they were away.

Having asked for Durrushehvar's hand, the deputation then inquired as to whether there was a girl to marry Moazzam Jah. Abdulmejid's nomination was Enver Pasha's daughter, Princess

Mahpeyker. But she wasn't keen on moving to India.[26] At that point Prince Osman Fuad, who was staying in Paris, took the initiative and swept in. Princess Adile was his elder sister, and Princess Niloufer his niece. He contrived for the two to visit Paris while the younger Jah was on a trip there, and sure enough fifteen-year-old Niloufer met the prince.

According to Vasib, the two 'soon warmed to each other and told Abdulmejid Efendi and the Nizam of their intention to marry.'[27] Princess Neslishah remembered Niloufer as a 'ravishing beauty' and recounted that Moazzam Jah was 'breathless' at the very sight of her.[28] Niloufer herself, recalling their first meeting years later after the couple's unhappy divorce, told a rather different story. She remembered that the prince had looked her up and down 'as if he were inspecting a racehorse'. Niloufer said she married him to escape poverty: 'I went to Hyderabad with just a small copy of the Qur'an clutched to my chest'.[29]

While Moazzam Jah was in Paris, he met up with one of the city's famous courtesans and hired an expensive photographer to take photos of Niloufer while the courtesan was hiding in the ladies' lavatory. The photographer then later took photos of the courtesan. The final bill was £1,000; when the Nizam saw it he was unsurprisingly furious.[30]

Meanwhile, Abdulmejid was attempting to dissuade the Hyderabadis from extending a proposal to Niloufer. He said she would be unsuitable because she had been given a modern, European upbringing, having been extremely young when she left Istanbul. She knew little of harem life and it was entirely foreseeable that she would come to hate the experience of being removed from her relatively free lifestyle and thrust into the Hyderabadi court, with all its strictures. But Moazzam Jah wasn't swayed. Osman Fuad had staged what Ali Vasib admiringly called a 'lightning operation'—very quickly the Nizam agreed to the marriage and the couple were engaged.[31]

The bewilderment of the British

Throughout this time, British officials were still unsuccessfully trying to identify Azam Jah's bride-to-be. But the Turkish government soon caught wind of the situation, and grasped it perfectly. On 13 October the Turkish ambassador in London, Ferid Bey, called on the Foreign Office to warn uncomprehending officials there about the exploits of Shaukat Ali, whom he informed them was planning a congress in Palestine at which a Caliph would be chosen.

The ambassador also noted, as per Turkish intelligence, that Ali had been in contact with the deposed Caliph in Nice, and alleged that 'it was Shaukat Ali's design to link the Indian Moslem Princes and Abdul Mejid'. The ambassador also disclosed that Ali was going to seek the British government's approval for his scheme. The officials, bemused, told him they had no idea about the plan.[32]

Investigations commenced at the Foreign Office. After an Ottoman family tree diagram was painstakingly created and studied, it was decided that someone called 'Princess Emine Monkhile' (Princess Emine Mukbile) seemed to best fit the bill.[33] In late October, the Foreign Office sent the British consulate in Nice a secret dispatch asking for information on 'Princess Emine Moukbille', the spelling having changed.

Colonel Stokes at the consulate sent the Foreign Office a polite report back on 26 October noting that Princess Emine Mukbile was in fact engaged to Prince Ali Vasib. The actual princess set to marry Azam Jah, Stokes explained, was Caliph Abdulmejid's daughter, Princess Durrushehvar, whom his spies assured him was 'highly accomplished and well educated', as well as 'musical and artistic'—and her father's 'constant companion.'[34]

Foreign Office officials were delighted. 'Identification has at last been achieved!' wrote one triumphantly, observing that the princess being the daughter of the deposed Caliph made Shaukat Ali's involvement in the affair 'more intelligible'.[35] He mused that the marriage 'would suit Shaukat Ali's work nicely and would be a very useful piece of propaganda in advocating his pan-Moslem ideals.'

It is a testament to just how large the British Empire's administration was that different offices had radically distinct understandings of the situation. Britain's India Office had a much better grasp of what was happening, and informed the (rather slow) Foreign Office that Ali was masterminding a scheme for a 'Pan-Islamic Federation, which is to be discussed' at the Congress—

where he 'desires to revive the Caliphate.' Sir Samuel Hoare, the secretary of state, ordered that the Turkish ambassador be told the British government considered Ali unimportant and his scheme implausible.[36]

The two dynasties united

All this time, ferocious marriage negotiations were being thrashed out in London between representatives of the Caliph on the one side and Hydari and Pickthall on the other.[37] These were lengthy and intense.[38] The Ottomans asked for a trousseau of £20,000; Hydari countered with £10,000 and the eventual agreement was £15,000. The Ottomans also asked that Durrushehvar be allowed to return to France annually to visit her father. British officials recorded another demand: 'Right of succession to be entailed on male issue of this marriage'.[39] This establishes the intensely political nature of the proceedings: Abdulmejid was intent on having his potential future grandson be the ruler of Hyderabad.

There is no record of the Nizam objecting to this demand, but he decided the others were too extravagant and dramatically broke off negotiations in mid-October.[40] At this point Sir Terence Keyes, opposed to the marriage, felt the Caliph should be told 'that unless he and his daughter are prepared for her to throw in her lot unreservedly with her husband's State he should give up all idea' of the match, and that Azam Jah should be informed that to marry a princess 'whose heart and interests lie outside India would be fatal to his future career and happiness'.[41]

Jah, who was genuinely taken with Durrushehvar, was utterly dismayed.[42] But the Nizam wasn't really willing to give up on the marriage. He sent a message to Hydari in London, telling him it was 'absolutely necessary' to 'go yourself to Nice in company of Pickthall' to speak to the Caliph. Hydari and Pickthall immediately headed to France. Their diplomatic prowess did the trick, and by 23 October the issues were resolved and Abdulmejid sent a cable to the Nizam.[43]

He expressed his sorrow at the 'misunderstanding which arose between our representatives in London'. Pickthall and Hydari had explained everything, he said; the Caliph was 'happy to address myself to my brother'. Abdulmejid told the Nizam that 'I confide the future and happiness of my daughter who will become yours to the fatherly love and protection of Your Exalted Highness.' He added: 'I am sure that you will do all that is necessary to ensure that happiness and defend the high prestige of our two ancient dynasties.'[44] A few days later, he sent another cable adding that it was 'unnecessary to discuss' other conditions for the marriage, since the Nizam would surely 'consider my daughter as his own daughter'.

By the end of October a definitive agreement had been reached. It was a clear triumph for the Nizam: the Caliph had completely dropped his more controversial extra conditions.[45] Abdulmejid also told the Nizam that the marriage of Durrushehvar and Azam 'will unite two Muslim dynasties by the intimate ties of family love; an event which cannot fail to have a very happy repercussion on the whole Muslim world.'[46] This was a significant statement; it shows that the Caliph understood the marriage as loaded with political significance.

'The honour of Hyderabad'

The second Round Table Conference of Indian politicians in London was in full flow, having started in September. It intended to succeed where the first conference had failed, but didn't, although this time Mahatma Gandhi was present, representing the Congress. Maulana Shaukat Ali spent his time giving details of the union of the Ottoman and Asaf Jahi dynasties to the London press. He briefed journalists that the wedding would take place at the Palais Carabacel, clarifying for posterity that the so-called palace 'is really a villa rented by the ex-Caliph'. Ali also revealed, taking on the role of cultural ambassador, that Durrushehvar would probably not attend the actual wedding ceremony, instead waiting behind a door. Male witnesses would ask her whether she accepted the marriage, at which point 'as a matter of form' she would hesitate, perhaps twice, before ultimately agreeing to the union.[47]

And so in London the marriages went from being an open secret to public knowledge, with newspapers reporting on details of the union before the official announcement was made. The Hyderabadi delegation at the conference, which included Azam Jah, hosted a dinner at which Sir Samuel Hoare, the recently appointed Secretary of State for India, loudly hinted at the wedding. The prince was openly enthusiastic; one journalist recorded the 'romance of the mutual attraction which clearly manifested itself between the young people themselves'.[48]

But the commentary was more than gossip about young love— the potential political implications of the union were not lost on London's commentators. Some saw the marriages as a potentially beneficial development for the British Empire and its status as a Muslim power. Hyderabad was accepted to be the 'traditional exponent of Islamic culture in India', as one paper put it, and the marriage, many thought, 'will do much to promote friendly relations' between the British and the 'Moslem world', by demonstrating that 'Islam in India and Islam in the Near East can meet together in cooperation for peaceful progress.'[49]

The *Daily Express* reported dramatically that it was 'able to reveal details of an impending marriage in London which will have social, political and religious significance the world over.' The marriage, the *Express* opined, 'will influence millions of Moslems both in the Indian Empire and throughout the rest of the Eastern world'; it would 'cement Anglo-Islamic friendship.' The paper falsely announced that the wedding would be held in London (and that it would 'provide for London a spectacle which it has never seen'), got Durrushehvar's age wrong, saying she was twenty-two—and included a photo of the Caliph with his 'holy beard'.[50]

TIME magazine reported on 9 November that the engagement 'struck many Moslems as a happy thought. Should these young people wed and have a man child, temporal and spiritual strains would richly blend in him. He could be proclaimed "The True Caliph."'[51] Clearly, word was flying around that Azam Jah and Durrushehvar's firstborn son, in line to be Nizam in the distant future, would also be a claimant to the Caliphate.

On 11 November, an extremely large Hyderabadi delegation arrived in Nice on an express train from London. Hydari was among them, along with other important Hyderabadi politicians, including the populist Nawab Bahadur Yar Jung. Pickthall and Ali were attendees too.[52] So was Keyes, who had opposed the whole affair.[53] They all stayed at the most expensive hotel in Nice, the Negresco, courtesy of the Nizam, and the merry entourage reserved an entire floor of the hotel for themselves. 'What is the point of so much expense?' a rather perplexed Prince Omer Faruk asked them. 'It is the honour of Hyderabad,' came the reply.[54]

The joint wedding ceremony was held at the Palais Carabacel on 12 November. Both princes wore 'richly-embroidered robes of Indian cloth', with turbans on their heads and garlands of flowers hung around their necks in the normal Indian way.[55] 'Flowers were strewn around,' Vasib later recalled, 'and all their suites at the Negresco were piled to the ceiling with baskets of them.'[56] Locals practically besieged the Palais Carabacel, fascinated by the prospect of an exotic Islamic wedding. Azam and Moazzam Jah drove from the Negresco to the villa each in their own convertible Mercedes—both cars yellow, Hyderabad's princely colour, and covered in flowers. Large hooters were placed on the front of each and 'hooted all the way to the villa'.[57]

The wedding was a small affair. There would later be a civil marriage at the British consulate, but the Islamic marriage in the villa was conducted by Caliph Abdulmejid himself, who quipped at the start of the proceedings, 'Do you know I have never performed a marriage before?'

Negotiations over how much the Caliph, Durrushehvar and Niloufer would receive continued even during the ceremony, so that 'Hyderabad's two princes knelt for more than 30 minutes before propped up pictures of their brides.' Eventually the contract was signed. 'With aching knees they rose at last.'[58] The brides donned their veils and there were several rounds of photos. Shaukat Ali was a big hit with the children of the Ottoman imperial family; five-year-old Princess Nejla, a granddaughter of the Caliph, kept declaring, 'I shall marry him' (she later married an Egyptian prince).[59] Afterwards there was a small tea party, and the whole affair was completed.[60]

'A DISTINGUISHED SON OF ISLAM'

Ankara strikes a blow

Parallel to the build-up to the marriage had been mounting controversy over the looming World Islamic Congress, due to start in December. Abdulmejid's plan was to travel to Palestine to address the congress and rally support for his claim to the Caliphate. It is likely that he aimed for a restoration of the Caliphate through a vote by the congress' delegates. Turkey decided Abdulmejid needed to be stopped at all costs from entering Palestine and tried to lobby France to prevent him from leaving the country. The French government refused, not wanting to become embroiled in the issue.[61]

At the same time Egypt's King Fuad, perturbed by the idea of a revived Ottoman Caliphate, made his opposition to the congress known.[62] Mufti Hussaini arrived in Cairo on 8 November to try to persuade the Egyptian government to attend the congress. The insurmountable problem he faced was that, despite the actual wording of the congress invitation being suitably vague on what was to be discussed, no one was fooled. Shaukat Ali, after all, had been publicly declaring not just that he wanted the Caliphate back but also that Abdulmejid was his preferred candidate for the role. This was nothing short of outrageous to King Fuad. If anyone was to be the Caliph, it would be himself.[63]

The congress's detractors in Egypt put forward multiple reasons for opposing Abdulmejid. For one, they argued, a Caliph needed to be an independent ruler. Abdulmejid was ruler only of the Palais Carabacel. This meant that his seat would have to be in Jerusalem under the British Mandate, which they thought was unacceptable. 'I can't see any good reason for convoking a Moslem Congress now in Jerusalem,' eighty-year-old Sheikh Mohammed Bakhit, formerly Egypt's Grand Mufti, bluntly said. He was particularly concerned that an Islamic university would be set up in Jerusalem which could rival Egypt's prestigious al-Azhar seminary.[64] Egypt was to have nothing to do with the conference. King Saud would also fail to attend, claiming that the invitation had simply reached him too late.[65]

Around the time of the weddings in Nice, the British Foreign Office (no doubt facing pleas from Ankara) was desperate to simply have the congress banned from taking place. But the British Mandate in Palestine refused to hear it, its officials fearing that stopping the event would trigger an 'Arab rebellion'. Ultimately, the Mandate made it known instead that Abdulmejid would be denied entry to Palestine. This was a serious blow that spelled the decisive end of any hope that Abdulmejid would be elected Caliph.[66]

For Hussaini, everything seemed to be going wrong. British pressure on him became so intense that he ultimately declared from Jerusalem that 'no caliph will be elected by the congress', although he was unable to resist adding mysteriously that 'we will deal with the question abstractly'. No one knew what this meant. In Nice, the monocled Hussein Nakib (one of the Caliph's secretaries) enigmatically briefed American journalists that Abdulmejid 'constantly corresponds with the Grand Mufti of Palestine'—before refusing to say any more.[67]

Real or fake? Experts debate the deed

It was in this fraught context that the sensational deed transferring the Caliphate to the Asaf Jahi dynasty was purportedly drawn up, on 19 November. The document reads (in Arabic) as follows:

> In the name of God the Compassionate the Merciful, and God gives His kingdom to whom He wills and God is All-Encompassing, Knowing. We offer thousands of congratulations and well-wishes to His Highness, Possessor of Splendour and Nobility, Sultan Mir Osman Ali Khan, Sultan of the Kingdom of Hyderabad Deccan, Governor of the Asafi Kingdom, Governor and Ruler of it all, especially as far as the Two Noble Sanctuaries. It has been established that I, Caliph Abdulmejid II, son of Commander of the Believers Sultan Abdulaziz, elect the Possessor of the State and Greatness, Mir Osman Ali Khan, Sultan of Hyderabad Deccan, may God eternalise his Kingdom and Sultanate, to the position of the Caliphate. Indeed this position fell to my most elevated grandfather Sultan Selim Shah son of Bayazid Khan, and the Abbasid Caliph al-Mutawakkil 'ala Allah III gave it to him. Indeed the Sultan of the Deccan shall be Commander of the Faithful.

'A DISTINGUISHED SON OF ISLAM'

> And I beseech God, splendid and glorious is He, that He grant victory to all the People of the Two Sanctuaries and the People of Islam and I trust that the firstborn son of this new kinship after you be suitable to the position of the Caliphate and rulership of Hyderabad in the Deccan.

Below the Arabic text, in red, is what appears to be the Caliph's signature. On the bottom of the page are the apparent signatures of the two princes and princesses.[68]

The Imam ul-Mulk family, who said they found the document in the papers of the Nizam's military secretary, Colonel Amiruddin, assured me they have no political agenda, no intentions for the document, despite what it suggests. 'Our custodianship of the deed is cultural, historical and apolitical,' Nawab Syed Ahmed Khan said, 'with no ambitions for the Caliphate's political revival.'[69]

Being no manuscript expert, I suspected that I would be unable to tell an authentic Caliphal deed from something scrawled down by an amateur forger in a dark shed. To try to understand the document, I went to see prominent academic Dr Syed Abdul Mohaimin Quadri, who is proficient in Arabic and had first told Khan what it said.

Quadri works from his cramped library, found within the shrine complex of a locally revered saint, Hazrat Pathar Wali Sahib, in Hyderabad's Old City. The space is dominated by a magnificent collection of manuscripts, including innumerable rare Urdu books and over 600 centuries-old Persian and Arabic manuscripts. A bearded scholar, complete with traditional skullcap and kurta, Quadri presents a serene and highly learned figure, with an undoubtedly deep commitment to his preservation work. During our visit, he received an almost constant stream of visitors, all of whom greeted him with reverence (the state of Telangana's home minister had recently dropped by, I was told).[70]

The scholar seemed excited by the document. 'It is authentic,' he said confidently, explaining that it transfers the Caliphate to the Nizam to hold in trust, the intention being that the Caliphal title should eventually be claimed by a potential first-born son from the dynastic union.[71] Quadri wasn't the only one to proclaim it authentic. I read a document written by Ahmed Ali, now retired, who had been a curator at the Indian government-owned Salar Jung

Museum, Hyderabad's largest museum (it has an entire gallery full of beautifully decorated hookah bowls), which proclaimed the deed to be real. On this basis, I published an article in late August in *Middle East Eye* reporting on the deed's emergence and Quadri's assessment of it. So far, so good, I thought.

But just a few days after my report, I was alerted to an article on Turkish news website *Haberturk* by prominent Turkish writer Murat Bardakçı calling the document a forgery: 'Let me just say this: this document was manufactured a few years ago, so it is a fake!'[72] Bardakçı, who regularly appears on Turkish television panels for historical discussions, wrote the magnificent biography of Princess Neslishah from which I have cited extensively in this book. I took the article seriously.

He noted that while he had not seen the deed, there 'is no need for me to give detailed information about the physical features of the document.' The signatures at the bottom, he said, 'had no connection with the real signatures of these people'. Friends with contacts in Hyderabad, Bardakçı added, had told him that their contacts knew the document 'was produced by a sensationalist journalist via Photoshop, and even found out the name of the journalist!' Bardakçı didn't name the journalist.[73]

Intrigued, I contacted Bardakçı to ask if he had any more information. He pointed me to Ayub Khan, a Toronto-based researcher who has published multiple academic articles on aspects of Indian history. Khan, who was immensely helpful and generous with his time, told me that when he saw the photo of the deed he immediately thought its authenticity was 'doubtful for a number of reasons'. Firstly, he said, 'it is missing essential stylistic elements of an official Ottoman document including the tughra, included specifically to prevent tampering.' The tughra was the seal Ottoman Sultans used. It is unclear whether Abdulmejid would have had it to hand in Nice at that time (he was, of course, not a Sultan either).

Khan also highlighted that official documents were usually written in diwani, an Arabic cursive script, unlike here. 'Caliph Abdulmejid was a skilled calligrapher and shouldn't have had any trouble in drafting the official deed in diwani even while in exile.' Khan noted that Abdulmejid's handwriting in private correspondences 'doesn't

'A DISTINGUISHED SON OF ISLAM'

match' the writing in the document, suggesting it was written by someone else. And the inclusion of the poetic pen names of Princes Azam and Moazzam Jah raised further doubts, given these weren't conventionally used in documents in Hyderabad or elsewhere. 'All these issues render the document doubtful to say the least,' Khan concluded.[74]

By this point I was fascinated. I asked Ahmed Ali, the retired curator, for his views. Ali has many accolades to his name—he has organised 120 exhibitions in India and abroad, including in Turkey and the Arab world, written eighty published articles on art, history and conservation and delivered more than forty-five research papers. He is also the author of four books, including the particularly relevant *Script, Calligraphy and Manuscripts*.

The curator stuck to his position that the deed is authentic. 'The document is scribed on thick wheat paper in Arabic naskh script with carbon black [ink],' he explained.[75] The naskh script was often used in Ottoman calligraphy, and in India for official purposes.[76] 'The document ends with prayers for the Nizamate of Hyderabad and the title of the Caliphate transfers to the first-born male of the union,' Ali noted. He said that the 'names along with the Caliph's signature are authentic and match those found on other documents' he had read. He added that 'the name of Azam Jah on the document is matched with his handwritten book of poetry,' found among Amiruddin's papers.[77]

I approached Dr Quadri again. He firmly rejected accusations that the deed was fake. 'If anyone is calling anything fake, then subject the documents and historical items found in the whole world's museums to the most rigorous tests,' he said. 'They would also all be cast into doubt.' Quadri proceeded to give me his views on the deed. He said that Abdulmejid's signature was 'exactly the same' as on other documents. 'You can see it exactly to the letter.'[78]

I asked about the ink. The signature, he said, used red ink from the night-blooming jasmine, which was very old. 'This ink was only used for titles or signatures or on very special occasions.' Meanwhile the ink used for the rest of the document 'is a strong carbon black ink. If we soaked it in water for fifteen days, the ink would not run. If we leave it a month in water, then a little difference occurs. This

165

ink also was only prepared for princes or rulers.' Quadri said of the other signatures, concurring with Ahmed Ali, that 'Azam Jah's name's penmanship corresponds with every name found in the manuscripts written by those same hands.'

As for the paper, he noted that it was very strong and made from wheat. 'Such paper was used around rulers and princes. It was beyond the means and reach of common people.' And the handwriting? 'The script is naskh, which would usually be selected for orders and edicts' in India.[79] This suggested that the deed would have been drawn up by the Hyderabadi delegation, not the Ottomans.[80] The naskh script was often used in Ottoman calligraphy, and in India for official purposes.[81] Finally, I asked about the content of the deed itself. 'From the manner of expression which is in the text,' Quadri replied, 'it is clear that these are the words of rulers.'[82]

But what did the family of the Caliph's late grandson, Prince Mukarram Jah, think? After months of trying to reach them, I finally made contact with Princess Esra, Jah's Turkish ex-wife—then eighty-nine years old. She told me over the phone from Turkey that she had 'no doubt that it is a false document'. The signatures 'of both my mother-in-law [Princess Durrushehvar] and Princess Niloufer are not theirs,' she said, adding that there would be no female witnesses on such a deed. 'The document is forged.'[83]

Shaukat Ali's designs

How did this extraordinary piece of paper end up among Colonel Amiruddin's private possessions? Its provenance remains a mystery. The Caliphate was never ultimately transferred to Hyderabad. The Nizam never claimed the title 'Caliph'. Abdulmejid never stopped using it. What could the motive have been for forging the document? If it was to claim the Caliphate, then nothing came of it.

There is certainly no evidence or suggestion that Nawab Syed Ahmed Khan or his family forged the deed. I put Princess Esra's assessment to Khan. 'I respectfully disagree with the princess,' he told me. 'But I'm not interested in trying to persuade anyone that the deed is real.' He said that his family accepted the views of Ali and Quadri. 'And the issue of the deed aside, all I want to see accepted is that the Caliph sought to transfer the title to his grandson. There is good evidence for this.' Khan questioned why the Caliph's would-be mausoleum had been left abandoned and in a state of disrepair. He reiterated that his family were custodians of the deed for apolitical, historical and cultural purposes.[84]

My own view is that it is impossible to proclaim the deed authentic. However, the document is ultimately so interesting because strong evidence does in fact exist that Abdulmejid wished the Caliphate to continue through the Asaf Jahi line. Most of the evidence emerged in the 1940s, but one indicator is from just days after the wedding—around the time that the purported deed would have been signed.

By 7 December, Sir Terence Keyes concluded that Shaukat Ali had come up with an 'elaborate scheme for dragging Indian princes into revival of Khilafat [Caliphate]' and that the marriages had been part of the plan, the aim being for Hyderabad to ultimately become the seat of a revived Caliphate. The Nizam, he wrote to Delhi, had nearly fallen into the trap 'but I think realises folly of scheme and resents way in which Shaukat tried to make cats-paw of him.'[85] This is hard to believe. Osman Ali Khan was a shrewd and canny operator who would have understood exactly who Ali was and why he was interested in brokering the marriage. As for Marmaduke Pickthall, Ali's fellow Khilafatist, he was no stranger; the Nizam had employed him. It seems implausible that the Nizam had fallen into a trap.

Far more likely is that the ruler had understood the significance of the marriage for enhancing his dynasty's position in the Islamic world—but wanted to keep talk of the Caliphate out of the headlines, due to political sensitivities. The Nizam was a potentate, not a populist, and this was where he clashed with Shaukat Ali. On 24 November, the Maulana published a letter in a Hyderabad paper pointing out that the marriages had implications for the Caliphate, though without specifying what they were. He also wrote to the Urdu newspapers in Bombay, urging Muslims to give the arriving couples a warm welcome to India.[86] British authorities soon caught wind of a plan among Muslims in Bombay to 'make a great occasion' of the arrival of the couples. One local paper stated that the marriages 'foreshadow the restoration of the Khalifa', Keyes recorded. The British Government of India, anxious not to anger Turkey, was keen to prevent these demonstrations.

The Nizam, for his part, was furious; the last thing he would have wanted was a public furore over the potential resurrection of the Caliphate. He sent Ali a telegram 'reproaching him with breach of confidence', Keyes reported, and 'telling him not to persuade Bombay Moslems to make demonstration.' Crucially, the Nizam never accused Ali of fabricating the idea that the marriage had implications for the Caliphate—only of being indiscreet. Under pressure, Ali quickly wrote to his contacts in Bombay asking them to cancel their plans for demonstrations.[87] The crisis was averted.

Ultimately, it is clear that both Abdulmejid and Shaukat Ali aimed to revive the Caliphate. Unable to attend the congress in Jerusalem, Abdulmejid nonetheless had a chance of securing a future for the Caliphal title—through the Asaf Jahi dynasty.

9

OTTOMANS IN HYDERABAD

Although the World Islamic Congress failed dismally at achieving its intended goals, it was a monumental moment in the history of the Palestinian cause. Beginning on 7 December 1931, it hosted 130 delegates from 22 countries.[1] Representatives came from places as far-flung as Turkestan, Java and Yugoslavia.[2] Notables included Riad al-Solh, the future prime minister of Lebanon, and Shukri al-Quwatli, who would become president of Syria. The famous Egyptian reformist thinker Rashid Rida also addressed the congress.[3]

Sir Muhammad Iqbal, who had left the Round Table Conference in London early for the occasion, arrived in Jerusalem to particular fanfare. He visited the grave of Maulana Mohamed Ali at al-Aqsa Mosque, composing a poem in his honour that referenced the Islamic belief that the Prophet Muhammad was taken on a visit to heaven from al-Aqsa:

> The Holy Land welcomed him in warm and eager embrace
> And he went the way of the Prophet to Heaven.
> Only a land which was not tainted with a sense of colour and smell
> Could have contained a servant of God, who had risen high above the criterion of colour.
> The light of the East alas has gone out of the East!
> But his vision will remain forever in the mind of Asia.[4]

The World Islamic Congress

The event proceeded under the watchful and increasingly concerned eye of the British Mandate. To begin the congress Mohammed

Hussein Kashif al-Ghita, a prominent Shi'a sheikh from Iraq, led the delegates in prayer at al-Aqsa Mosque in a show of Shi'a-Sunni unity.[5] Mufti Hajj Amin al-Hussaini then gave the presidential address, describing the delegates as 'friends of all and enemy of none'. The congress's goal, he proclaimed, was 'to provide a common platform for the Muslims of the world so that united they may fulfil the mission of Islam'.[6]

The delegates took an oath to 'defend the holy places with every bit of strength' and called for a boycott of 'Zionist goods'. They resolved to create an Islamic university in Jerusalem to attract Muslims from across the world and establish Palestine as a global hub of Muslim intellectual activity. Most significantly, they agreed to form an Islamic company to buy up Palestinian land, as a counterweight to the Zionist settlement project.[7]

British officials had been assured by Hussaini before the congress began that delegates wouldn't discuss controversial topics. They were therefore horrified when delegates not only discussed all manner of contentious political issues in great detail, but even carried a general resolution condemning colonialism and decreeing that Zionism 'directly or indirectly alienates Muslims from control over Islamic lands and Muslim holy places'.[8] When British High Commissioner Arthur Grenfell Wauchope asked the Mufti for an explanation, Hussaini blithely replied that he was unable to control what the delegates said.[9]

The last straw was a particularly fiery speech delivered by Abd al-Rahman Azzam, later to become the first secretary general of the League of Arab States, condemning Italian atrocities in Libya. The High Commission quickly ordered his deportation and Azzam was taken to the Egyptian border with a police escort. He was greeted everywhere as a hero along the way, especially in Gaza, where crowds of Palestinians gathered to honour him as he passed through.[10] Back in Jerusalem, Palestinian nationalist Awni Abd al-Hadi then gave one of the most popular speeches of the congress, outlining what he described as a colonialist plot to take over Palestine. He proposed a rejection of the British Mandate, to great enthusiasm from most delegates—although the Mufti, anxious not to be arrested, kept it out of the official list of resolutions.[11]

Another notable address was delivered by Iqbal on 14 December. Urging delegates to 'inculcate the spirit of Muslim brotherhood in all parts of the world', Iqbal declared that the 'World Islamic Congress has great responsibilities.' He warned of two 'great dangers', materialism and excessive nationalism: 'I am not afraid of the enemies of Islam. My fear is from the Muslims themselves. Whenever I ponder, I bow my head in shame over the thought that we are not worthy of the great Prophet of Islam.'[12]

Today, Iqbal is considered among the most influential Muslim philosophers of the modern age. He was also recognised as such at the time, and was a veritable hero to many of the Muslims at the congress. Iqbal also championed the cause of Palestine. In an Urdu poem, 'The Trap of Civilisation', he made his views on the British Mandate's replacement of Ottoman rule in Palestine quite clear, saying of the Palestinians:

> Having been rescued from the 'tyranny' of the Turk,
> These poor men have been caught in the clutches of "civilisation!"[13]

Although there were significant points of consensus, the congress was disrupted by internal disagreement. Voting blocs formed almost immediately and Egyptian delegates from rival parties heckled each other during speeches. At one point, newspaper editor Sulaiman Fawzi had to be protected from a physical attack by the Jordanian delegate, Hamid Pasha bin Jazi.[14] There was no substantial resolution for Islamic unity and the conference ended in failure.[15]

The Mufti followed up with an Indian tour in 1933, during which the Nizam of Hyderabad donated money towards the proposed Islamic university in Jerusalem. Osman Ali Khan had previously given towards the upkeep of al-Aqsa compound, and he funded an endowed hospice in Jerusalem dedicated to the revered twelfth-century Indian saint Baba Farid Gangshakar, who had once visited the city.[16] However, within a few years the university project shuddered to a halt because of a lack of funds.[17]

After an Arab Revolt against the British in Palestine began in 1936, the Mufti stopped collaborating with the Mandate and fled the territory under threat of arrest. Hussaini became so anti-

British that he ended up in Italy during the early years of the Second World War, making connections with the Nazis to try to secure a commitment to the independence of Arab states by the Axis powers.[18] In doing this Hussaini was part of a trend of unlikely anti-colonial radicals collaborating with the fascist powers out of opposition to the British; Subhas Chandra Bose, one of India's most revered freedom fighters, not only met Adolf Hitler but also went to Japan in a submarine to raise an army to invade India.[19]

Despite all this, the congress was in its own way immensely important. It established the Palestinian cause as a pan-Arab and global Islamic one for the first time. Never before had an international body of Muslim notables gathered to declare the Palestinian struggle a cause for Islam. After the event, several Arab delegates stayed in Jerusalem to draft an Arab National Charter, another unprecedented development.[20] Delegates were photographed displaying an early version of the Palestinian flag, which had the al-Aqsa mosque drawn in the middle. The flag was dedicated to Maulana Shaukat Ali.[21]

Over the decades, links between Indian Muslims and Palestine remained strong. Hyderabad's Imam ul-Mulk family, custodians of Abdulmejid's purported deed, established ties with the Palestinian Liberation Organization after 1967.[22] Syed Vicaruddin, then the family's head, hosted Palestinian leader Yasser Arafat in Hyderabad twice and in 1998 the then Mufti of Jerusalem, Shaykh Ekrama Sabri, laid the foundation stone of a mosque in Hyderabad. The State of Palestine even awarded Vicaruddin the Star of Jerusalem, one of the highest Palestinian honours given to a foreign national, in 2015.

The geopolitical legacy of the World Islamic Congress was also significant. In 1949, Hussaini convened an international conference in Karachi, in recently established Pakistan, as a sequel to the 1931 congress. In 1951, also in Karachi, he chaired the World Muslim Congress, attended by representatives of thirty-two Muslim countries. Its findings provided the foundation for the eventual establishment of the Organisation of the Islamic Conference in 1969, eventually renamed the Organisation of Islamic Cooperation, which still exists to this day.[23]

The Ottomans leave Europe

The Nizam had agreed in December 1931 for Princess Durrushehvar's mother to go to Hyderabad with her, along with Hussein Nakib, Abdulmejid's secretary. But he also wanted to invite the Caliph to visit Hyderabad and stay for a few weeks. After the row caused by the press coverage in Bombay, however, the British government put a quick stop to this plan. Keyes informed the Nizam that considering Shaukat Ali's 'indiscretions', the Caliph turning up in Hyderabad 'would perturb' Ankara and embarrass Britain. He also added that it would 'increase animosity of Hindu politicians [elsewhere in India] for Hyderabad… Hindu agitators are turning their attention to Hyderabad's heavy expenditure on outside Moslem concerns'. The Nizam had no choice but to postpone the Caliph's visit (in the end, it would never happen).[24] Keyes further advised the Nizam to defer the visit of the Caliph's wife, at which point Prince Azam Jah intervened, insisting that Durrushehvar's mother was a 'gentle retiring lady unconcerned with politics'. He got his way and she was given permission to go with her daughter.[25]

The evening after the weddings, Prince Ali Vasib and Prince Osman Fuad attended one of the oddest dinners of their lives: Prince Moazzam Jah invited the two to dine at his suite in the Negresco. When they arrived, they were taken to the sitting room to join a table with the prince and his aide-de-camp. No sooner had they been seated than Jah turned to the aide and began speaking to him in Urdu, resulting in an extended conversation (which the two Ottomans were unable to understand) that lasted for the entire two-hour meal. Eventually Ali Vasib and Osman Fuad began to speak to each other in Turkish, so that 'two separate conversations were going on in mutually incomprehensible languages until it was time for us to go home.' It was a strange evening.[26]

Vasib had mixed feelings about the Hyderabadi princes. 'Never before had I seen anyone throw money around in so profligate a fashion,' he later recalled. Their rooms were so full of items they had bought that they looked like shops. Azam Jah had a 'large number of decorative plates', which he would give out as presents, and he bought jewellery for Durrushehvar. Moazzam, meanwhile, presented Niloufer with new presents on a daily basis, including luxury dresses and furs. Vasib had to admit he was a 'man of impeccable taste'. Over the few weeks before they departed for India, the newly married couples threw a series of banquets at music halls and hotels across the Riviera.[27]

On 9 or 10 December, the couples and those accompanying them set sail on a steamer to Venice. From there they were bound for India.[28] The couples happened to be on the same liner as none other than Mahatma Gandhi, who was returning from the Round Table Conference in London. The Ottomans and Hyderabadis were first-class passengers; Gandhi, as was his style, travelled in steerage. He requested to meet the princesses, and a rendezvous was arranged in the second-class area of the liner.

What transpired is unknown—but it is clear that Niloufer came to admire the leader greatly. Years later, in February 1948 when Gandhi was assassinated, she wrote to Nehru—then India's prime minister—that a 'great silence' had set in after the Mahatma's passing. She expressed her hope that 'the house for which he [Gandhi] lived—for which he sacrificed and died will soon chime—the endless, the beautiful, the serene, and the realised hours of peace, love, and understanding.'[29] Evidently, Gandhi had made an impression on her.

When the couples arrived in Hyderabad on 31 December, the Nizam was at the station to greet them. He was fond of Azam Jah ('in his own queer way', Keyes thought) and when the two met they hugged, in a startling break from conventional decorum, 'patting each other on the back and weeping copiously'. In between sobs, the Nizam would turn to the crowd and explain: 'Fatherly affection; fatherly affection' and 'family greeting; family greeting'. Keyes reflected that the Nizam 'has really a very tender spot in his heart'.[30]

The Resident then set to work trying to head off any potential political controversies. So keen was he to dispel persistent rumours of an impending restoration of the Caliphate, that at a state banquet at the Chowmahalla Palace on 4 January 1932 in honour of the newlyweds, he gave a speech in which he specifically stressed that there was no 'deep-seated plan' behind the marriages.[31]

The Nizam was discomforted by the fact that his sons didn't officially hold the title Highness, meaning the Ottoman princesses were of a higher status: 'it will surely be derogatory to the status of my sons in the eyes of the Public if this invidious distinction is allowed to exist', he worried.[32] As a compromise, the British allowed Azam Jah to be titled Prince of Berar, a region which had been part of Hyderabad State but was taken over by the British in 1853, although the Nizam retained nominal sovereignty over the province.[33]

Despite his concern for his heir apparent's status, the Nizam was particularly impressed with Durrushehvar and her charm; so was everyone else. 'She has great dignity and self-possession,' thought Keyes admiringly. Most importantly, she showed 'every promise of being able to hold her own.'[34] But problems had already begun between Moazzam Jah and Niloufer. When they had stopped in Bombay on the way to Hyderabad, the prince devoted himself to his customary nightlife as though he had no bride; in Hyderabad he continued to ignore her. Keyes thought Niloufer was 'very attractive' and well educated, but was told she was somewhat 'difficult'. Yet there is no doubt that her husband quite severely neglected her.[35]

Azam Jah found his brother's conduct repulsive and wanted him pensioned off so he would leave Hyderabad. The Nizam, similarly furious with Moazzam Jah, threatened to withhold finances from him—at which point he suddenly began treating Niloufer much better, and 'there was a marked change in their relations.'[36] Azam Jah, meanwhile, was devoted to Durrushehvar, 'though he is of course quite incapable of appreciating her literary and musical tastes,' Keyes remarked.[37]

But rumours began swirling around the Nizam's wife, Dulhan Pasha. They were spread by Moazzam Jah, who was telling anyone that would listen that she planned to rule Hyderabad as Regent upon the Nizam's death: 'Mother is always experimenting with poisons,' he would add darkly, 'and there are no cats left in King Kothi'. Soon enough, talk of poisoning was everywhere and Azam Jah became convinced that his mother, who had opposed the marriages, would try to poison his wife.[38]

Keyes highly doubted that Durrushehvar was in any danger from Dulhan Pasha, and thought if there was any risk it would be from Moazzam Jah.[39] His colleague S.B. Patterson disagreed and speculated wildly that Dulhan Pasha (whom he called 'little better than [an] educated savage') was perfectly capable of poisoning not just the princesses but her own sons too. But Moazzam Jah, he was sure, would not kill his older brother, for the same reason that there had been no chance of Charles II of England being killed by his brother James: 'They would never murder me, James, to make you King.'[40]

Life in the capital

The Ottomans had mixed experiences in Hyderabad. Hussein Nakib, the Caliph's secretary, quickly realised that he was (for some unknown reason) tremendously unpopular at the Nizam's court, where people kept asking him when he was going back to France. Given that Abdulmejid hadn't ordered him back, Nakib was forced to keep saying 'very soon' and assuring people that he was preparing to leave.

One day, after he injured his heel, one of the Nizam's men grimly warned him that he would die if he stayed in Hyderabad. The secretary took the hint, left and went back to Nice, which turned out well for him; he fell in love with a housekeeper at the villa, Madame Grandjean. The two quickly married and rented a nearby house, continuing to work for Abdulmejid.[41]

In contrast, Niloufer's mother Princess Adile was a hit in Hyderabad. She brought gifts originally from Istanbul for the Nizam, including a Qur'an, some prayer mats and an array of vases. The Nizam was extremely pleased and made a note of each item on a small piece of paper, telling his orderlies to watch them overnight before they were transported to the treasury. The Nizam respected Adile and treated her well.[42] Over the next several years other members of the Ottoman family would visit from time to time, including Prince Osman Fuad, who loved to holiday there: there is a photo of him—looking extremely satisfied—posing gun in hand next to a dead bear he had killed on a hunting expedition.[43]

Caliph Abdulmejid had agreed before the weddings that Durrushehvar and Niloufer would go into purdah, traditional seclusion, in Hyderabad—and officially they did. But Keyes was pleased to see that 'the Nizam prescribes only a very nominal adherence to custom', so that in practice the princesses appeared at public events.[44]

Sultana Walajahi, aged eighty-six, lives in Surrey in south east England. Her late father, Hussain Abdul Munim, worked as a financial secretary for Hyderabad's treasury during the state's final decades. When I interviewed Walajahi on her recollections of Hyderabad, she recalled as a child seeing Durrushehvar and Niloufer at the Lady Hydari Club, an exclusive ladies' club set up by Lady Amina Hydari, Sir Akbar's wife. The building that hosted it is now derelict, with shattered windows, but it was once magnificent. 'I have wonderful memories of it,' Walajahi said. 'It was a very elegant, huge building made of stones, with gardens and tennis courts and badminton courts.'[45]

The ladies of the club attended regular tea parties at which 'the two princesses were the chief guests'. She remembered going to one with her mother as a child; everyone had to wait for the princesses to start eating before the food could be touched, although 'I would whisper, "Ammi [Mother], can I have one pastry?"' (the answer was invariably no). The princesses were bona fide celebrities. 'If they wore saris with beautiful brocade borders, everybody would try to copy that. If they wore chiffon saris with some gold or silver work, everyone would. They were trendsetters.'[46]

Describing her 'Indian country of adoption' as a 'land of beauty and romance', Durrushehvar told the English readers of the *Nottingham Evening News* in June 1933 that she was happy there (of course, it is hard to imagine her saying anything different in public). She lived with Azam Jah like a modern wife, without a harem: 'We share each other's lives, for I am my husband's only wife'. In writing for a British audience—accustomed to often sensationalised and lurid descriptions of Indian life by Western observers—Durrushehvar was playing a sort of ambassadorial role for Hyderabad.[47]

The women of the state, she explained, lived in a completely different way to their European counterparts. She found the habits of elite and poor women alike 'fascinatingly interesting, whether they are full of romance or full of hardship.' Durrushehvar pitied the poor working women for whom 'even age arrives too soon… Mate and mother before fifteen, the woman of the poor class is often grey, with wrinkles on her mahogany face, at the age of thirty!' These were people who worked from childhood until death: 'They live and die uncomplaining.'

In contrast, for a woman of the middle classes, her home was her dominion; 'her ambition—for she has ambitions—is imbibed by her children.' Aristocratic women, those with whom Durrushehvar had the most contact, led a comfortable existence in their exquisitely designed houses. The archetypal Indian lady of the aristocracy, Durrushehvar wrote, would have 'long black hair' and 'enormous black eyes', a 'shapefully chiselled nose' and 'amber-coloured cheeks, forming the characteristic oval face.' She would wear luxury jewellery, and a bracelet on each wrist if she was married. She might play the sitar, and sing in a musical motif which 'would seem monotonous to Western ears, but its poetic, beautiful words and melancholy melody have peculiar properties, and never fail to have their effect on the soul of the singer and audience alike'.

The lady would certainly walk with a 'sliding gait, her head held high' ('I have often tried and have never been able to master it,' the princess lamented).[48] Yet Durrushehvar observed that Hyderabad's society, like elsewhere, was in flux. She met women who had married in their early teens but later broke 'the ancient bonds of family slavery' by travelling to Europe to study. When they came back they worked, often as teachers.

The princess' writings are a fascinating window into Hyderabad's society at the time. Despite the reforms and transformations, Durrushehvar was at pains to stress to her British readers that Hyderabad wasn't losing its culture—for 'modern progress merely improves, but does not kill' the old ways. Hyderabadi women continued to wear their traditional dress. For a wealthy Muslim woman at home, this would be tight trousers, a blouse and a piece of muslin draped over the shoulder which could also be used to cover her head; 'its comforts cannot be disputed'.

Out and about, women wore saris—invariably richly embroidered, and 'no brocade and no embroidery equals the Indian product.' Not just Muslims, either—a Hindu woman would wear the sari 'in the same fashion as her Mohammedan sister.' Western makeup was rare among Hyderabad's women, which relieved Durrushehvar ('I have met a few who tried it, with no success at all. They looked grey under the generous dab of white powder, while the rouge on their brown lips was a visitor who had intruded with much indiscretion...'). Instead, women used paan (betel-leaf), the 'chewing-gum of India', to redden their lips.[49]

Elizabeth Cooper, a British writer who spent time in the capital, hit back against the idea—common in her country—that Hyderabadi women (at least the elites) were all miserable. She recorded that the mother reigned supreme in the women's quarters of every house. One noblewoman Cooper knew had a bodyguard of women soldiers who would salute and present arms at the arrival of every visitor. Cooper also met the wife of one of the Nizam's colonels, who had travelled across Europe and spent time in both Turkey and Egypt—all the while going about 'freely as any European'. On her return to Hyderabad she had become a secluded housewife; her daughter, by contrast, would go out as she wished.[50]

Cooper once went to a racetrack with the Congress politician Sarojini Naidu, where she was infatuated with the Indian riders: 'I think there is no handsomer man in the world than the high-class Indian gentleman,' she gushed. 'With his clear brown skin, his large black eyes, his stately carriage, and magnificent physique, accentuated by the pugaree or turban on his head, he is a picture that, once seen, cannot easily be forgotten'. The average Englishman, she complained, was 'either too fat or too thin', with a 'most unhealthy complexion'.[51]

At the race, English women watched from the stand whereas Indian women looked on from an upstairs room. They were dressed in the 'most brilliant colours' and one woman had no fewer than seven ear piercings, as well as a diamond in her right nostril, a ruby in her left and five diamond necklaces around her neck for good measure.[52] Cooper thought them 'extremely pretty' with 'exquisitely shaped mouths'. They all, she noted, seemed to be having much more fun than the English women in the stand below; they were 'chatting and laughing with the utmost freedom and goodfellowship'. She concluded that whatever the English view might be, these women didn't feel particularly hard done by.[53]

Princess Durrushehvar might have started off in Hyderabad by merely commentating on societal changes, but she soon began leading them. Sir Arthur Lothian, the Resident in the 1940s, recorded that Durrushehvar had 'done much for the advancement of women in Hyderabad', so 'now in no part of India will one see a greater number of educated and good-looking ladies at public functions'.[54] The princess patronised new nursing schools and colleges for women, a maternity hospital and schools for orphan girls.[55]

She believed no woman should have to beg to survive, but 'should be able to preserve her feminine pride and dignity with the dexterity of her hands and her own labour.' To this end, Durrushehvar talked constantly about domestic production and self-sufficiency. 'Whether she follows the old tradition or gets involved in new movements; whether she becomes poor or rich, every woman can serve her state and nation in proportion to her strength,' she declared. 'One of the most useful and comprehensive things that can be done for this purpose is the promotion of local industries.'[56] Her efforts won her plaudits from far and wide; in 1944 Gandhi himself wrote to her to praise 'how you are serving the poor in your part of India. May God bless you.'[57]

The princesses went back to Europe at regular intervals. In 1935, King George V celebrated his twenty-fifth anniversary on the throne and high-ranking dignitaries from across the British Empire were summoned to London for the celebrations. Azam Jah and Durrushehvar went as representatives of Hyderabad, and Durrushehvar wore the grand medal of the Order of the Ottoman Dynasty around her neck. As she entered the reception room, she encountered Turkey's prime minister, Ismet Pasha, who had been as complicit as anyone in the expulsion of the House of Osman. Rather smoothly, the prime minister politely greeted her and leaned forward to kiss her hand. But the princess rebuffed him, moved her hand to her chest, gripped the medal and waved it at him, before turning around and walking away. Durrushehvar was unwilling to play nice with the people who had forced her out of her home.⁵⁸

The nocturnal court

Princess Niloufer despised her time in Hyderabad. She had been used to the relatively modern and Western lifestyle she lived in France, and as the Caliph had foreseen, being transported to Hyderabad was like being thrust back in time. To be a princess was to be practically imprisoned, with one's lifestyle regulated and heavily surveilled.⁵⁹ Niloufer constantly worried that servants would report her conversations to the Nizam.⁶⁰

One day the ruler decided his daughters-in-law should have nose rings, like many Indian women. Niloufer's mother was horrified and threatened to disown her if she did such a thing (the Nizam ultimately dropped his plan). 'I never heard the nizam speak softly: he always screamed at the top of his voice,' Niloufer recalled.⁶¹ Despite the difficulties she faced, however, the princess took up charitable work alongside Durrushehvar, and had a hospital and a cancer research centre built in her name.

Later, during the Second World War amid an outbreak of venereal disease among Hyderabad's poor women, Niloufer would go 'from village to village' educating women on preventing it.⁶² During that time she caught typhoid fever and the Nizam sent her his personal healers. 'Instead of medicine, they tried to make me swallow crushed pearls,' she recalled decades later. 'Thank God I didn't take any of that, and I am still alive today.'⁶³

Descriptions of the princess from men who knew her invariably focus on her legendary beauty. Lothian declared that she was 'one of the loveliest women in the world'.⁶⁴ Much of civil servant Sir Conrad Corfield's account of his time in Hyderabad is dedicated purely to praising her attractiveness. In 1932 Corfield was stunned when he met the princess at a dinner. He felt she was the 'loveliest creature I had ever set my eyes on'. He was seated next to Niloufer; her 'violet eyes and blue black Circassian hair were enough to ruin a man's appetite'. Corfield hardly ate a thing and instead spent the evening gazing 'surreptitiously' (he himself judged) at her 'perfect features, her creamy complexion and the dimples in her cheeks'. Niloufer conversed with everyone in broken English, which she had only recently started learning. When dessert was served, Corfield 'pressed her to have a chocolate', at which point she looked across the table at Moazzam Jah and said, 'Please no, he say I already too fat'. Corfield 'couldn't see anything wrong with her figure myself'.[65]

A few years later he was overjoyed to see Niloufer again at a dinner in Delhi. He hurried up to speak to her but soon a whole queue of men had congregated, asking to be introduced to the princess one by one, until Niloufer found herself 'surrounded by a circle of admiring young officers', who Corfield complained 'were gradually edging me out'.[66]

On another occasion at a party thrown in honour of the Viceroy, Lord Willingdon, and his wife, Lady Willingdon, the Viceroy asked for Niloufer to sit with him. Corfield wrote that Niloufer sat demurely by his side and 'fixed her gorgeous eyes like headlamps full on his face'. Their conversation went on so long that Lady Willingdon eventually brought the Nizam with her to disrupt their discussion, saying, 'It's quite time we left!' The Viceroy reluctantly replied, 'Very well, my dear,' before turning to the Nizam and remarking, 'I haven't enjoyed myself so much for years!'[67] Least infatuated with Niloufer, it seems, was her own husband. She never bore Moazzam Jah children, much to the Nizam's disappointment.

One evening during my stay in Hyderabad, I asked Nawab Akram Abbas Syed, son of the Nizam's military secretary Colonel Amiruddin, about his memories of the two princes. We were sitting with his son Nawab Sayyid Ahmed Khan and my friend James at the dining table in his Hyderabad residence. Every second of the conversation felt like gold dust, as Syed, eighty-two, revisited his childhood. He has a short white beard and sharp eyes; with a purposeful gait and dignified—almost regal—posture, he speaks in the elegant and cultivated English of the Indian upper echelons, albeit with a subtle twang picked up from his time in Canada. His eyes lit up as he remembered the old days. It was like being transported into the past.

Syed recalled that even much later in Azam Jah's life, the prince would have his concubines dressed in riding breeches, and second

Syed's father Amiruddin to chaperone them. 'I remember I did ride with the concubines, and I was about eighteen or nineteen,' the Nawab said. By contrast, Moazzam Jah would call the elite of Hyderabad to fancy dress parties, and would have elite women sit and sing for him. Syed recalled that Jah once held a ball in the Banjara Hills, an upscale area of the capital, at which 'everyone had to be in fancy dress'. The Nawab remembered that his father 'was dressed as Rama, and my mother was dressed as Sita' (Rama and Sita are divine figures in Hinduism and central to the story behind the festival of Diwali, indicating the cosmopolitanism of Hyderabad's high society).[68]

While in Europe he had frequented cabaret bars, casinos and nightclubs, in the 1930s—still a young man—Moazzam Jah transformed himself into a sophisticated poet-prince. Every night he held a 'Nocturnal Court', as it was popularly known, at the Hill Fort Palace, his residence. His permanent courtiers slept during the day and spent each night immersed in poetry, music and fine dining. When the poet Sidq Jaisi first met Jah, he thought him 'handsome, delicate, gentle, and cultured'.[69] Being in his presence was no mean feat, though, since every time the prince praised a courtier, the latter would be expected to thank him by giving a 'salaam' (a salutation which involved dropping to the floor in an elaborate bow) seven times in quick succession.[70]

Once, Jaisi was summoned to see the prince, who began extolling the poet's skills to a courtesan companion, so that 'At every word of praise, I had to do seven floor salaams… there was no escape'. The prince forgot to explicitly invite him to sit down, meaning he was forced by etiquette to remain standing. Finally, after a full and strenuous hour, the courtesan took pity on him and asked Jah why Jaisi was still standing. The prince, shocked, asked him; 'Why don't you sit down?'[71] The poet then performed a final seven salaams in thanks and 'collapsed into a chair'.[72]

Court itself was an intense experience. It began at eleven o'clock every night. There were around thirty-five courtiers, who sat on elegant furniture around a great hall, with the prince at the head of the proceedings. The walls were 'adorned with exquisitely beautiful paintings', and between every two courtiers a teapoy held tins of the finest cigarettes. As Jaisi put it, 'there was such refinement in everything there and such an abundance of luxuries… Scenes from the Arabian Nights seemed to be brought alive in that court.'[73]

Moazzam Jah spent 'recklessly' on courtesans, especially for his Eid celebrations. One year a dozen were paid to come to Hyderabad, where they were put up in a bungalow, and at court a girl was sat next to each courtier.[74] But it wasn't just the courtesans who would dance—one courtier was a young male Hindu dancer whom Jaisi described as 'fair and delicate'. One night he was called up from his seat to perform—and 'was the cynosure of all eyes in the hall'.[75]

The prince was himself a poet, his pen name being 'Shahji'. His poems were often sung in the court to the accompaniment of a harmonium and tabla, which was tough work for the courtiers, who would vie with each other to shout praise of escalating vehemence after each verse ('This line has no parallel' / 'God be praised' / 'an invaluable addition to Urdu literature' / 'It is not the opening of a poem; it is the rising of the sun!' / 'Such felicity can't be humanly acquired').[76]

Despite the required hyperbole, Jah was in fact a genuinely talented poet and produced several masterpieces, some of which are sung by classical musicians to this day.[77] One such Urdu poem is titled 'The Night of Parting', here in English translation:

> That night of parting haunts my every breath,
> Though my memories are many, for more I yearn.
>
> Such time did I pass in separation's realm,
> Neither you did I think of, nor even myself.
>
> My eyes and heart were devoted to your kindness, yet
> More than that, your cruelty I remembered.
>
> When thought of you came, it was lonesome indeed.
> To neither joy nor sorrow did it lead.
>
> The one who destroys the world of my heart,
> For that heartless one, this heart still yearns.
>
> When trials he does craft with art,
> It is I he first calls to play the part.

My rivals he turns to for sweet embrace,
To test his sorrows, I take their place.

Time remembers you,
But when you are recalled, so am I.

Shahji alone to the garden did stray,
The memory of your footprints torments him to this day.[78]

Sometimes, Jah would add unexpected twists to his customary rituals. According to the poet Fani, there was one night on which the prince decided to arrange dinner on the lawn outside, with differently coloured light bulbs hanging from the branches of every tree in the vicinity. That it was monsoon season and the sky was overcast didn't deter Jah. Niloufer also joined him and his courtiers for the dinner.

As soon as the first course (soup) was served, rain began pouring down, filling up the bowls with water. Jah nonchalantly remarked that 'the soup is delicious today'. The courtiers sounded their agreement. As the rain intensified, the princess was allowed to go inside and dine in her chambers, but the courtiers weren't so fortunate. The rain poured down in torrents and still the courses came out, one by one: 'The dishes as they were served up were so watery that they were completely bland and unfit for consumption.' At dinner's end, the prince 'washed his hands with great composure'.[79]

The birth of Prince Mukarram Jah

Durrushehvar became pregnant just over a year after marrying Azam Jah, and headed to Nice for the later stages of the pregnancy. On 7 October 1933 came the longed-for moment—the baby was born, and it was a boy. He was named Mukarram Jah.[80] In Nice the Caliph was delighted; in Hyderabad cannons fired from the Chowmahalla Palace, fireworks lit up the sky and sweets were distributed across the capital. The Nizam treated the birth as an event of monumental importance.[81]

Extraordinarily, in the first year of the baby's life, Osman Ali Khan privately decided that his son Azam Jah would not, in fact, succeed him. Hyderabad's heir apparent was to be rubbed out of the succession—and it wouldn't pass to his brother either. Instead, the Nizam secretly appointed Mukarram Jah his successor.

'The reason why Azam Jah was not given the successorship was because of his flamboyancy,' Nawab Akram Abbas Syed told us. He recalled going with his father, the colonel, as a teenager to see Princess Durrushehvar in the 1950s. This was after the fall of Hyderabad, but before the princely titles were abolished. 'She was a very beautiful lady; she was always dressed in a sari and the sari would come over her head. Durrushehvar would stand there and say how the Nizam was, and how the successorship would be coming to Mukarram Jah.' Colonel Amiruddin was 'consulted as to how Mukarram Jah would take over and what his royal duties were going to be, and how he would behave on a royal platform.' The prince was groomed to take on the position of Nizam, even though it was merely ceremonial and power was with the Indian government.[82]

In the 1930s, though, there was special significance to the Nizam throwing Asaf Jahi custom out of the window and designating his baby grandson his successor as Nizam. The child was the living result of the marital union that had caused such a furore in 1931. That meant that decades into the future, as ruler of India's largest princely state and with Ottoman blood flowing through his veins, Prince Mukarram Jah would be perfectly placed to claim succession to the Prophet Muhammad and leadership of the Islamic world. Then, Hyderabad could ascend to unprecedented global prominence.

10

THE CALIPHAL SUCCESSION

In 1945, the Raja of Kotwara sent two women to a convent in France to find his young daughter. The Second World War had just ended and Syed Sajid Hussain Ali, the ruler of the northern Indian princely state, was busy campaigning with the Congress Party for Indian independence. Now that France was no longer under Nazi occupation, the Raja was intent on having his child—whom he had never met—found and brought to India.

The young girl, Princess Kenize, was born in France on 14 November 1939 to the exiled granddaughter of the Ottoman Sultan Murad V, Princess Selma. Less than two years later, Selma died and her young daughter was left in the care of a convent. Princess Kenize would not make it to India in 1945. The nuns who raised the girl were horrified at the thought of her being brought up by a Muslim prince and hid her. The Raja's rescue mission failed, and the child, who might have been raised in an Indian princely court, was instead brought up French.

'And so my life was predetermined by racism,' Princess Kenize told me eighty years later in Paris. 'The nuns hid me because in no way were they willing to give this nice little girl to a Muslim father. It was just that,' she reflected. 'Muslim for them meant devil.'

When I interviewed her in April 2025, the princess—better known today as Kenize Mourad—was sharp, perceptive and delightfully talkative. Stylishly dressed, she spoke English with an elegant French accent and a twinkle in her eye. Aged eighty-five, she was about to receive the most prestigious award in the country, the Légion d'Honneur—not in recognition of her royal status, but of her writing. Princess Kenize, with several books to her name, is in fact a distinguished author. She was once one of France's most fashionable novelists and the darling of its literary establishment. No longer: the royal explained to me that she had become thoroughly disenchanted with the country of her birth, and was only in Paris to receive the award. She would then leave for Turkey.

For years, Princess Kenize has effectively been persona non grata in the French media, a far cry from the days when her bestselling novels won her regular newspaper coverage and television appearances. The reason, she explained, was that she has written extensively on the Palestinian struggle against dispossession and occupation. This topic has always been distinctly out of fashion in French literary circles: 'I'm an idealist,' the princess told me. 'I'm fighting for the Palestinians, and I've paid for it dearly in France.'

After working for years as a left-wing journalist, she was made famous in the 1980s and 1990s through her novels. But her 2005 book *Our Sacred Land: Voices of the Palestine-Israeli Conflict* was the turning point—it marked the princess' return to journalism and was based on a journey she took through Israel and the occupied Palestinian territories. It was a collection of testimonies from Palestinians and Israelis alike and documented the iniquities of the occupation in the West Bank. 'The book was balanced,' Princess Kenize told me. 'I depicted Jews who were heroes and helped the Palestinians, standing against their government. I showed settlers who were very nasty.'

After its publication, she found herself subject to a press boycott. 'Before that book, I was always on television and my books were in all the papers. But afterwards it all stopped, and even my next novels were boycotted.' Her most recent book, a geopolitical thriller about Pakistan released in 2024, was widely reviewed in Pakistan but ignored in France. 'Nobody knows about it. Even many of my friends don't know I wrote it. My life has been really wounded by my position on Palestine.'

Although she was to be awarded the Légion d'Honneur, a search for her name online demonstrated that the press boycott remained in place. The environment in France had become so suffocating, Princess Kenize told me, that she had recently moved to Turkey—

from where her mother was exiled around a century ago. 'There are many problems in Turkey but it's not anti-Palestinian, it's not anti-Muslim.'

The princess appeared saddened by the situation, but not bitter. She didn't regret her writing on Palestine, she insisted, and would certainly not stop speaking about it. This uncompromising approach seemed fitting, given the extensive pro-Palestinian work of the man who had brokered her parents' marriage: Maulana Shaukat Ali.

Princess Kenize's first novel, *Regards from the Dead Princess*, was published in 1987. An intensely personal work, it was based on four years of research and told the tragic story of her mother, Princess Selma, the granddaughter of Sultan Murad. The princess was exiled from Istanbul with the rest of the Ottoman imperial family in 1924, and was among those who went to Beirut in Lebanon. 'They had little money,' Princess Kenize explained to me, 'and my grandmother was looking for my mother to marry a Muslim, a prince and somebody with money. There were two reservoirs of these sorts of people: the Egyptian monarchy and the Indian princes. She contacted Maulana Shaukat Ali, and he had my father in mind.'

The Maulana's success at brokering the marriages of Princess Durrushehvar and Princess Niloufer had made him a trusted ally of the House of Osman. He proposed that Selma should marry the Raja of Kotwara, a cosmopolitan potentate with a love of sports cars and a British education. The Raja went to university in Edinburgh, Princess Kenize laughingly told me, having decided against Oxford because 'students in their first year there could not have a car'. He was an unconventional figure—an avowed communist, despite his royal position, who threw his support behind the Congress Party.

'For the Maulana, it was very good for somebody in Indian politics to have a connection with the Ottoman family,' Princess Kenize said. Her mother travelled to Lucknow in north India in 1937 to be married. Like Princess Niloufer, she struggled with the demands and strictures of courtly life. 'My father was not religious, he was very progressive. But being in India, his wife had to obey all the customs—and my mother could not stand it.' When she was pregnant in 1939, Princess Selma travelled to Paris, accompanied only by a eunuch, to have her baby. She was stranded there when the war began, and Princess Kenize was born on 11 November that year. Two years later, Selma died in Paris of sepsis. Thus her daughter was raised in a convent as a Christian and a Frenchwoman, completely alienated from her heritage.

As a young woman, Princess Kenize discovered Islam, and she finally made it to India when she was twenty-one, meeting her father for the first time. I asked how she looked back on her upbringing. 'I've had an interesting life,' she reflected. 'But it has been very difficult to overcome all of this. I spent many years in depression trying to find my identity.' She added that she felt her life experiences had influenced and informed her writing on the Palestinian struggle: 'I experienced injustice, loneliness and poverty when I was young.' The princess paused to think. 'I think my whole life has been to fight by writing for the dispossessed and for minorities. The other important aspect has been to explain my native countries, Turkey and India, to my adopted country.'[1]

She may now feel alienated from France, which had been home to many Ottoman exiles, but Princess Kenize still has a devoted readership in India and Pakistan. And she remains an active and respected commentator in Turkey, where her ancestors ruled.

'India must pay homage'

Brokering the marriage of Princess Kenize's parents in 1937 was one of Maulana Shaukat Ali's final significant acts. By the time of his death the following year, he had made his mark on history.

The Khilafat Movement had failed but nonetheless transformed India as the first chapter of the mass movement for independence, while Ali's aim to join Islam's wealthiest dynasty with its Caliphal family had succeeded. But Ali was not going to retire quietly—instead, in his final years he entered a new phase of his political career, plunging himself into Muslim League politics as a close ally of Muhammad Ali Jinnah.

In 1935, the Maulana was elected in northern Uttar Pradesh for the Central Legislative Assembly, turning from a campaigner into a parliamentarian.[2] During that time, it seems he reconciled with the Nizam, who started paying him monthly to help fund his activities. Ali never did things by halves: he had the old Khilafat House repurposed into a Muslim League campaigning office and flew both the Khilafat Committee flag and the Muslim League flag there. 'Mohamed Ali was my younger brother but I had accepted him as my leader,' he told Jinnah. 'Now, you are my leader, and I will work as a soldier under your leadership.'[3] Unquestionably, he did. The 1937 elections went disastrously for the Muslim League, which lost badly everywhere and failed to win a single seat in Punjab, but Ali was an exception. He was indefatigable and enormously effective on the campaign trail; 'God had given him such magnetic attraction that thousands of people would come just on hearing his name,' one Leaguer said admiringly.[4] The veteran politician never lost hope that India would overcome its religious conflict. In 1938, shortly before his death, Ali predicted that soon all of India's communities would 'bury the hatchet and face their white rulers with one common demand.'[5] It was not to be.

On 6 November 1938 Ali's only surviving daughter, Sultana, died. He was devastated, and in Delhi fell ill and was told he had bronchitis. On the morning of 27 November, Ali asked his nephew to set out a chair for him on his house's verandah. He sat down and enjoyed the winter morning air. Then, at half past nine, the Maulana uttered the word 'Allah' and breathed his last. Ali's grandson later recalled that he 'used to tell his grandchildren, in a good humoured way, that as and when the angel of death came to him, there would be a long and furious wrestling match between them. But when that moment came, Shaukat Ali went away quickly, whispering the name that had sustained him at every juncture of his eventful life.'[6]

There was an outpouring of grief. Ali's funeral procession to Delhi's grand Jama Masjid was attended by thousands of people from all religious communities. 'My personal association with him was that of a dear friend,' said Jinnah, 'and his loyalty to the All India Muslim League and to me, personally, was unswerving, staunch, and he stood by us like a rock. By the passing away of such a man, I feel that it would be difficult to fill the gap, and his loss has been a great blow, almost irreparable.'[7]

The League's political enemy, Jawaharlal Nehru, also praised Ali. 'I had the privilege of close comradeship with him,' Nehru told the

Associated Press, 'and the subsequent differences of opinion with him cannot take away the bright memory or lessen the grief at the passing away of one who played a great part in India's struggles. Essentially a fighter, he has died in harness, and India must pay homage to him.' Congress leader Bhulabhai Desai called Ali 'magnificently endowed in mind, emotions and physique', a man of 'abounding energy'. Congressman Madhav Aney added that Ali was 'big in every sense of the word', adding that there was 'bigness in his mind and in the magnificent physique, beside which I looked like a dwarf.'[8]

In death, Ali was a veritable Indian hero. He didn't live to see just how dark the subcontinent's politics were about to become.

The death of the Caliph

Abdulmejid II spent his final years in Paris, the city in which Princess Kenize was born. Seventy years old in November 1938 and still a Francophile, he sang the praises of the 'sublime institutions and advancements' in that 'preposterously civilised place'.[9] He rented a villa in Paris close to the forest, while one of his secretaries, Huseyin Nakib, lived near the Eiffel Tower.[10]

The following year, the Second World War broke out. Under German occupation Abdulmejid barely saw anyone and spent his days writing his memoirs, whose whereabouts are unknown. He also immersed himself in his art and the house was filled with his paintings, mostly of family members he missed dearly.[11] 'Enemy planes come and fly over our heads,' Abdulmejid complained in May 1940. But he would ignore air raid sirens when they sounded at night, remaining in his bed 'even when everybody runs to the basements', since the 'unsettling sound does not terrify me'.[12]

In 1942, an unsuspecting Nakib was arrested by the occupying Germans, accused of being a spy and thrown into the notorious Fresnes prison. The experience was traumatic: 'I heard shots every morning as the Germans regularly carried out executions,' he recounted. He was kept in solitary confinement 'without pencil, paper or reading matter', and the Germans 'took everything I possessed.' Nakib had seen a lot of brutality in his life, having once been a soldier. 'But never in forty years have I seen anything so savage as the Germans,' he proclaimed, stressing that 'I say this in all objectivity.'[13]

The Caliph was in severe financial difficulty; the Nizam's money was unable to reach him owing to the occupation.[14] He began making arrangements in the event of his death, and was set against being buried in the Ottoman family tomb in Damascus, because of his old enmity towards his cousin Sultan Mehmed Vahideddin, who was buried there; he 'was the cause of our downfall'. On 2 May 1939, the Caliph wrote to the Nizam expressing a wish to be buried either in Beirut, where much of the Ottoman imperial family had moved, or in India.[15]

His death came in 1944. Abdulmejid's final days were devastating. His life had been often joyous and always interesting, but ultimately tragic. Raised in confinement, he knew only a brief spell of freedom in Istanbul before the hardship of the Great War. Then, during the national struggle, he was placed in confinement once more. And although he ascended to the Caliphate, it was only briefly and he was soon forced out of his country. While he loved the French, neither Nice nor Paris could substitute for his beloved Istanbul. The Caliph was doomed to live and die in exile. He would never see his home again.

But still he never lost hope that the situation would improve—if not for himself then for future generations. Abdulmejid never accepted the abolition of the Caliphate, and was evidently committed to the institution and to Islam until his final breath. Old and sick under German occupation, he placed his hopes in Hyderabad. There the Ottoman legacy might live on; there the Caliphate could be declared once more.

The last Ottoman Caliph breathed his last on the evening of 23 August 1944. He was seventy-six years old. American troops, trying to liberate France, were fighting the Germans nearby: when stray bullets flew into the villa, Abdulmejid had a heart attack. Word was sent to Hussein Nakib, no longer in prison. His trusty secretary, who had been loyal throughout all those long years of exile, picked up a doctor and the two rushed as fast as they could to the villa, with bullets 'whistling over their heads'. By the time they arrived, Caliph Abdulmejid was dead and there was nothing to be done.[16]

After the last Caliph

Abdulmejid had one surviving sister, Princess Nazime, who was in Beirut. In the summer of 1945, the Caliph's granddaughter Princess Neslishah visited her there. Neslishah later recalled that Abdulmejid's death had made Nazime lose her mind with grief—she was 'totally demented, and her eyes were the eyes of a madwoman.' Nazime took Neslishah around the house, leading her by the hand, until they came to one room containing just a piano, a chair and a framed picture of Abdulmejid.

The elderly princess sat down and began pressing the keys, her eyes dead and expressionless. Then, catching sight of the Caliph's photograph, her whole face lit up. She suddenly seemed to be woken out of a stupor. 'Her eyes, her mouth, her whole aspect became normal again.' Smiling at the photograph, Nazime's fingers relaxed and she began to play Chopin perfectly. After a while the smile faded, and Nazime seemed lost once more. 'I felt like crying, but I didn't,' Neslishah remembered. 'I was just trembling all over.'[17]

At that point Abdulmejid was still not buried, his body having been embalmed and interred in the Paris Mosque.[18] He would be there for nearly a decade more. As soon as the Caliph died, his daughter Princess Durrushehvar—then in her thirties—had taken it upon herself to arrange his affairs. 'News has just reached me,' she wrote in a telegram to her mother as soon as she heard of the death. 'You are not alone in your sorrow.'[19]

Durrushehvar was intent on going to Paris, which would be no mean feat considering the war and occupation. The Nizam was initially set against the idea, but the princess stood her ground and persuaded him. 'My father is not buried,' she stressed to the Nizam, adding pointedly that 'I know you will not prevent me from carrying out my last duty to my father.'[20]

Osman Ali Khan reluctantly agreed.[21] He ordered a day of mourning in Hyderabad, with all the offices and schools in the capital to be closed and a memorial service held at the Mecca Masjid. He advised Durrushehvar to bear the loss 'with fortitude and courage as death is nothing new or unexpected in this transient world.'[22] Practical difficulties meant she wasn't able to go to Paris until February the next year.[23]

I ploughed through records of correspondence between the Nizam, Durrushehvar and British officials in the British Library to try to piece together what happened after the Caliph's death. More than anything else, I was looking for a crucial telegram written by the then Resident in Hyderabad, Sir Arthur Lothian. It was on the topic of Abdulmejid's final wishes. The telegram had been mentioned in *The Last Nizam* (2005), a biography of Prince Mukarram Jah written by the Australian historian John Zubrzycki.[24] When I came across the reference, I was stunned. I resolved to find it in the British Library archives and discover exactly what it said.

The letter concerned the issue of succession. The Ottoman succession was a matter of considerable contention at the time, since the Empire and the Caliphate had ended. Succession had occurred in myriad ways throughout Ottoman history, some of which involved fratricide and others janissaries hauling bewildered princes out of the harem and placing them on the throne based on their perceived pliability. Towards the end of the Empire, a convention was established that the eldest prince would become the head of the Ottoman dynasty upon the ruler's death; this was how Abdulmejid was labelled Crown Prince and successor to Mehmed Vahideddin, although he was only recognised as Caliph through the unprecedented process of election by the Grand National Assembly. Now that he had died, the Ottomans saw Abdulmejid's eldest cousin Prince Ahmed Nihad as the natural head of the family. He was in Beirut, where he lived until his death in 1954.[25]

But Nihad didn't claim the Caliphal title, and it was only in 1948 that the family decided they should appoint a family head on an official basis, giving Nihad a list of duties, a salary and a car. At that point Prince Omer Faruk stepped forward and argued that he, not Nihad, should be the family's head because he was Abdulmejid's son.[26] Unhappily for him, his candidacy received no support— not even from his wife Princess Sabiha, whom he divorced soon afterwards.[27] Evidently, the question of how the succession should properly have been done was contested. This was a time of flux and all convention had broken down, as it had done when Abdulmejid was elected Caliph.

But what had Abdulmejid actually wanted? Princess Durrushehvar held his wish in the form of a *wassiyat*, a type of will intended for a specific person, in this case the Nizam. The princess treated it as greatly important; while in Dehradun, a city in northern India, she sent a telegram to the Nizam on 19 October 1944 telling him her father had 'made Vassiat to you'. She would, she promised, 'present the letter urgent [upon] my arrival in Hyderabad.'[28]

The whereabouts of the document, which was closely guarded, are unknown. But the message sent by Sir Arthur Lothian to his colleagues in Delhi refers to its extraordinary contents.

The Caliph's final wishes

In the British Library archives, I pored through bundles of documents in search of the telegram until I found it, buried in a weighty file. It was on a piece of paper marked 'confidential'. Lothian sent the message on 20 November 1944, three months after Abdulmejid had died in Paris.[29]

In the bombshell dispatch, Lothian disclosed that he had discovered the Nizam was withholding information from the British about the late Caliph's 'wassiyat'. He informed the Government of India in New Delhi that the Nizam (who by then had seen the *wassiyat*) had informed him that the Caliph wanted to be 'buried either in Hyderabad or in one of the holy cities of Arabia'.

He explained that the Nizam said that Lothian's predecessor Sir Duncan Mackenzie had advised against allowing the Caliph to come and live in Hyderabad State, warning of the 'political dangers' it would bring. And so, the Nizam concluded, he was opposed to the Caliph being buried in the state, 'as he had nothing to do with Hyderabad in his life'. It is easy to see the logic here: the situation was febrile, with Indian independence on the horizon and Hindu-Muslim tensions at fever pitch.

But Lothian then disclosed that he had spoken to the Nawab of Chhatari—at that point the president of the Nizam's executive council, the state's prime minister. Chhatari revealed two key points to Lothian. The first was that he had seen a copy of the *wassiyat* in the possession of Princess Durrushehvar, and that the Caliph's 'expressed preference was for burial in Hyderabad'. This wasn't what the Nizam had told Lothian. The Resident learned something else about the *wassiyat*, too: 'The Nizam also omitted to tell me the interesting fact that the ex-Sultan had named therein Mukarram Jah, son of the Prince and Princess of Berar, as his successor in the Khalifate [Caliphate].'[30] Lothian refers to Abdulmejid as the 'ex-Sultan' rather than the ex-Caliph, a common mistake made by British officials.

This extraordinary communiqué shows that the British learned that Caliph Abdulmejid aimed for Hyderabad to be the future seat of the Caliphate. Lothian thought the revelation was 'interesting' and informed New Delhi.[31] He saw no cause for concern or alarm; after all, the British expected to pull out of India imminently and did so less than three years later. Mukarram Jah was still a child. His Indian grandfather was only sixty (he would live for another twenty years). Mukarram Jah wouldn't become the Nizam in the foreseeable future—and so the Caliphal succession was simply not considered a problem for the British government, as long as it remained a secret.

Months later I discussed the topic with Ayub Khan, the researcher who argued that the purported Caliphal deed of 1931 was of questionable provenance. He highlighted something crucial: in 1974 Chhatari, a reform-minded politician who had formerly governed the United Provinces in the north, published his memoirs.[32] That was three decades on from the events following the Caliph's death.

In this obscure Urdu text, Chhatari wrote that the Nizam told him Abdulmejid had named his son-in-law, Prince Azam Jah, as the next Caliph. The *wassiyat* said that 'there has been detailed discussion with his son-in-law, His Highness, Prince [Azam] Jah'. The Nizam 'instructed me that His Highness Prince Azam Jah said that the discussion with Prince Azam Jah which the late Caliph has mentioned in his will, the upshot of it was that after the late Caliph, Prince Azam Jah should become the Caliph of the Muslims.'[33]

This flatly contradicts Lothian's letter, which refers to Mukarram Jah, Azam's son. The memoirs also indicate why Chhatari might have been indiscreet and spoken to Lothian about the issue: he was opposed to any Caliphal scheme. The prime minister wrote in his memoirs that the Nizam asked for his opinion. Chhatari reflected that the Caliphate 'is no landed title, that should the Caliph not have a son, the son-in-law should inherit.'[34] Abdulmejid, however, did have a son, which makes this an irrelevant argument.

While Chhatari's correspondence further establishes that Abdulmejid wanted the Caliphal line to pass through the Asaf Jahi dynasty in Hyderabad, it introduces a new mystery. Which generation of the Asaf Jahi dynasty did Abdulmejid wish the Caliphal line to pass through: father or son? Why would the last Caliph choose his son-in-law, who was not a direct descendant and member of the Ottoman dynasty, as his successor? After all, Abdulmejid must have known that the Nizam had quietly designated Mukarram Jah as his heir.

Chhatari never mentioned in his memoirs, which cover events until 1948, that Mukarram Jah had been selected as the Nizam's heir when he was still young—a significant omission. While it would not have been public knowledge at the time, it was crucial as to whom Abdulmejid would have designated his successor. One reason for the contradiction between the accounts may thus be their intended audiences. Lothian's letter was private correspondence, ultimately for the Viceroy of India, on a matter of government intelligence. In contrast, Chhatari's book was published for public consumption. It is also possible Azam Jah was arguing that he should hold the Caliphal title until his son reached adulthood, at which point it could then be transferred to him. The whereabouts of Abdulmejid's wasiyyat are still unknown. The precise truth is, for now, beyond reach. But on the balance of probabilities, it is reasonable to conclude that Abdulmejid wanted his grandson Mukarram Jah, rather than Azam Jah, to claim the Caliphal title.

In July 2025, I spoke to a man who had known Mukarram Jah more intimately than nearly anyone else. Shahid Husain Zuberi, now in his seventies, began working for Jah in 1969 at the age of twenty-three and knew him for nearly half a century. He became a close confidante of the Prince, who was the eighth titular Nizam, and served as the chairman of his private estate. I asked Zuberi about

THE CALIPHAL SUCCESSION

the purported Caliphal deed which had surfaced in Hyderabad. 'I am not competent enough to give my opinion on it', he said.

However, he told me, he clearly recalled Jah speaking about the Caliphate. 'Prince Mukarram Jah himself told me that he was to be the successor of the Caliphate', Zuberi said. The intention behind the 1931 marital union, he strongly believes, was that the Caliphate should be transferred to Hyderabad. How did Jah feel about his maternal grandfather's legacy? Zuberi said the Prince never spoke in detail about it, but 'he must have surely revered it'. He added that the Prince 'was never proud of anything in his life. Instead he was always thankful to the Almighty'.[35]

The abandoned mausoleum

There is one final and remarkable component to the death of the last Caliph and his final wishes. In February 1945, Durrushehvar finally returned to her home city, Istanbul. She got around the ban on the House of Osman by entering as the Princess of Berar, her title in India. But her return was far from victorious; she was a petitioner, asking if her father could be buried in the city. Durrushehvar was invited to Ankara to meet the president, who unfortunately turned out to be the former prime minister, Ismet Pasha—the man Durrushehvar had insulted in London years earlier. Neither of them mentioned the incident, but Ismet denied the princess' request to have the Caliph buried in Turkey.[36]

Shortly afterwards, the Nizam made a move and asked the British whether he could build a tomb for Abdulmejid in Hyderabad State. On 1 February the following year, the Government of India's Secretary of State, Frederick Pethick-Lawrence, wrote to the Viceroy, Lord Archibald Wavell, about the issue. 'I can think of only one ground on which burial in Hyderabad might cause us embarrassment,' he said, 'and that is the possible effect of the question of the succession to the Khalifate [Caliphate].' He noted Lothian's 1944 dispatch, which had reported that Abdulmejid had 'named as his successor Mukarram Jah, the heir presumptive of Hyderabad.'[37] At this point the official heir apparent was still Azam

THE INDIAN CALIPHATE

Jah, so the description of Mukarram Jah as 'heir presumptive' makes it clear that the British were aware of the Nizam's plans.

The Secretary of State weighed up the risk and mused:

> Certainly 25 years ago Muslims in India would have considered this an important fact. While I am not in a position to know how much the Khalifate is now a burning question in India I can conceive that, if it remains potentially so, the bringing of this body with some ceremony for burial in Hyderabad, and the news, if it were to leak out, that the heir presumptive had inherited the Khalife [Caliphate] might be an embarrassment not only in India, but in the Muslim world generally.[38]

However, he calculated, 'there seems a reasonable chance that neither the Nizam nor, in his turn, the Prince of Berar [Azam Jah], will disclose the terms of the "Wassiyat" as they would probably dislike the idea of distracting attention from themselves to Mukarram Jah.' This appears to reference the fact that Mukarram Jah being the Nizam's designated heir was a secret. He added with a dash of caution that 'we cannot exclude the possibility that the princess [Durrushehvar] will make the disclosure', but noted that the Foreign Office had been consulted informally and had no objection to the Caliph being buried in Hyderabad. Unless the Viceroy thought otherwise, he concluded, 'I agree that Lothian may be authorised to tell the Nizam should he raise the matter again, that His Majesty's Government see no objection to the body being buried in Hyderabad.'[39] Since the mausoleum was built, it appears that the British gave permission for the Nizam to honour the Caliph's wishes.

This correspondence demonstrates that a year and a half after Lothian's dispatch, the British considered it a matter of fact that Abdulmejid had appointed Mukarram Jah his Caliphal heir—and were making decisions on that basis. Nothing had happened to make Lothian revise his view. Had the Resident discussed the issue further with Chhatari or other members of the Hyderabadi government in the time since his original message was sent? It seems plausible.

In April 2024, James and I flew from Hyderabad early one morning to Aurangabad, in the western state of Maharashtra. There we visited the abandoned mausoleum in Khuldabad, an area that had been part of the Nizam's state. Today, the mausoleum feels remote, yet its location is anything but random. Aurangabad is a region of deep political significance: it was once home to the capital of the Delhi Sultanate, a medieval Indo-Islamic empire. The magisterial Daulatabad Fort, still standing, serves as testament to this. In Khuldabad, too, stands the tomb of the last powerful Emperor of the Mughal Empire, Aurangzeb Alamgir—the historical ruler who was most revered by the seventh Nizam. Also in the area is the resting place of Asaf Jah I, the first Nizam of Hyderabad.

Khuldabad is further imbued with spiritual significance: numerous Muslim saints are buried there. A well-known shrine to the famous saint Hazrat Amir Hasan Sanjari is close to the Ottoman mausoleum. An obscure book in Urdu published in 2001 entitled *Gulistan-e-Khuldabad* documents the area's history.[40] Its author, Mohammad Abdul Hai, knew the region well: 'Nature has blessed this area with all its gifts,' he wrote in Urdu. 'Whoever comes here for spiritual elevation would surely be imprinted with lasting effects from nature.'[41]

In 1971, decades after the fall of Hyderabad State, Princess Durrushehvar visited the region. Abdul Hai accompanied her. He recalls in his book how, having paid her respects at the tomb of the first Nizam, the princess 'expressed a desire to see her father's empty tomb and went directly from there' to the Caliph's mausoleum. It must have been a moving experience. 'Upon seeing the tomb, she remarked that the dome was built in the design of Turkey's Istanbul.'[42]

Abdul Hai provides illuminating details about the story behind the tomb: the Nizam ordered that a place be selected in Khuldabad for the structure 'with special care that the chosen spot should be lower than all the tombs of the buried saints'. A place was selected on a hillock three kilometres west of Khuldabad city. Construction began (it is unclear exactly when) 'on fifteen acres of land'.[43]

It was to be an ambitious project, 'including a domed structure, mosque, garden, and a khanqah [place of retreat] for pilgrims'. A paved road was even built between the shrine of the saint Hazrat Amir Hasan Sanjari and the tomb. By 1948, the mausoleum itself had been built and a grand door fitted at the entrance, made of carved sheesham wood. Work on the surrounding complex was about to begin.[44]

Then came the fall of Hyderabad.

Prince Mukarram Jah

At this point, Prince Mukarram Jah was still a boy. He had spent his childhood summers in Nice with his mother and the Caliph, of whom he later remembered little apart from his 'always stern expression'. As a child there he would play in the Roman ruins and go on walks in the idyllic surrounding area.[45]

The Nizam opposed Princess Durrushehvar's wishes for her son, which were for him to attend Eton and become a cultivated cosmopolitan—and Europeanised—gentleman. This would make him far too foreign, Osman Ali Khan reasoned. Instead he was tutored in Hyderabad as a young child.[46] In 1944, he was sent to a Western-style school in the foothills of the Himalayas, which Durrushehvar was more pleased about.[47]

By age thirteen Mukarram Jah could speak English, French, Turkish and Urdu. He was a skilled horse rider, and liked to drive jeeps and disassemble engines. Some abilities he lacked; he 'could not catch a ball' and was unable to do simple arithmetic. He had, however, shot a tiger.[48] Once he was back in Hyderabad a British tutor was sought for himself and his younger brother Muffakham.

Philip Mason, who had worked in the Defence Department of the Government of India, was brought to Hyderabad in 1947 where he met Durrushehvar. She thought he was a good fit and he was appointed tutor and governor to the two princes.[49] Mason was hugely admiring of Durrushehvar, whom he described as a 'commanding figure, handsome of feature, with a clear fair complexion and auburn hair'—and an 'imposing figure'. She wore 'superb' saris and was quite in command; no one 'could ignore her or slight her'.

Mason reflected years later that

> if fate had so willed she might have been one of the great queens of the world. She would have been as imperious as Elizabeth I of

England and she would have demanded as much from the young men of her court, sent them as readily to their death on the Spanish Main, teased them as merrily and as cruelly.

He added that she 'would not have seen so clearly the virtues of compromise' as the sixteenth-century queen.⁵⁰

One great mystery is what exactly the Nizam thought of Caliph Abdulmejid's designs for the Caliphate. Philip Mason provides an indication.

As tutor to the young princes, he spent considerable time not just with Durrushehvar but also with British and Hyderabadi officials in the state. Mason came to believe that the Nizam aspired to make Hyderabad the seat of the Caliphate, recalling in the 1970s that the Nizam 'had long cherished the ambition to be regarded one day as the Khalif [Caliph] of Islam, the Shadow of God upon Earth, an office which had fallen into abeyance when the last Emperor of Turkey was forced from the throne.' He asserted that it was with 'this in mind' that the Nizam 'had married his elder son to the daughter of the last Emperor.'⁵¹ Mason might have been hazy on the details, but this indicates that he heard talk of Hyderabad's government aspiring to the Caliphate.

This is further corroborated by the English travel writer and novelist Rosita Forbes: visiting Hyderabad in 1939 (before the Caliph's death), she had spent considerable time in conversation with the state's then prime minister, Sir Akbar Hydari, whom she found not only clever and wise but also 'reasonably democratic' in character, and 'immensely hospitable'.⁵² Hydari, lunching with Forbes by the city's Marble Arch, invited her to study Hyderabad under his guidance and 'shoot unnumbered tigers' to relax.⁵³ She took him up on the offer and eventually came to think that 'Hyderabad may well remain a contended State tending towards constitutional if not yet democratic government under the aegis of intelligent Princes whose Faith is their own private affair, but whose position as leader of that Faith must add to the prestige of their country.'⁵⁴ This referred to the Nizam as an Islamic—and tolerant—ruler.

Having spent time with Hydari, Forbes asserted that the Nizam was 'the predominating religious personality in orthodox Islam'.

The Muslims of India who would have looked to a Caliph in Istanbul, she wrote, were now 'inclined to transfer their traditional allegiance, spiritual and cultural, to the Ruler of Hyderabad'.[55] In fact, she understood, the Asaf Jahi dynasty was 'irrevocably allied with the fountain-head of orthodox Islam and committed to the principle of the Caliphate'.[56]

It is quite possible—especially considering that the Nizam aspired to make Hyderabad independent in the 1940s—that Mason and Forbes were quite correct, and that the world's richest Muslim aimed ultimately to have his lineage claim the Caliphal title.

The road to Partition

In the 1940s, everyone expected that the British would shortly leave India. The real question was what the subcontinent would look like once they were gone. Secular Indian nationalists, claiming to represent all Indians, continued to reject the Muslim League's proposals for constitutional safeguards for Muslims. Pakistan became a serious proposition only when the League's offer of a coalition in 1937 was rejected by the Congress, which had taken power in seven out of eleven provinces but won no Muslim-reserved seats.[57] Congress ministries began introducing laws to please Hindu nationalists, like bans on cow slaughter. In 1940 the League (which claimed to represent all Muslims) passed the famous Lahore Resolution, ambiguous enough to be interpreted as calling for a separate Muslim state but also, potentially, for a Muslim state within an Indian federation.[58]

Where were the princely states to fit in? Congress heavyweight Sarojini Naidu believed India had a 'federated national life' and culture. This meant that only through a federation could it be united. In 1925 she told the Congress that 'when we have the great federation of free India, the Indian [princely] states will come in as an integral unit of Greater India working on the same basis of democratic freedom with the people of [British] India.'[59] A federation would be quite unlike a modern nation state—and unlike British rule too. Federal proposals represented attempts to conceptualise an alternative political arrangement to a unitary, centralised nation state.

But at the same time, Hyderabadi politics were being transformed. The 1930s had seen the rise of the Majlis-e Ittehad al-Muslimin, an Islamic party which promoted a populist brand of Muslim politics. The Ittehad's idea of Islamic governance bore little resemblance to Mughal-style rule, which saw no problem in the majority of the population being Hindu. By contrast, the Ittehad began a massive drive to increase the Muslim population of the state through proselytising Islam to lower-caste Hindus and Dalits.[60] In July 1939 a raft of political reforms came into effect: a legislature was set up with eighty-five members. Forty-three were to be elected; of those, seats were reserved for different economic interests and half were reserved for Muslims, who would be vastly overrrepresented. The aim was to preserve Muslim rule in the state, which was fatally threatened by the prospect of any genuine democratisation.[61]

The Ittehad's rise in popularity was due to Congress agitation in Hyderabad, some of which was violent and took on a Hindu nationalist and anti-Muslim flavour. According to British intelligence in 1939, rather than there being a danger of civil war in Hyderabad, the real risk was from outside agitators: 'any danger that there might have at one time been of civil disturbance in the State was due to Muslim resentment' against agitators who were 'invading the State'.[62]

That same year the Nizam signalled he would accept a federation—but with the proviso that he would have total autonomy within the state, and a guarantee of British protection. In March 1939 the British offered up a half-hearted and deliberately vague statement saying Britain would give it 'if it could'. The Nizam couldn't accept this.

Meanwhile elsewhere in India, an eclectic mixture of ideas was circulating. A pro-Muslim League group of Islamic scholars in the north west frontier provinces passed a resolution in 1940 calling for the Nizam to be made the King of Pakistan.[63] The following year, a group within the League, which called itself the 'Muslim League Foreign Sub-Committee' (despite Jinnah refusing to commit to any constitutional proposals), called for two federated Muslim states in the north, with Hyderabad as a 'Third Zone of Muslim Influence and Power' on the grounds that it was not the creation of the British and had existed before British rule—and that it was the 'principal seat of the culture of Muslim India'.[64] Moreover Choudhary Rahmat Ali, who had coined the name Pakistan, argued for an independent Muslim zone in the Deccan named 'Osmanistan' after the Nizam, although he was sceptical of dynastic rule.[65]

In 1946 the recently elected Labour government under Clement Attlee, keen to pull Britain out of India, sent a Cabinet Mission to try to formulate an agreement for a political structure post-independence. The resulting plan recommended an Indian federation with a central government responsible for defence, foreign affairs and communications. There were to be three groups of provinces—two of them Muslim (in the west and the east) and one, the largest, Hindu.[66] The princely states would remain autonomous. At that point the British believed the Nizam was 'not unprepared' to have Hyderabad enter a federation.[67]

The problem was that the two most important players—Jinnah and Nehru—had completely incompatible political visions. Nehru was very clear what he wanted: India as a socialist, democratic and modernising republic—a unitary nation state. A federation would make his state-building ambitions impossible, especially because of the princely states. Better give away some of the land to Jinnah for Pakistan, Nehru reasoned, than lose much more to a federation, which he thought would mean not Partition but 'an indefinite number of partitions'.[68] Although Jinnah had accepted the Cabinet Mission Plan, it fell apart later that year when Nehru succeeded Maulana Abdul Kalam Azad as Congress president. Nehru said he opposed grouping provinces together, which threatened Jinnah's desire to control the two Muslim provinces and effectively establish Pakistan within the Indian federation. Jinnah accused Nehru of betraying the terms of the Cabinet Mission Plan and rescinded his acceptance of it. The stage was set for Partition.

On 9 September 1946, the Nizam made the British aware that 'I am not one of the believers in Pakistan… [Jinnah] should ask for the proper share of the Muslim community in the administration of the country along [with] other communities who no doubt are the equal share-holders of their "communal property".'[69] The leader of the Muslim League had a rocky relationship with the Nizam. In 1946, their meeting in Hyderabad to discuss the state's future had failed miserably when Jinnah sauntered into the meeting smoking a cigar, before casually sitting in front of the Nizam with his legs outstretched ('Do you know who I am?' the Nizam shouted, at which point Jinnah hurriedly threw his cigar away).[70]

But as independence drew closer, Jinnah initially tried to persuade the Nizam to join Pakistan, which could have worked if Pakistan had been a component of an Indian federation, which Jinnah had likely wanted. Now the idea was entirely implausible. The Congress could not possibly accept a giant state in the heart of the Indian Union being a part of Pakistan.[71] Jinnah eventually encouraged the Nizam to aim for independence. To that end, Hyderabad tried to acquire port facilities in Portuguese Goa and build a rail link from the state to the sea, which would facilitate trade.[72] The Nizam agreed to a proposal in July for the Indian Union to control Hyderabad's foreign relations, defence and communications, with the Nizam's government having autonomy on everything else. But this compromise fell by the wayside when India insisted that Hyderabad formally accede.[73]

All the while Jinnah encouraged the Nizam, warning the Viceroy hyperbolically that if the Indian government 'attempted to exert any pressure on Hyderabad, every Muslim throughout the whole of India, yes, all the hundred million Muslims, would rise as one man to defend the oldest Muslim dynasty in India'.[74]

All the Nizam's men

After Partition, Hyderabad experienced a momentous demographic upheaval: around 750,000 Muslims, fleeing violence, poured into the state as refugees. At the same time around 400,000—mostly Hindus—left for neighbouring regions.[75] The state was divided between those who wanted accession to the Indian Union and those who opposed it. While many Hindus supported the former option, both the main Dalit political parties, the Depressed Classes Association and the Depressed Classes Conference, firmly backed Hyderabadi independence, believing that joining the Union meant falling prey to the majoritarian domination of caste Hindus.[76] Prominent Dalit leader B.S. Venkatrao praised 'cosmopolitan Hyderabad culture and expression of lasting harmony between the different races and creeds who have flourished here happily for ages together.'[77] Parts of the Hindu landed elite also backed Hyderabadi independence, since their power had depended on the Nizam's rule.[78]

But by this point the Nizam was losing control of his own state. Before independence the Ittehad had created a paramilitary squad, the Razakars, which sent tens of thousands of ill-trained young Muslims armed with old muzzle-loaders into the outlying areas of Hyderabad to stave off anti-Muslim attacks by outside agitators.[79] 'Not even half could fire a shot,' Hyderabad's last prime minister, Mir Laik Ali observed ruefully of the Razakars. Of those who could, some 'were as much a source of danger to the user as to the target'.[80] Ali had replaced the Nawab of Chhatari, who had resigned from the role in November 1947 under Razakar duress.[81] The Razakars began launching vicious attacks on Hindu communities and others, including Muslims, who opposed their vision for the state.[82]

Important figures within the Indian government came to believe that the Nizam was working with the Razakars to systematically assault Hyderabad's Hindus. This belief provided the justification and impetus for the ultimate invasion, but it was inaccurate. Lothian, who maintained that 'there has been little evidence of bigotry or anti-Hindu bias' on the Nizam's part, believed that Osman Ali Khan was simply unable to appease any faction: 'He is thus between the devil and the deep sea; and one cannot but be sorry for him.'[83] Not only did the Razakars attack Muslims who opposed them, they even attacked members of the Nizam's forces. General El Edroos, commander of the Hyderabad army, was a firm opponent of the Razakars.[84]

The militants committed horrifying atrocities against rural Hindu communities. In some cases, however, false propaganda whipped up outrage in India. On 22 May 1948, the press reported that a Muslim mob attacked Hindus at Gangapur station, killing at least two people as the police looked on. Yet a *Daily Express* correspondent, Maurice Cheesewright, interviewed people at Gangapur station and reported that, in fact, no Hindus had been killed. He traced 'fabricated reports' back to India's agent to Hyderabad, K.M. Munshi. 'The stories of attacks on Hindus, eagerly and naively reported by the Indian press,' Cheesewright told his British readers, 'nearly all came from the big house in Bolarum, ten miles from Hyderabad city, where Munshi used to curl up on a water-cooled verandah to gather tittle-tattle from his own political agitators'.[85]

The fledgling Indian state placed a blockade on Hyderabad. In his monumental book *The Destruction of Hyderabad*, which on its publication in 2013 laid bare the truth about the Indian invasion for the first time in the public domain, A.G. Noorani argues that invasion was never the only solution to the crisis. The blockade was having an impact, and an increasing number of men in Hyderabad's government were realising they couldn't hope for independence. So why did India launch the invasion, misleadingly labelled the Police Action? Prime Minister Nehru opposed the idea.[86] But his home minister, Vallabhbhai Patel, was heavily anti-Muslim, even openly distrusting Muslims in the Congress.[87] As Noorani put it, Patel's goal with Hyderabad was 'to remove what he saw as an "alien state" with an alien culture.'[88]

By late April Patel was laying the groundwork for an invasion, unsubtly stationing troops near Hyderabad's borders and even constructing airstrips around them. Privately, Patel had actually set a date for the invasion, 13 September.[89] By 31 August, Indian soldiers had completely encircled Hyderabad. Hyderabad's prime minister, Laik Ali ramped up his bombastic rhetoric, declaring that 'We have 100,000 bombers in South Arabia ready to bomb Bombay', which was untrue.

Patel was raring to go ahead with the invasion as scheduled, but Nehru objected. He felt that Patel's anti-Muslim bigotry was impacting his approach. At one meeting, Nehru even said to Patel's face: 'You are a complete communalist and I'll never be a party to your suggestions and proposals.' Patel sat for a while in silence, then left the room without a word, suffered a heart palpitation and had to be put on oxygen.[90]

THE INDIAN CALIPHATE

Matters came to a head when Hyderabad, citing India's threats of invasion, boldly asked the United Nations Security Council to mediate the situation on 24 August. The issue was set to be discussed in a council meeting on 16 September. By then it was too late.[91] At 4 a.m. on 13 September, just after Jinnah had died, the orders were given and the invasion started. As Indian troops entered Hyderabad, the sheer imbalance of power became obvious to everyone. Hyderabad's army had no chance. Most of the recently arrived weaponry was still in the military warehouses—and while the Indian army had tanks, the Razakars could only use crude guns, spears and stones. Just four days later, at 4:18 in the afternoon on 17 September, Laik Ali announced Hyderabad's surrender on the Nizam's behalf, noting that 'there was no point in sacrificing human blood against heavy odds'.[92]

With Ali's announcement the last Caliph's ambition for a revived Caliphate was well and truly dashed. It could have come to pass if Hyderabad became independent, or an autonomous state within a loose federation. In the end, Partition had made it impossible. Abdulmejid's designs, formulated after the Caliphate fell amid the forging of a new Turkish nation, failed amid the construction of a new Indian one.

Bloodshed and secrecy

Philip Mason understood that Asaf Jahi rule could never withstand the Congress, and he felt this to be a tragedy. He had been won over by Hyderabad's nobles and their culture, and felt a sentimental attachment to them: 'Their courtesy and good humour were unfailing; their clothes were enchanting. There was a special pleasure in talking to the ladies…' In the end, Mason believed that the British had betrayed Hyderabad 'with such contempt for past obligations and such callous disregard for the decencies of diplomacy.'[93]

Sultana Walajahi, whose father Hussain Abdul Munim worked for the treasury, was still a child when the Nizam was forced from power. Her family's experience perfectly illustrates the destruction of Hyderabad's Muslim elite, many of whom moved to Pakistan. She told me she remembered that her brother-in-law was the manager of a Bank of India branch in the district of Gulbarga. 'One day he was sitting in his office when he heard soldiers marching.' He went to the window and saw rows of soldiers outside. Then came a knock on the door. It opened and soldiers burst into the office. 'What is this?' he asked. No answer. The soldiers pointed their guns at him and forced him out of the building.

'He walked down the road and down the steps and walked towards his house, and he had to cross quite a number of dead bodies while crossing the road from his office to the house,' Walajahi recalled. He told his family, 'Look, this place is not for us. This is not for Muslims.' They decided to migrate. So did Walajahi's eldest brother, who was a soldier. 'I cannot serve an enemy country,' he decided. 'I will go to Pakistan.'[94]

The official Indian figures claimed that the so-called Police Action saw little bloodshed, counting the deaths of 1,273 Razakars and 807 of Hyderabad's soldiers (along with just ten Indian soldiers).[95] Nehru boasted that 'not a single communal incident' had taken place. This, of course, was nonsense—as the prime minister would soon find out after he was pressured by Maulana Azad, then education minister, to investigate what really happened.[96] The team sent to find out, which produced what was known as the Sunderlal Report after one of its authors, found that large-scale anti-Muslim massacres had swept the state. At a 'very conservative estimate', the report concluded, at least '27 thousand to 40 thousand people' were killed.[97]

For many in Hyderabad, the aftermath of the invasion was apocalyptic. The investigators found 'wells still full of corpses', one in which there was a 'woman with a small child sticking to her breast'. Elsewhere bodies had been burnt and reduced to 'charred bones and skulls'. There was ample evidence of forcible conversions—a 'universal factor, almost everywhere we went. After the adult males of a locality had been killed, the women and children were generally "persuaded" to adopt the Hindu faith.' And Indian soldiers had participated in the atrocities: 'At a number of places members of the armed forces brought out Muslim adult males from villages and towns and massacred them in cold blood.'[98]

According to scholar Wilfred Cantwell Smith, who visited Hyderabad in 1949, between one-tenth and one-fifth of the male Muslim population was killed off. Muslims were purged from the government and administration. He noted that some 'estimates by responsible observers' were that up to 200,000 had died. 'In some areas, all the men were stood in a line, and done to death... there was widespread rape, arson, looting, and expropriation.'[99]

Laik Ali and his cabinet were all arrested after Hyderabad's surrender (Laik Ali would later make a daring escape from prison in March 1949 and travel to Pakistan disguised as a woman).[100] The Indian army also rounded up and detained thousands of people—not just the Nizam's soldiers but civilians as well, mostly Muslims accused of opposing Hyderabad's accession to the Union. The state's cosmopolitanism was decisively crushed. Up to 25,000 Arabs were identified and thrown into prison, as well as thousands of Pathan and Afghan migrants.[101] The army simply wanted 'to get rid of the Pathan and Arab outsiders in Hyderabad as quickly as possible'. They were kept in vast detention camps and many were eventually deported, while others were freed and left India. Children of migrants—born in Hyderabad—faced the same fate.[102]

The Police Action, Noorani argued, 'was the annihilation of a certain way of life, the uprooting of a people, and the sweeping away of a culture, swiftly and almost completely.'[103] There was to be no accountability. Nehru suppressed the Sunderlal Report, no doubt fearing the political and social consequences it would have had if it was made public. Following Patel's advice, he removed one of its authors from an ambassadorial role in the Middle East. The report's existence only emerged into the public realm twenty years later, at which point Nehru's daughter, Prime Minister Indira Gandhi, swiftly banned its publication. The report was finally published in 2013 as an appendix to Noorani's book.[104]

Yet even since then, there has been no public reckoning in India with this gruesome episode. The museums I toured in Hyderabad in 2024 contained no mention anywhere in any exhibition of the massacres. Historical displays either omitted any mention of how the Nizam's state joined independent India, or noted its incorporation

THE CALIPHAL SUCCESSION

into the nation without including any details. Officially, this was an atrocity that never happened.

After the fall

The Republic of Turkey had expelled the House of Osman once the Caliphate was abolished. The Indian government, by contrast, allowed the Asaf Jahi dynasty to retain its palaces and titles, even as people were rounded up and massacred. But when Patel arrived in Hyderabad after the invasion, there was no false courtesy. Upon seeing the Nizam, whose title was His Exalted Highness, Patel quipped, 'So, His Exhausted Highness is here.' During that meeting, the Nizam was reduced to pleading for clemency. Patel was smug, cold and harsh.[105]

The Nizam, with a title but no power, was utterly dejected. The British, he felt, had betrayed him. Sultan Ghalib al-Qu'aiti, born in 1948, told me that years later when he paid his respects to the Nizam in 1966, he saw the Nizam look up to the sky while recalling the British. 'His eyes turned moist. "What promises did they not make to me and then turn away?" he said.'[106] An Urdu verse ascribed to the Nizam which he probably wrote soon after the invasion may indicate his state of mind:

> By the cruelty of fate all pleasure is gone out of my life, Osman
> Neither that wine remains, nor that company, nor the beloved.[107]

By this point, Durrushehvar was gone from Hyderabad, having left days before the invasion. She had seen the end of the Ottoman Empire and been exiled from Istanbul; now Hyderabad, too, seemed likely to fall. She wasn't going to stay and see it happen. The princess took her two sons to London and moved into a suite at the Savoy Hotel, where they would live for two years.[108]

Mukarram Jah was sent to Harrow, despite the Nizam's protestations that he be sent back to Hyderabad. One of England's most exclusive and elite schools, Harrow was famous for educating young eastern royals and elites, including many Indian princes and Jawaharlal Nehru himself. Jah was there with the future King of

Iraq, Faisal, and his cousin Hussein, who would be King of Jordan. The three became good friends.[109]

In September 1952 Mukarram Jah matriculated at Peterhouse College, Cambridge University's oldest college. He studied English and history but had a lot of time for fun—specifically explosives, once unexpectedly producing a grenade on a fishing trip ('there was this big explosion and all these dead fish floated to the surface'). He often went to Paris to visit his aunt, Princess Niloufer, who was much happier after Asaf Jahi rule had ended.[110]

Soon after the invasion the princess had moved to divorce Prince Moazzam Jah, writing to Nehru to ask him to speak to the Nizam about it. Nehru did so, but the Nizam refused to get involved. Jah flew to Paris, where Niloufer endured the prince's entreaties for ten long days; 'he coaxed me and threatened me'. Eventually, Niloufer won out and Jah reluctantly agreed to the divorce.[111] In many ways Niloufer was the polar opposite of Durrushehvar. She made Mukarram Jah work a holiday job as a nightclub bouncer, and if he came home before three in the morning 'I had to go to sleep in the bathtub with a pillow and a blanket as punishment,' he later recalled. 'My aunt would always tell me, "Your mother hasn't brought you up properly, my boy".'[112]

At one point while the prince was a student, he was attending an event in Cambridge with his mother when the two of them ran into a rather awkward Lord Mountbatten, who had been the last Viceroy of India. He could say nothing to Durrushehvar besides, 'Sorry, ma'am.'[113] Mukarram Jah graduated from Cambridge with third-class honours in 1955 and trained as an officer cadet at the Royal Military College at Sandhurst, much like any upper-class English gentleman.[114]

For most of this time his late grandfather, Caliph Abdulmejid, had been interred in the Paris Mosque. After the collapse of Asaf Jahi rule, all plans to have Abdulmejid's body taken to Khuldabad were dropped. Salih Keramet, a secretary of the Caliph, made several valiant attempts to persuade Turkey to permit his burial in Istanbul. In 1951 he asked the prime minister to take the issue to the Grand National Assembly. This was ignored.[115] Then in 1952, he wrote a long letter to the government listing several reasons why Abdulmejid should be buried in Istanbul—including that the Ottoman Empire was no longer a live issue and that Abdulmejid had been a fine artist.[116]

By March 1953, Keramet was citing the UN Declaration of Human Rights. He appealed 'to the fairness and the humanity of our Grand National Assembly', calling for the Caliph's rights 'as per the 10th, 14th and 16th articles of the UN declaration of human rights approved by the Turkish Republic, the right of consolidation and protection, and even after his death, the right of reuniting with his homeland.' This, too, was completely ignored.[117]

Finally the Nizam decided that the best option was to have the Caliph buried in Medina, one of Islam's holy cities in Saudi Arabia—where the Prophet Muhammad was buried. The Saudi government agreed to the plan.[118] On 25 March 1954, the Caliph's wife, daughter and son went to the Paris Mosque to pray by Abdulmejid's body and say their farewells.[119] Three days later, the body was put on a plane and taken to Saudi Arabia.[120] The Nizam's representatives in Medina oversaw the burial. The funeral prayer was performed at the Prophet's mosque in the evening, and at dusk the coffin was taken to the Jannat al-Baqi graveyard, where many of the Prophet's relatives and close companions were buried.[121]

The Caliph's secretary, who had served him for decades, reflected on Abdulmejid's life. The self-proclaimed 'democrat prince' had, he concluded,

> tried to enlighten himself throughout his youth, learned foreign languages, prepared to serve the nation and the country, and now sees the spiritual reward for whatever he suffered for this great ambition of his, and reached the privilege of being buried with the manifestation of providence and near the Prophet and his kin, something his predecessors couldn't achieve.[122]

The area picked for the grave was stony, and digging it took a while. Finally, the coffin was lowered into the grave as the onlookers prayed. The puritanical interpretation of Islam followed by the Saudi rulers meant that the grave could have no structure built over it; the mausoleums of many of Islam's early heroes had already been destroyed after Ottoman rule ended. Caliph Abdulmejid's coffin was covered with stones and dirt until no traces of it were visible.[123] The humble grave was a far cry from the majestic Ottoman mausoleum which stood abandoned and desolate in the countryside of Khuldabad, and which stands there now, derelict and hollow.

EPILOGUE

The seventh Nizam of Hyderabad lost his power but remained fabulously rich. After 1948, he moved mountains to ensure that Prince Mukarram Jah could easily be his successor. In the agreement he entered into with the Indian government, he bypassed the Shari'a dictate which required his grandson to share the Nizam's estate with his immediate family. Instead, he made Jah the sole heir to his vast wealth.[1]

It was in June 1954 that the Nizam officially declared that Mukarram Jah was his successor, by putting it in writing in a letter to Nehru. He cited Prince Azam Jah's 'extravagant mode of life and addiction to drinks, etc.' as the reason.[2] Later, in October 1956, the Nizam wrote to Nehru declaring that his son had 'sadistic tastes' and was a 'moral pervert'. Azam Jah would have disputed this description of him, which was designed to convince Nehru to demand that Jah pay his debts to the Nizam and have his allowance reduced (the plan worked). The former heir apparent would die in 1970 a lonely man. Mukarram Jah and Durrushehvar were in England and didn't return to Hyderabad for the funeral.[3]

Prime Minister Nehru came to have big plans for Mukarram Jah. He saw him as a potential figurehead for India's Muslims, based on the prestige of his lineage. In an echo of Gandhi's support for the Khilafat Movement in the 1920s, Nehru thought that Jah could be a Muslim poster-boy for India, boosting India's standing in the Islamic world. Like Gandhi, Nehru wanted to use Islam to help India geopolitically.[4]

He made Jah his aide-de-camp as a step towards giving him a bigger role. But Jah was instead obsessed with becoming a soldier and tried to join the Indian army, which the prime minister covertly obstructed.[5] Nehru died in 1964, before Jah became Nizam. Osman

Ali Khan breathed his last aged eighty on Friday 24 February 1967 with Durrushehvar by his bedside, just as the call to the Friday prayer sounded from the Mecca Masjid.[6] Later that year, on 6 April, Mukarram Jah was appointed the eighth Nizam of Hyderabad at the Chowmahalla Palace.[7] He wore Caliph Abdulmejid's sword during the ceremony, in a gesture to his Ottoman ancestry.

Nehru's daughter Indira Gandhi was prime minister, and she saw the princely order in a different light. She started a populist campaign for the abolition of the princely privileges, privy purses and titles. That required changing the constitution, which needed a two-thirds majority in parliament.[8] And yet abolishing the privy purses, which cost the exchequer only around 0.2 per cent of the national budget, would barely make a dent in inequality in India. Indira Gandhi ignored this, declaring in 1971 that the reform would be 'an important step in the further democratisation of our society'.[9] Bangladesh's war of independence that year distracted the government for a while, but the prime minister found the time to push through the bill in December. It altered the constitution, derecognised the princes and abolished their privy purse and privileges.[10] This was the final blow for the princely order.

Mukarram Jah opted for an unconventional solution to his troubles, moving to western Australia in 1973, where he bought a 200,000-hectare sheep farm. Jah once told a journalist that Abu Bakr, Islam's first Caliph, had been a shepherd; 'I see no reason why I shouldn't be one.'[11] He bought a gold mine in western Australia during the mining rush, naming it the Majeed Mine after Caliph Abdulmejid. It never made a profit.[12]

In the late 1950s or early 1960s, a poet staying with Prince Moazzam Jah recalls him strolling around on the terrace of his house in the Banjara Hills, called 'Mount Pleasant', one evening. He was melancholy. 'How times have changed!' Jah mourned. 'There was a time when all this belonged to us. And now...!'[13] The poet-prince lived until 1987. On 15 September, he composed five devotional Urdu poems dedicated to Imam Hussein, the Prophet's grandson. That night, he fell into a coma and died.[14]

His former wife Princess Niloufer died two years later, aged seventy-three, in Paris, having lived happily since 1963 with film

EPILOGUE

producer Edward Julius Pope Jr, whom she married after divorcing Jah.[15] In the 1960s, Niloufer had been the first fellow member of the Ottoman imperial family that French-born Princess Kenize met. 'I was a student at the Sorbonne,' she told me. 'Aunt Niloufer called me to have tea.' Niloufer introduced her to one of her distant cousins—'a young, plump Indian man,' Princess Kenize recalled fondly. He was Prince Muffakham Jah, Princess Durrushehvar's second son, known as Keramet by the family. 'He was very nice and we talked. He asked me to have lunch the day after, so we did. We talked about what I wanted to do—at the time I wished to be a medical doctor.'

A few days later, Princess Niloufer telephoned her. 'She tells me, "Keramet is asking if he can hope".' Princess Kenize laughed at the memory. 'I say, "hope for what?" She says, "Don't be ridiculous, for your hand!"' This came as a shock: 'I didn't understand the culture. I had never been to the east. How could this man ask someone else if he could marry me and not ask me?' She turned down the proposal, which annoyed Princess Durrushehvar. 'She was so cross that this little girl dared to refuse her son that when we would meet, which was normally at funerals, she did not even look at me,' Princess Kenize remembered, adding that 'Keramet was a nice person.'[16]

Durrushehvar lived the rest of her life in London, where Nawab Akram Abbas Syed recalled she would host Hyderabadi students in England for dinner parties.[17] She died in 2006 aged ninety-two and was buried in Brookwood Cemetery, just south west of the capital; the princess refused to be buried in Turkey because the government had denied permission for her father to be buried there sixty-two years earlier.[18]

In 1996 Mukarram Jah, by then in his sixties, moved to Turkey, from where his grandfather and mother had been exiled. There, the heir to the Ottoman Caliphate took up residence in a small apartment in Antalya overlooking the Mediterranean, living in relative anonymity for the rest of his life. Historian John Zubrzycki tracked him down and interviewed him in his apartment in 2005. Zubrzycki told me he agreed with my assessment of the Ottoman-Asaf Jahi union. 'Behind his bluster and eccentricities,' he noted, 'Osman Ali Khan was a shrewd tactician who wanted to consolidate the legacy of the Asaf Jahi dynasty by cementing an alliance, through marriage, with the exiled Ottoman royalty. His intention to designate his grandson, Mukarram Jah, as the Caliph of Islam, was part of this grand scheme.' Zubrzycki had argued this in his biography of Jah, which he told me the prince read and liked.

But what had he thought of the titular eighth Nizam when he met him? 'I found a man deeply saddened by the cards that life had dealt him, thrust by his grandfather into a position of responsibility that he wasn't prepared for and ultimately was unable to fulfil,' Zubrzycki said. He remembered Jah as 'unquestionably charismatic and cultured, generous and gentle'.[19] Princess Esra, who had married Jah in 1959 and divorced him in 1974 shortly after he moved to Australia, told me that 'Prince Mukarram Jah was proud of belonging both to the Hyderabad dynasty as well as the Ottoman dynasty.'[20]

When Jah died in Istanbul in January 2023, his body was taken to Hyderabad and buried at the Mecca Masjid, alongside several of his forebears. I visited his grave there in April 2024. His eldest son Prince Azmet Jah, who has become the titular ninth Nizam, is a British filmmaker who has worked with Steven Spielberg and lives in London.[21]

The legacy of the Ottoman-Asaf Jahi union

The twentieth century saw the near-total destruction of the Islamic world's old cosmopolitan elite network, as ruling classes in several countries were dismembered and replaced. The fall of the Ottomans paved the way for the creation of a new Middle East and eastern Europe, of new nation states and novel conflicts to go with them. In that context, the plan to tie the House of Osman's future to Hyderabad was a last-ditch attempt to salvage the Ottoman legacy, preserve some continuity between the old and new eras and establish new connections between far-flung regions of the Islamic world.

This history testifies to the fact that among a mass of surging nationalisms, there was indeed a coherent Islamic world in the early twentieth century. In fact, it was perhaps more connected

EPILOGUE

than it had ever been. And the story's key political players—the last Caliph, the seventh Nizam, Maulana Shaukat Ali, Marmaduke Pickthall and others—weren't simply tired restorationists or quirky traditionalists. Each in their own way aimed to fashion a new order for Muslims in the modern world.

It is barely remembered today that several Arab states in the Persian Gulf were governed by the British Raj, effectively as Indian princely states, in the early twentieth century. As the Viceroy of India put it in 1903, 'To all intents and appearances the State [of Oman] is as much a Native State of the Indian Empire as Lus Beyla or Kelat [in Princely India].' Oman was given a twenty-one gun salute, on a par with Hyderabad, while Qatar, Kuwait and Bahrain received only seven guns—and Abu Dhabi a paltry five.[22]

These states, which weren't absorbed into the Indian Union in 1947 and instead remained under British protection, eventually gaining independence, survive today. Having discovered copious amounts of oil and natural gas, they are dizzyingly wealthy and some, like Qatar and the United Arab Emirates (which is formed of multiple former princely states), are tremendously powerful. They present a marked contrast to the princely states in the subcontinent, like Hyderabad, which were all destroyed amid the formation of India and Pakistan.

It is one of history's great ironies that while Indians often administered these Gulf states in the early twentieth century, they now form large sections of the populations of those same states as a labouring underclass. This points to the fact that the subcontinent is far from being a focal point of the Islamic world today. Neither Pakistan nor Bangladesh are considered great powers, while India isn't even seen as part of the Islamic world, partially because it refuses to perceive itself as such—particularly under its current Hindu nationalist government.

As I have sought to demonstrate in this book, the situation was once radically different. The Indian subcontinent defined the British Empire's engagement with Islam. During the Balkan Wars of 1912 and 1913, through the First World War and then the occupation of Anatolia, Indian Muslims often influenced British policy. They helped to install Abdulmejid as Caliph after the Ottoman Empire's demise, since it was Indian concern that initially made Mustafa Kemal Atatürk reluctant to do away with the Caliphate. Then, when the institution was abolished, India was primed to become the new seat of the Caliphate.

Today, most people would consider the idea that the last Ottoman Caliph looked to the subcontinent to continue his line completely implausible. But it wasn't. If there had been some sort of Indian federation and Hyderabad ended up as an independent or at least highly autonomous state, Prince Mukarram Jah as Nizam, with the wealth and power of Hyderabad and the prestige of the Ottoman dynasty, could have been better placed than anyone else to lay claim to the Caliphal title.

Caliph Abdulmejid had envisaged a reconstituted, modern Caliphate deriving its legitimacy not from imperial might but from the recognition of the world's Muslims. His vision might have come to fruition if Jah gained that recognition, and Hyderabad became a symbol of transnational Muslim unity. The fact that Abdulmejid looked to Hyderabad itself indicates that India was in important ways the epicentre of the Islamic world in the early twentieth century.

How would an Indian Caliphate have worked, given that Muslims were a demographic minority in the subcontinent? That independent India tried to join the Organisation of Islamic Cooperation (itself a descendant of the congress that Maulana Shaukat Ali instigated), although Pakistan thwarted its attempts to do so, indicates that a federal and Hindu-majority India could have quite comfortably used the Asaf Jahi dynasty to project soft power and stake its claim to importance in the Islamic world.[23] Of course, it could have simultaneously retained its Hindu and other identities, since a federal India would have been too diverse and capacious to claim only one.

Equally, of course, it is quite possible that a federation would have led to civil war in the subcontinent (although civil war happened anyway amid Partition). Moreover, most of the world's Muslims might have rejected or simply ignored an Ottoman Caliph in Hyderabad. We will never know. Ultimately, Partition carved up

EPILOGUE

the Indo-Islamic world and left Muslims in the new Indian nation an unprotected and proportionally much smaller minority.

For decades the tale of the union of the Ottoman and Asaf Jahi dynasties and the Indian Caliphate that never was has been consigned to almost total oblivion in popular consciousness—in the subcontinent, Turkey and the world at large. My aim in writing this book has been to set the record straight. The last Caliph's would-be mausoleum is an abandoned ruin, but perhaps, if the truth behind it becomes well known, that may not always be so. It is a chapter in our extraordinary, often unexpected and always interconnected global history. It deserves to be remembered.

NOTES

INTRODUCTION

1. 'Abdulmecid II: Artist, musician and the last caliph of Islam' in *Middle East Eye*, 18 March 2022. https://www.middleeasteye.net/discover/turkey-ottoman-Abdulmecid-ii-last-caliph-islam-artist-musician
2. 'Muslim leaders reject Baghdadi's caliphate' in *Al Jazeera*, 7 July 2014. https://www.aljazeera.com/news/2014/7/7/muslim-leaders-reject-baghdadis-caliphate
3. 'Iraq: UK acknowledges Islamic State committed genocide against Yazidis' in *Middle East Eye*, 1 August 2023. https://www.middleeasteye.net/news/iraq-uk-acknowledges-yazidi-genocide-islamic-state
4. 'Why the West cannot afford to ignore political Islam' in *Middle East Eye*, 11 November 2016.
5. Reza Pankhurst, *The Inevitable Caliphate: A History of the Struggle for Global Islamic Union, 1924 to the Present* (New York: Oxford University Press, 2013), 2–3.
6. 'The Lingering Dream of an Islamic State' in *The New York Times*, 12 January 2018. https://www.nytimes.com/2018/01/12/opinion/sunday/post-isis-muslim-homeland.html
7. 'Abdulmecid II: Artist, musician and the last caliph of Islam'.
8. 'The Nizam of Hyderabad' in *Time*, 22 February 1973. https://content.time.com/time/covers/0,16641,19370222,00.html
9. 'Sir Muhammad Iqbal's 1930 Presidential Address to the 25th Session of the All-India Muslim League Allahabad, 29 December 1930' in *Speeches, Writings, and Statements of Iqbal*, ed. Latif Ahmed Sherwani (Lahore: Iqbal Academy, 1977 [1944]). https://franpritchett.com/00islamlinks/txt_iqbal_1930.html
10. Ibid.

NOTES

1. THE DEMOCRAT PRINCE

1. Alain Quella-Villéger, 'Pierre Loti and Abdülmecid: A Little-Known Franco-Turkish Friendship' in *The Prince's Extraordinary World: Abdülmecid Efendi*, ed. Nazan Ölcer (Istanbul: Sabancı University/Sakıp Sabancı Museum, 2022), 94.
2. Edhem Eldem, 'From *The History Lesson* to *Beethoven in the Harem:* An Ambitious and Bourgeois Prince' in *The Prince's Extraordinary World*, 54.
3. Murat Bardakçı, *Neslishah: The Last Ottoman Princess* (Cairo: The American University in Cairo Press, 2019), 20.
4. Eldem, 'From *The History Lesson*', 54.
5. Alain Quella-Villéger, 'Pierre Loti and Abdülmecid', 95.
6. Eldem, 'Prince', 54.
7. Marc David Baer, *The Ottomans: Khans, Caesars and Caliphs* (New York: Basic Books, 2021), 378.
8. Eldem, 50.
9. Ibid, 52.
10. Ömer Faruk Şerifoğlu, 'The Society of Ottoman Painters and Its Founder Abdülmecid Efendi' in *The Prince's Extraordinary World*, 114.
11. Zeynep İnankur, 'Women in the Courtyard' in *The Prince's Extraordinary World*, 122.
12. Ibid, 128.
13. Ibid, 130.
14. Ibid.
15. Eldem, 53.
16. Ibid, 55.
17. Zeynep İnankur, 'Women in the Courtyard', 130.
18. Şerifoğlu, 'The Society of Ottoman Painters', 123.
19. Ali Surat Ürgüplü, 'A Life Dedicated to Art' in *The Prince's Extraordinary World*, 64.
20. Eldem, 56.
21. Alain Quella-Villéger, 'Pierre Loti and Abdülmecid', 95.
22. Şerifoğlu, 'The Society of Ottoman Painters', 115.
23. Ürgüplü, 'A Life Dedicated to Art', 65.
24. Ibid, 63.
25. Omer Faruk Şerifoğlu, 'Two Art-Loving Artists in the Ottoman Dynasty: Sultan Abdülaziz and His Son Abdülmecid Efendi' in *The Prince's Extraordinary World*, 73.

26. Şerifoğlu, 'The Society of Ottoman Painters', 116.
27. Ürgüplü, 'A Life Dedicated to Art', 64.
28. Evren Kutlay, 'The Ottoman Caliph Who Painted (His) History: Şahâne-i Üstâd Abdülmecid Efendi' in *The Prince's Extraordinary World*, 101.
29. Emre Aracı, 'Giuseppe Donizetti at the Ottoman Court: A Levantine Life' in *The Musical Times*, vol. 143, no. 1880 (2002), 49.
30. Kutlay, 'The Ottoman Caliph Who Painted (His) History', 104.
31. Ibid, 106.
32. Ibid, 83.
33. Ibid, 78.
34. Ibid, 200.
35. Marshall G.S. Hodgson, *The Venture of Islam: Conscience and History in a World Civilization*, vol. 1 (Chicago and London: The University of Chicago Press, 1974), 276.
36. Ibid, 750.
37. Gail Minault, *The Khilafat Movement: Religious Symbolism and Political Mobilization in India* (Delhi: Oxford University Press, 1982), 4.
38. Hüseyin Yılmaz, *Caliphate Redefined: The Mystical Turn in Ottoman Political Thought* (Princeton: Princeton University Press, 2018), 101.
39. Ibid, 234.
40. Ibid, 1.
41. Shahab Ahmed, *What Is Islam? The Importance of Being Islamic* (Princeton: Princeton University Press, 2016), 475.
42. Yilmaz, *Caliphate Redefined*, 2.
43. Ibid, 3.
44. Ibid, 237.
45. Baer, *The Ottomans*, 20.
46. Ahmed, *What Is Islam?*, 467–468.
47. Ibid, 473.
48. Baer, *The Ottomans*, 190.
49. Seydi Ali Reis, *The Travels and Adventures of the Turkish Admiral Sidi Ali Reïs in India, Afghanistan, Central Asia, and Persia, During the Years 1553–1556*, trans. A. Vambery (London: Forgotten Books, 2010 [1899]), 26.
50. Ibid, 32.
51. Suraiya Faroqhi, *The Ottoman and Mughal Empires: Social History in the Early Modern World* (London: I.B. Tauris, 2019), 123.
52. Ahmed, *What Is Islam?*, 67.

53. Karen Barkey, *Empire of Difference: The Ottomans in Comparative Perspective* (New York: Cambridge University Press, 2008), 267.
54. Jason Goodwin, *Lords of the Horizons: A History of the Ottoman Empire* (London: Vintage Books, 1999), 298.
55. Ibid, 302.
56. Baer, *The Ottomans*, 361.
57. Butrus Abu-Manneh, 'The Islamic Roots of the Gülhane Rescript' in *Die Welt des Islams*, vol. 34, no. 2 (1994), 196.
58. Ibid, 369.
59. Ünver Rüstem, *Ottoman Baroque: The Architectural Refashioning of Eighteenth-Century Istanbul* (Princeton: Princeton University Press, 2019), 2.
60. Ibid, 4.
61. Baer, *The Ottomans*, 361.
62. Rüstem, *Ottoman Baroque*, 10.
63. Goodwin, *Lords of the Horizons*, 309.
64. Baer, *The Ottomans*, 375.
65. Ibid, 376.
66. Ibid, 380.
67. Ibid.
68. Ibid, 384.
69. Minault, *The Khilafat Movement*, 5.
70. Ibid, 6.
71. Azmi Özcan, *Pan-Islamism: Indian Muslims, the Ottomans and Britain (1877–1924)* (Leiden: Brill, 1997), 105.
72. Joseph A. Massad, *Islam in Liberalism* (Chicago and London: The University of Chicago Press, 2015), 66.
73. Ibid, 64.
74. Ibid.
75. Ibid, 68.
76. Faisal Devji, 'Islam and British Imperial Thought' in *Islam and the European Empires*, ed. David Motadel (Oxford: Oxford University Press, 2014), 443.
77. Ibid, 449.
78. Ibid, 446–447.
79. Ibid, 451.
80. Baer, *The Ottomans*, 418.
81. Yakoob Ahmed, *The Role of the Ottoman SunniUlema During the*

Constitutional Revolution of 1908-1909/1326-1327 and the Ottoman Constitutional Debates (SOAS, 2019), 14.

82. Ibid, 117.
83. Ibid, 46.
84. Ibid, 122.
85. Baer, *The Ottomans*, 426.
86. Ibid, 427.
87. Ibid, 442.
88. Eldem, 51.
89. Ibid, 50.
90. Bardakçı, *Neslishah*, 22.
91. Eldem, 55.
92. Durru Shehvar Azam Jah, 'Life of an Eastern Princess: From Turkey to Hyderabad' in *Nottingham Evening News*, 6 June 1933.

2. ANGLICISED RADICALS

1. M. Raisur Rahman, '"We Can Leave Neither": Mohamed Ali, Islam and Nationalism in Colonial India' in *South Asian History and Culture*, vol. 3, no. 2 (2012), 260.
2. Khalid Ali, *Ali Brothers: The Life and Times of Maulana Mohammed Ali and Shaukat Ali* (Karachi: Royal Book Company, 2011), 13.
3. Rahman, '"We Can Leave Neither"', 255.
4. Ali, *Life and Times*, 22.
5. Rahman, '"We Can Leave Neither"', 255.
6. Ibid.
7. Peter Chappell, 'How a small society of Indian Cambridge students helped destroy the British Raj' in *Varsity*, 16 September 2018. https://www.varsity.co.uk/features/15993
8. Ali, *Life and Times*, 48.
9. Ibid, 49.
10. Ibid, 51.
11. Ibid, 54.
12. Ibid, 55.
13. Ibid.
14. Maulana Muhammad Ali, Speech at the Fourth Plenary Session of the Round Table Conference, London, 19 November 1930, in *Pakistan Movement: Historical Documents*, ed. G. Allana (Karachi: University of Karachi, 1969).

15. Ali, *Life and Times*, 61.
16. Shan Muhammad, *Unpublished Letters of the Ali Brothers* (Delhi: Idarah-i Adabiyat-i Delli, 1979), xi.
17. Ibid.
18. Rahman, "'We Can Leave Neither'", 255.
19. Ibid, 258.
20. Ali, *Life and Times*, 140.
21. Rahman, "'We Can Leave Neither'", 255.
22. Ibid.
23. Ali, *Life and Times*, 463.
24. Gail Minault, *The Khilafat Movement: Religious Symbolism and Political Mobilization in India* (Delhi: Oxford University Press, 1982), 49.
25. Ali, *Life and Times*, 194.
26. Minault, *The Khilafat Movement*, 50.
27. Ibid.
28. Ali, *Life and Times*, 70.
29. Ibid, 10.
30. Ibid.
31. Ali, *Life and Times*, 121.
32. Ibid, 112.
33. Özcan, *Pan-Islamism*, 128.
34. Ibid.
35. Rahman, "'We Can Leave Neither'", 259.
36. Özcan, *Pan-Islamism*, 139.
37. Ibid, 141.
38. Ibid, 145.
39. Rahman, "'We Can Leave Neither'", 259.
40. Özcan, *Pan-Islamism*, 144.
41. Ibid, 148.
42. Ibid.
43. Ibid, 149.
44. Ibid, 154.
45. Ibid, 147.
46. Ibid, 167.
47. Ibid, 139.
48. Ibid, 169.
49. Ibid, 170.
50. Abdal Hakim Murad, 'Marmaduke Pickthall: A Brief Biography' in

British Muslim Heritage. http://www.masud.co.uk/ISLAM/bmh/BMM-AHM-pickthall_bio.htm.
51. Ibid.
52. K. Humayun Ansari, 'Pickthall, Muslims of South Asia, and the British Muslim Community of the Early 1900s' in *Marmaduke Pickthall: Islam and the Modern World*, ed. Geoffrey P. Nash (Leiden and Boston: Brill, 2017), 27.
53. Marmaduke Pickthall, 'The Muslims in the Modern World' (speech, 1936), in *Journal of the Royal Central Asian Society* 23, no. 2 (1936), 221.
54. Ansari, 'Muslims of South Asia', 36.
55. Özcan, *Pan-Islamism*, 170.
56. Ibid, 171–172.
57. Ibid, 174.
58. Ibid, 176–178.
59. Margrit Pernau-Reifeld, 'Reaping the Whirlwind: Nizam and the Khilafat Movement' in *Economic and Political Weekly* 34, no. 38 (September 18–24, 1999), 2746.
60. *Unpublished Letters*, xv.
61. Rahman, '"We Can Leave Neither"', 259.
62. Minault, *The Khilafat Movement*, 51.
63. Faisal Devji, 'Islam and British Imperial Thought' in *Islam and the European Empires*, ed. David Motadel (Oxford: Oxford University Press, 2014), 463.
64. *Unpublished Letters*, xvi.
65. Eugene Rogan, *The Fall of the Ottomans: The Great War in the Middle East, 1914–1920* (London: Penguin Books, 2015), 48.
66. Ibid, 70.
67. Joseph A. Massad, *Islam in Liberalism* (Chicago and London: The University of Chicago Press, 2015), 90.
68. Rogan, *Fall of the Ottomans*, 302.
69. Ibid, 404.
70. See John Buchan, *Greenmantle* (Harmondsworth: Peacock Press, 1964.)
71. Özcan, *Pan-Islamism*, 180.
72. Ibid, 181.
73. Ibid, 182.
74. Ibid, 183.
75. Rogan, *Fall of the Ottomans*, 71.
76. Ibid, 74.

77. Ibid, 249.
78. Mohammad Siddique Seddon, 'Pickthall's Anti-Ottoman Dissent: The Politics of Religious Conversion' in *Islam and the Modern World*, 97.
79. Minault, *The Khilafat Movement*, 51.
80. Mohamed Ali, letter to Gandhiji, 20 February 1918, Chhindwara, C.P., in *Unpublished Letters*, 136.
81. Mohamed Ali and Shaukat Ali, letter to the Viceroy, 24 April 1919, Chhindwara, C.P., in *Unpublished Letters*, 153.
82. Mohamed Ali, letter to Gandhiji, 20 February 1918, Chhindwara, C.P., in *Unpublished Letters*, 137.
83. Minault, *The Khilafat Movement*, 56.
84. Mother of Mohamed Ali, letter to Sir Subramaniam Iyer, President of the Madras Home Rule League, 4 August 1917, Chhindwara, C.P., in *Unpublished Letters*, 88.
85. Mother of Mohamed Ali, letter to Mrs Anne Besant, 11 December 1917, Chhindwara, C.P., in *Unpublished Letters*, 126.
86. Ibid, 127.
87. Ibid, 129.
88. Mohamed Ali and Shaukat Ali, letter to the Viceroy, 24 April 1919, Chhindwara, C.P., in *Unpublished Letters*, 155.
89. Ibid, 156–157.
90. Minault, *The Khilafat Movement*, 58.
91. Ozcan, *Pan-Islamism*, 184.
92. Ibid, 185.
93. Ibid, 185.
94. Eldem, 51.
95. Murat Bardakçı, *Neslishah: The Last Ottoman Princess* (Cairo: The American University in Cairo Press, 2019), 29.
96. Ali, *Life and Times*, 250.
97. *Unpublished Letters*, xvii.

3. 'GOD VERSUS MAN'

1. George W. Gawrych, *Atatürk: Father of the Republic of Turkey* (London: I.B. Tauris, 2023), 5.
2. Ibid, 7–9.
3. Ibid, 18
4. Ibid, 20.
5. Ibid, 24.

6. Ibid, 20.
7. Ibid, 22.
8. H.I.H. Prince Ali Vâsib, *Memoirs of an Ottoman Prince: What I Saw and Heard in My Homeland and in Exile*, prepared by H.I.H. Prince Osman Selaheddin, with contributions by H.I.H. Princess Ayse Gülnev and H.I.H. Prince Selim Süleyman, translated and edited by John Shakespeare Dyson (Istanbul: Timas Publishing, 2017), 226.
9. Ibid, 230.
10. Murat Bardakçı, *Neslishah: The Last Ottoman Princess* (Cairo: The American University in Cairo Press, 2019), 25.
11. Ibid, 27.
12. Ibid, 28.
13. Gawrych, *Father of the Republic*, 30.
14. Vâsib, *Memoirs*, 227.
15. Gawrych, *Father of the Republic*, 33.
16. Ibid, 34.
17. Vâsib, *Memoirs*, 228.
18. Ibid, 265.
19. Ibid, 266.
20. Ibid, 185.
21. Ali Satan, 'Abdülmecid Efendi: From the National Struggle to the Caliphate' in *The Prince's Extraordinary World*, 26.
22. Ibid.
23. Ibid.
24. Ibid, 27.
25. Ibid, 29.
26. Ibid, 30.
27. Alain Quella-Villéger, 'Pierre Loti and Abdülmecid: A Little-Known Franco-Turkish Friendship' in *The Prince's Extraordinary World*, 98.
28. *The Prince's Extraordinary World*, 191.
29. Bardakçı, *Neslishah*, 36.
30. Satan, 'Abdülmecid Efendi', 30.
31. Joseph A. Massad, *Islam in Liberalism* (Chicago and London: The University of Chicago Press, 2015), 93.
32. Ibid, 242.
33. Azmi Özcan, *Pan-Islamism: Indian Muslims, the Ottomans and Britain (1877–1924)* (Leiden: Brill, 1997), 91.

34. Khalid Ali, *Ali Brothers: The Life and Times of Maulana Mohammed Ali and Shaukat Ali* (Karachi: Royal Book Company, 2011), 242.
35. Özcan, *Pan-Islamism*, 190.
36. Ibid, 191.
37. Faisal Devji, *Muslim Zion: Pakistan as a Political Idea* (Cambridge, Massachusetts: Harvard University Press, 2013), 81.
38. 'INDIA A GREAT MOSLEM STATE IS BRIGHT MOHAMMEDAN DREAM; Religious Supremacy Means More to Gandhi's Islamic Allies Than His Idea of Political Independence—Bonds With Hindus Weakening' in *The New York Times*, 20 May 1923, 7.
39. Shan Muhammad, *Unpublished Letters of the Ali Brothers* (Delhi: Idarah-i Adabiyat-i Delli, 1979), xix.
40. *Khilafat Movement (1920–1921)*, vol. 10 of *Source Material for a History of Freedom Movement in India*, ed. K.K. Chaudhari (Mumbai: Government of Maharashtra, 1982), 54.
41. Mary S. Lovell, *The Riviera Set; 1920–1960: The golden years of glamour and excess* (London: Abacus, 2016), 238.
42. Ibid, 239–240.
43. Ibid.
44. Ibid, 241.
45. Tripurdaman Singh and Adeel Hussain, *Nehru: The Debates That Defined India* (London: William Collins, 2021), 23.
46. Ibid, 70.
47. Chaudhari, *Khilafat Movement*, 50.
48. Ibid, 51.
49. Ibid, 52.
50. Ibid, 29.
51. Ibid, 66.
52. Ibid, 71.
53. Ibid, 72.
54. Ibid, 72.
55. Faisal Devji, 'Islam and British Imperial Thought' in *Islam and the European Empires*, ed. David Motadel (Oxford: Oxford University Press, 2014), 463.
56. Rahman, '"We Can Leave Neither"', 261.
57. Chaudhari, *Khilafat Movement*, 77–78.
58. Ibid, 88.
59. Ibid, 87.

60. Ibid, 97.
61. Margrit Pernau-Reifield, 'Reaping the Whirlwind: Nizam and the Khilafat Movement' in *Economic and Political Weekly* 34, no. 38 (September 18–24, 1999), 2747–2748.
62. Ibid, 2749.
63. Özcan, *Pan-Islamism*, 191.
64. K. Humayun Ansari, 'Pickthall, Muslims of South Asia, and the British Muslim Community of the Early 1900s' in *Marmaduke Pickthall: Islam and the Modern World*, ed. Geoffrey P. Nash (Leiden and Boston: Brill, 2017), 41.
65. Ibid, 38.
66. Özcan, *Pan-Islamism*, 192.
67. Ibid, 192–193.
68. Mohamed Ali, letter to Raghupati Under Secretary and Treasurer, 16 February undated (1925), Delhi, in *Unpublished Letters*, 262.
69. Ali, *Life and Times*, 259.
70. Ibid, 260.
71. Ibid, 264.
72. Özcan, *Pan-Islamism*, 192.
73. Mohamed Ali and other members of the Indian Khilafat Delegation, letter to the Khilafa, 28 May 1920, Paris, in *Unpublished Letters*, 191.
74. Ibid, 193.
75. Ibid, 198.
76. Ibid, 200.
77. Ali, *Life and Times*, 265.
78. Ibid, 267.
79. Ibid.
80. Ibid.
81. Ibid.
82. Ibid.
83. Ibid, 268.
84. Özcan, *Pan-Islamism*, 192–193.
85. Ibid, 194.
86. M. Raisur Rahman, '"We Can Leave Neither": Mohamed Ali, Islam and Nationalism in Colonial India' in *South Asian History and Culture*, Vol 3, 2 (Oxford: Routledge, 2012), 262.
87. Özcan, *Pan-Islamism*, 169.
88. Ali, *Life and Times*, 336.

89. Özcan, *Pan-Islamism*, 173–174.
90. Ibid.
91. Rahman, '"We Can Leave Neither"', 263.
92. Özcan, *Pan-Islamism*, 173–174.
93. Ali, *Life and Times*, 316.
94. Özcan, *Pan-Islamism*, 236.
95. Ali, *Life and Times*, 241.
96. Ibid, 146.
97. Ibid, 148.
98. Özcan, *Pan-Islamism*, 195.

4. THE LAST CALIPHATE

1. Cenk Alper, 'Foreword' in *The Prince's Extraordinary World*, 11.
2. George W. Gawrych, *Atatürk: Father of the Republic of Turkey* (London: I.B. Tauris, 2023), 46.
3. Ibid, 49.
4. Murat Bardakçı, *Neslishah: The Last Ottoman Princess* (Cairo: The American University in Cairo Press, 2019), 41.
5. H.I.H. Prince Ali Vâsib, *Memoirs of an Ottoman Prince: What I Saw and Heard in My Homeland and in Exile*, prepared by H.I.H. Prince Osman Selaheddin, with contributions by H.I.H. Princess Ayse Gülnev and H.I.H. Prince Selim Süleyman, translated and edited by John Shakespeare Dyson (Istanbul: Timas Publishing, 2017), 266.
6. Bardakçı, *Neslishah*, 41.
7. Ibid, 41.
8. Ibid, 42.
9. Ibid, 43.
10. Ibid.
11. Ali Satan, 'Abdülmecid Efendi: From the National Struggle to the Caliphate' in *The Prince's Extraordinary World*, 32.
12. Ibid.
13. Vâsib, *Memoirs*, 42.
14. Satan, 'Abdülmecid Efendi', 29.
15. Ibid, 32.
16. Bardakçı, *Neslishah*, 44.
17. Satan, 'Abdülmecid Efendi', 32.
18. Ibid, 33.

19. Ibid.
20. Ibid, 32.
21. Özcan, *Pan-Islamism*, 198.
22. 'INDIA A GREAT MOSLEM STATE IS BRIGHT MOHAMMEDAN DREAM; Religious Supremacy Means More to Gandhi's Islamic Allies Than His Idea of Political Independence—Bonds With Hindus Weakening' in *The New York Times*, 20 May 1923, 7.
23. 'TO ERECT KEMAL STATUE.; Constantinople Will Honor Turkish Leader Despite the Koran' in *The New York Times*, 20 July 1925, 2.
24. Satan, 'Abdülmecid Efendi', 33.
25. Ibid, 36.
26. Ibid.
27. Ibid.
28. Ibid.
29. Ibid, 37.
30. Bardakçı, *Neslishah*, 44.
31. Ibid.
32. Ibid, 45.
33. Vâsib, *Memoirs*, 257.
34. Ibid.
35. Ibid, 175–175.
36. Ibid, 268.
37. Bardakçı, *Neslishah*, 49.
38. 'DISSENT IN TURKEY' in *The New York Times*, 11 April 1923, 20.
39. Vâsib, *Memoirs*, 258.
40. Ibid.
41. Ibid, 262.
42. 'NEW CALIPH REVIVES POMP AT SELAMLIK; Crosses the Basporus in an Ancient Pointed Barge, Flying His Personal Standard' in *The New York Times*, 17 March 1923, 4.
43. Bardakçı, *Neslishah*, 49.
44. Ibid, 71.
45. Vâsib, *Memoirs*, 262.
46. Ibid, 261–262.
47. Ibid, 262.
48. 'SAW A NEW TURKEY BORN AT ANGORA; Dr. John H. Finley Witnessed Opening of Her First Real Parliament' in *The New York Times*, 26 August 1923, 1.

49. Gawrych, *Father of the Republic*, 69.
50. Khalid Ali, *Ali Brothers: The Life and Times of Maulana Mohammed Ali and Shaukat Ali* (Karachi: Royal Book Company, 2011), 49.
51. Bardakçı, *Neslishah*, 49.
52. Satan, 'Abdülmecid Efendi', 38.
53. 'Caliph, as a Citizen, Lowers Flag' in *The New York Times*, 6 February 1924, 2.
54. 'TURKS STIR ALL ISLAM BY DEPOSING CALIPH; 300,000,000 Moslems Affected by Angora's Action—Constantinople Loses in Struggle' in *The New York Times*, 9 March 1924, 4.
55. Özcan, *Pan-Islamism*, 200.
56. 'TURKS STIR ALL ISLAM BY DEPOSING CALIPH'.
57. Ibid.
58. 'TURKEY IN TURMOIL OVER CALIPHATE; Letter of Aga Khan, Criticizing It, Resented by Angora Government' in *The New York Times*, 6 January 1924, 7.
59. Tripurdaman Singh and Adeel Hussain, *Nehru: The Debates That Defined India* (London: William Collins, 2021), 25.
60. Ali, *Life and Times*, 353.
61. Gawrych, *Father of the Republic*, 55.
62. 'TURKS STIR ALL ISLAM BY DEPOSING CALIPH'.
63. Özcan, *Pan-Islamism*, 201.
64. 'TURKS STIR ALL ISLAM BY DEPOSING CALIPH'.
65. Vâsib, *Memoirs*, 273.
66. Bardakçı, *Neslishah*, 52.
67. 'CALIPH'S FATE IN BALANCE; Constantinople Believes He and All Imperial House Will Be Expelled' in *The New York Times*, 1 March 1924, 15.
68. Vâsib, *Memoirs*, 270–271.
69. Bardakçı, *Neslishah*, 50.
70. Ibid, 59.
71. Ibid.

5. SLINGS AND ARROWS

1. 'Angora Moves to Drive Caliph Into Exile; Police Act to Prevent His Taking Treasures' in *The New York Times*, 3 March 1924, 1.
2. Ibid.

3. Murat Bardakçı, *Neslishah:The Last Ottoman Princess* (Cairo:The American University in Cairo Press, 2019), 53.
4. 'EXILED CALIPH OFF FOR SWITZERLAND; Ascends Throne at 2 o'Clock in the Morning to Hear the Deposition Order Read' in *The New York Times*, 5 March 1924, 3.
5. Bardakçı, *Neslishah*, 53.
6. Ibid, 55.
7. Ali Satan, 'Abdülmecid Efendi: From the National Struggle to the Caliphate' in *The Prince's Extraordinary World*, 39.
8. Bardakçı, *Neslishah*, 55.
9. H.I.H. Prince Ali Vâsib, *Memoirs of an Ottoman Prince: What I Saw and Heard in My Homeland and in Exile*, prepared by H.I.H. Prince Osman Selaheddin, with contributions by H.I.H. Princess Ayse Gülnev and H.I.H. Prince Selim Süleyman, translated and edited by John Shakespeare Dyson (Istanbul: Timas Publishing, 2017), 272.
10. Bardakçı, *Neslishah*, 60.
11. Ibid, 59.
12. Satan, 'Abdülmecid Efendi', 39.
13. 'CALIPH'S HAREM IN PLIGHT; His Departure in Exile Leaves Women Penniless' in *The New York Times*, 7 March 1924, 18.
14. Bardakçı, *Neslishah*, 62.
15. Vâsib, *Memoirs*, 272.
16. Bardakçı, *Neslishah*, 56.
17. Trans. Deniz Erdem, Salih Keramet Nigâr, *Caliph Abdülmecid II* (Kerestecibaşı Library; additional collections, Istanbul: İnkılap ve Aka Publishing House, 1964), 8.
18. Bardakçı, *Neslishah*, 63.
19. Nigâr, *Caliph Abdülmecid II*, 8.
20. Bardakçı, *Neslishah*, 64.
21. Nigâr, *Caliph Abdülmecid II*, 8.
22. Ibid, 9.
23. Vâsib, *Memoirs*, 272.
24. Ibid, 279.
25. Bardakçı, *Neslishah*, 68.
26. Ibid, 67.
27. Ibid, 68.
28. Nigâr, *Caliph Abdülmecid II*, 9.
29. Bardakçı, *Neslishah*, 58.

30. Ibid.
31. Ibid, 75.
32. Nigâr, *Caliph Abdülmecid II*, 9.
33. Ibid, 10.
34. Bardakçı, *Neslishah*, 76.
35. Ibid.
36. Ibid.
37. Ibid.
38. Nigâr, *Caliph Abdülmecid II*, 10.
39. Ibid, 12.
40. Ibid, 10.
41. Bardakçı, *Neslishah*, 76.
42. Ibid, 78.
43. Ibid, 79.
44. Ibid, 81.
45. 'EX-CALIPH NEEDS MONEY; So He Is Painting and Composing, Hoping to Sell His Work' in *The New York Times*, 20 April 1924, 8.
46. Bardakçı, *Neslishah*, 79.
47. 'FRENCH DISAPPROVE HUSSEIN AS CALIPH; They Are Fearful of England's Getting Advantage in Influence Over Arab Kingdoms' in *The New York Times*, 9 March 1924, 6.
48. 'Sees Disaster To Islam' in *The New York Times*, 5 March 1924, 3.
49. Ibid.
50. 'Works' in *The Prince's Extraordinary World*, 225.
51. 'EXILED CALIPH OFF FOR SWITZERLAND; Ascends Throne at 2 o'Clock in the Morning to Hear the Deposition Order Read' in *The New York Times*, 5 March 1924, 3.
52. 'ANGORA BANS THE NAME OF CALIPH IN PRAYERS; Government Orders Clergy to Substitute a Plea to Allah to Favor the Republic' in *The New York Times*, 10 March 1924, 3.
53. 'ANGORA NOW CLAIMS POWERS OF CALIPH; Mustapha Kemal Notifies India's Moslems That Authority Is Vested in Assembly' in *The New York Times*, 11 March 1924, 3.
54. Ibid.
55. 'GREAT BRITAIN AND THE CALIPHATE' in *The New York Times*, 5 March 1924, 6.
56. 'FRENCH DISAPPROVE HUSSEIN AS CALIPH; They Are Fearful of

England's Getting Advantage in Influence Over Arab Kingdoms' in *The New York Times*, 9 March 1924, 6.
57. Ibid.
58. 'RIFF CHIEF FOR CALIPH.; Moslem Leaders Consider Abd-el-Krim, Spain's Foe in Morocco' in *The New York Times*, 19 February 1925, 11.
59. Nigâr, *Caliph Abdülmecid II*, 13.
60. Ibid.
61. Ibid.,
62. 'CALIPH APPEALS TO MOSLEM WORLD; Calls for an Inter-Islamic Conference to Consider Action Concerning His Exile' in *The New York Times*, 12 March 1924, 3.
63. Nigâr, *Caliph Abdülmecid II*, 16.
64. Ibid, 14/15.
65. 'CALIPH APPEALS TO MOSLEM WORLD'.
66. 'Sees Disaster To Islam' in *The New York Times*, 5 March 1924, 3.
67. Khalid Ali, *Ali Brothers: The Life and Times of Maulana Mohammed Ali and Shaukat Ali* (Karachi: Royal Book Company, 2011), 354.
68. 'CALIPH APPEALS TO MOSLEM WORLD'.
69. Azmi Özcan, *Pan-Islamism: Indian Muslims, the Ottomans and Britain (1877–1924)* (Leiden: Brill, 1997), 203.
70. Muhammad Iqbal, *The Reconstruction of Religious Thought in Islam* (Moscow: Dodo Press, 1930), 183.
71. Ibid, 184.
72. Ibid, 188.
73. Ibid, 184.
74. George W. Gawrych, *Atatürk: Father of the Republic of Turkey* (London: I.B. Tauris, 2023), 1.
75. Ibid, 74.
76. Ibid, 70.
77. Ibid, 221.
78. Robert W. Olson and William F. Tucker, 'The Sheikh Sait Rebellion in Turkey (1925): A Study in the Consolidation of a Developed Uninstitutionalized Nationalism and the Rise of Incipient (Kurdish) Nationalism' in *Die Welt des Islams* 18, no. 3/4 (Leiden: Brill, 1978)
79. Shahab Ahmed, *What Is Islam? The Importance of Being Islamic* (Princeton: Princeton University Press, 2016), 210.
80. Gawrych, *Father of the Republic*, 100.

81. Philip Mansel, *Constantinople: City of the World's Desire, 1455–1924* (London: Penguin Books, 1997), 418.
82. 'Turkey Separates Religion From the State; Deputies to Swear "On Honor," Not "Before God"' in *The New York Times*, 12 April 1924, 3.
83. Ibid.
84. 'REPUBLICAN TURKEY LEANS TO FEASTING; Little Observance of Moslem Lent, but Bairam, or Easter, Was Holiday Time. SOCIAL FEATURES SURVIVE Calls Paid and Gifts Exchanged as in Caliphate Days, With Dancing Added. "Night of Power" Loses Strength. Bairam a Holiday Season. Kemal's Republican Reception' in *The New York Times*, 22 April 1928, 60.
85. 'KEMAL TELLS TURKS TO DRINK ALCOHOL; Also to Take Up Western Music and Dances as Well as Latin Characters' in *The New York Times*, 12 August 1928, 23.
86. Marmaduke Pickthall, 'The Muslims in the Modern World' (speech, 1936), in *Journal of the Royal Central Asian Society* 23, no. 2 (London: Taylor and Francis, 2011), 223.
87. Ibid, 224.
88. Ibid, 225.
89. Evren Kutlay, 'The Ottoman Caliph Who Painted (His) History: Şahâne-i Üstâd Abdülmecid Efendi' in *The Prince's Extraordinary World*, 102–103.
90. İnci Enginün, 'Abdülmecid Efendi and Literature' in *The Prince's Extraordinary World*, 92.
91. Ibid.
92. Nigâr, *Caliph Abdülmecid II*, 19/20.
93. Ibid, 23/24/25.
94. Ibid, 16.
95. Ibid, 17.
96. Ibid.
97. Ibid, 18/19.
98. Ibid, 27.
99. Ibid.
100. Ibid, 27.

6. AN ORIENTAL DREAM

1. Philip Mason, *A Shaft of Sunlight: Memories of a Varied Life* (Chatham: W&J Mackay Limited, 1978), 207.

2. Ibid.
3. Barney White-Spunner, *Partition: The Story of Indian Independence and the Creation of Pakistan in 1947* (London: Simon & Schuster, 2017), 185.
4. A.G. Noorani, *The Destruction of Hyderabad* (New Delhi: Tulika Books, 2013), 1.
5. John Zubrzycki, *Dethroned: The Downfall of India's Princely States* (London: C Hurst & Co Publishers Ltd, 2023), 90.
6. Narendra Luther, *Hyderabad: A Biography* (New Delhi: Oxford University Press, 2012), 219.
7. D.F. Karaka, *Fabulous Mogul: Nizam VII of Hyderabad* (London: Derek Verschoyle Ltd, 1955), 79.
8. Ibid, 80.
9. Elizabeth Cooper, *The Harim and the Purdah* (New York: The Century Company, 1915), 154–155.
10. Arthur Cunningham Lothian, *Kingdoms of Yesterday* (London: Butler & Tanner Ltd, 1951), 77.
11. Zubrzycki, *Dethroned*, 11.
12. Eric Lewis Beverly, *Hyderabad, British India, and the World: Muslim Networks and Minor Sovereignty, c.1830–1959* (Cambridge: Cambridge University Press, 2015), 74.
13. Ibid, 22.
14. Luther, *Hyderabad*, 200.
15. Ibid, 210.
16. Beverly, *Hyderabad, British India, and the World*, 232–234.
17. Lothian, *Kingdoms*, 78.
18. Beverly, *Hyderabad, British India, and the World*, 172.
19. Ibid, 169.
20. Ibid, 170.
21. Ibid, 174.
22. Ibid.
23. Ibid, 176.
24. Luther, *Hyderabad*, 203.
25. Beverly, *Hyderabad, British India, and the World*, 109.
26. Ibid, 110.
27. Luther, *Hyderabad*, 251.
28. Ibid.
29. Beverly, *Hyderabad, British India, and the World*, 267.

30. William Barton, *The Princes of India* (London: Nisbet & Co Ltd, 1934), 205.
31. Ibid, 102.
32. Ibid, 124.
33. Taylor C. Sherman, 'Migration, Citizenship and Belonging in Hyderabad (Deccan), 1946–1956' in *Modern Asian Studies* 45, no. 1 (London: Cambridge University Press, 2011), 85.
34. Ibid, 86.
35. Beverly, *Hyderabad, British India, and the World*, 124.
36. Sam Dalrymple, *Shattered Lands: Five Partitions and the Making of Modern Asia* (London: William Collins, 2025), 3.
37. Ursula Sims-Williams, 'Curzon's Durbars and the Alqabnamah: The Persian Gulf as Part of the Indian Empire' in *Asian and African Studies Blog*, 30 December 2014. https://blogs.bl.uk/asian-and-african/2014/12/curzons-durbars-and-the-alqabnamah-the-persian-gulf-as-part-of-the-indian-empire.html
38. Personal Interview.
39. Abdal Hakim Murad, 'Marmaduke Pickthall: A Brief Biography' in *Masud*, 6 January 2015. http://masud.co.uk/marmaduke-pickthall-a-brief-biography/
40. Ibid.
41. Marmaduke Pickthall, 'The Muslims in the Modern World' (speech, 1936), in *Journal of the Royal Central Asian Society* 23, no. 2 (London: Taylor and Francis, 2011), 230.
42. Narendra Luther, introduction to *The Nocturnal Court: Darbaar-e-Diirbaar, The Life of a Prince of Hyderabad*, Sidq Jaisi (New Delhi: Oxford University Press, 2004), xxxv.
43. Ibid, xxxvii.
44. Taylor C. Sherman, *Muslim Belonging in Secular India: Negotiating Citizenship in Postcolonial Hyderabad* (Cambridge: Cambridge University Press, 2015)
45. Ibid, 5.
46. Ibid, 7.
47. Noorani, *Destruction of Hyderabad*, 10.
48. Mason, 200.
49. Luther, *Hyderabad*, 195.
50. 'Hyderabad: Silver Jubilee Durbar' in *TIME Magazine*, 22 February 1937.

51. 'Nizam of Hyderabad Orders Huge Barbecue of 1,000 Oxen and 10,000 Sheep for Jubilee' in *The New York Times*, 23 December 1935, 11.
52. 'THE NIZAM OF HYDERABAD RIVALS KING SOLOMON IN HIS GLORY; Lives in Feudal Magnificence and Guards His Enormous Harem with Amazons—Recently Had Tilt with Indian Government' in *The New York Times*, 22 August 1926, 5.
53. Karaka, *Fabulous Mogul*, 52.
54. Luther, Hyderabad, 217.
55. 'Nizam of Hyderabad Orders Huge Barbecue of 1,000 Oxen and 10,000 Sheep for Jubilee', 11.
56. Ibid.
57. Luther, *Hyderabad*, 246.
58. Conrad Corfield, *The Princely India I Knew, From Reading to Mountbatten* (Madras: Indo British Historical Society, 1975.
59. Ibid.
60. Lothian, *Kingdoms*, 179.
61. Personal Interview.
62. Karaka, *Fabulous Mogul*, 152.
63. Ibid, 39–40.
64. Ibid, 40.
65. Ibid, 57–59.
66. Ibid, 81.
67. Ibid, 85.
68. Ibid, 86.
69. Ibid, 87.
70. Ibid, 53.
71. 'THE NIZAM OF HYDERABAD RIVALS KING SOLOMON IN HIS GLORY', 5.
72. Barton, *The Princes of India*, 208.
73. Karaka, *Fabulous Mogul*, 55.
74. Cooper, *The Harim and the Purdah*, 156.
75. 'THE NIZAM OF HYDERABAD RIVALS KING SOLOMON IN HIS GLORY', 5.
76. Ibid.
77. Sarojini Naidu, 'Letters Too Tell Stories' in *The Untold Charminar: Writings on Hyderabad*, ed. Syeda Imam (Delhi: Penguin Random House India, 2008), 140.

78. 'THE NIZAM OF HYDERABAD RIVALS KING SOLOMON IN HIS GLORY', 5.
79. Ibid.
80. Mason, *A Shaft of Sunlight*, 200–201.
81. Personal Interview.
82. Karaka, *Fabulous Mogul*, 52.
83. Personal Interview.
84. 'The Nizam of Hyderabad Rivals King Solomon in His Glory', 5.
85. Karen Leonard, 'Political Players: Courtesans of Hyderabad' in *The Indian Economic and Social History Review* 50, no. 4 (Sage Publications: 2013), 429.
86. Mehr Afshan Farooqi, 'Will Gujarat Mourn Adil Mansuri?' in *Outlook*, 20 November 2008. https://www.outlookindia.com/books/will-gujarat-mourn-adil-mansuri-news–238983
87. Syed Sirajuddin, 'For Better and for Verse' in *The Untold Charminar*, 105–107.
88. Ibid, 112–113.
89. Luther, *Hyderabad*, 204.
90. Syed Sirajuddin, 'For Better and for Verse', 112.
91. Abhijit Sen Gupta, 'Rabindranath Tagore loved Hyderabad so much that he wanted to make City his second home' in *The Siasat Daily*, 6 May 2023.
92. Syed Sirajuddin, 'For Better and for Verse', 126.
93. Narendra Luther, introduction to *The Nocturnal Court*, XI.
94. Isaac Sequeira, 'The Mystique of the Mushaira' in *The Untold Charminar*, 133.
95. Luther, *Hyderabad*, 208.
96. Ibid, 211.
97. Ibid, 209.
98. Karaka, *Fabulous Mogul*, 101.
99. Luther, *Hyderabad*, 210.

7. 'I WILL NOT GO BACK TO A SLAVE COUNTRY'

1. Trans. Deniz Erdem, Salih Keramet Nigâr, *Caliph Abdülmecid II* (Kerestecibaşı Library; additional collections, Istanbul: İnkılap ve Aka Publishing House, 1964), 27.
2. John Zubrzycki, *The Last Nizam: An Indian Prince in the Australian Outback* (Sydney: Pan Macmillan, 2006), 153.

3. Cemil Kutlutürk, 'The Nizams of Hyderabad in India and the Support They Provided the Ottoman Empire' in *Turkish Journal of History* 78, no. 3 (Istanbul: Istanbul University Press, 2022), 76.
4. Omar Khalidi, 'The Caliph's Daughter' in *Cornucopia*, 31 (2004).
5. Mary S. Lovell, *The Riviera Set; 1920–1960: The Golden Years of Glamour and Excess* (London: Abacus, 2016), 2–3.
6. Anne De Courcy, *Chanel's Riviera: Glamour, Decadence, and Survival in Peace and War, 1930–1944* (New York: St Martin's Press, 2019), 3.
7. Maureen Emerson, *Riviera Dreaming: Love and War on the Cote D'Azur* (London; New York: I.B. Tauris, 2018), 3.
8. H.I.H. Prince Ali Vâsib, *Memoirs of an Ottoman Prince: What I Saw and Heard in My Homeland and in Exile*, prepared by H.I.H. Prince Osman Selaheddin, with contributions by H.I.H. Princess Ayse Gülnev and H.I.H. Prince Selim Süleyman, translated and edited by John Shakespeare Dyson (Istanbul: Timas Publishing, 2017), 325.
9. Ibid, 323.
10. Ibid, 330.
11. Murat Bardakçı, *Neslishah: The Last Ottoman Princess* (Cairo: The American University in Cairo Press, 2019), 83.
12. Bardakçı, *Neslishah*, 104.
13. Ibid, 111.
14. Ibid, 108.
15. Ibid, 93.
16. Ibid, 109–110.
17. Ibid, 93.
18. Durru Shehvar Azam Jah, 'Life of an Eastern Princess: From Turkey to Hyderabad' in *Nottingham Evening News*, June 6, 1933.
19. 'Marriage of the sons of HEH the Nizam to Turkish princesses', 21 January 1932, file no. 54, British Library.
20. Bardakçı, *Neslishah*, 115.
21. Ibid, 112.
22. Ibid, 115.
23. Vâsib, *Memoirs*, 347.
24. De Courcy, *Chanel's Riviera*, 7.
25. Vâsib, *Memoirs*, 350.
26. Metro-Goldwin-Mayer, *The Garden of Allah* (1972)
27. Bardakçı, *Neslishah*, 86.
28. Ibid, 391.

29. Vâsib, *Memoirs*, 393.
30. Ibid, 394.
31. Bardakçı, *Neslishah*, 120.
32. Ibid, 122.
33. Vâsib, *Memoirs*, 331.
34. Ibid, 328.
35. Ibid, 324.
36. Ibid, 326.
37. Emerson, *Riviera Dreaming*, 37–38.
38. Vâsib, *Memoirs*, 337.
39. Ibid, 338.
40. Ibid, 369.
41. Ibid, 349.
42. Ibid, 338.
43. M.Raisur Rahman, '"We Can Leave Neither": Mohamed Ali, Islam and Nationalism in Colonial India' in *South Asian History and Culture*, 3, no. 2 (Oxford: Routledge, 2012), 264.
44. Vasudha Dalmia, *The Nationalization of Hindu Tradition: Bhartendu Harischandra and Nineteenth-Century Banaras* (Oxford: Oxford University Press, 1997), 34–35.
45. Audrey Truschke, *The Language of History: Sanskrit Narratives of Indo-Muslim Rule* (New York: Columbia University Press, 2021), 3.
46. Christoffe Jaffrelot, *Hindu Nationalism: A Reader* (Princeton: Princeton University Press, 2007), 11.
47. A.G. Noorani, 'Assessing Jinnah' in *Frontline*, 26 August 2005. https://frontline.thehindu.com/the-nation/article30205988.ece
48. Jaffrelot, *Hindu Nationalism*, 11.
49. Christophe Jaffrelot, *The Hindu Nationalist Movement and Indian Politics, 1925 to the 1990s: Strategies of Identity-Building, Implantation and Mobilisation* (London: Hurst & Company, 1996), 19–29
50. Vanya Vaidehi Bhargav, 'A Hindu Champion of Pan-Islamism: Lajpat Rai and the Khilafat Movement' in *The Journal of Asian Studies* 81 (Cambridge: Cambridge University Press, 2022), 690.
51. V.D. Savarkar, *Essentials of Hindutva* ((Pune: Savarkar Bhavan, 1923), 29.
52. Ibid, 42.
53. Ibid, 20.
54. Jaffrelot, *The Hindu Nationalist Movement*, 26.

55. Vikram Sampath, *Savarkar: A Contested Legacy, 1924–1966* (London: Penguin Books, 2021), 35–39.
56. Ibid.
57. Khalid Ali, *Ali Brothers: The Life and Times of Maulana Mohammed Ali and Shaukat Ali* (Karachi: Royal Book Company, 2011), 112.
58. Ibid, 121.
59. Aakar Patel, *Our Hindu Rashtra: What It Is. How We Got Here* (Chennai: Westland Publications, 2020), 22.
60. Ibid, 23.
61. Mohamed Ali, letter to the prime minister of England, 1 January 1931, London, in *Unpublished Letters*, In *Unpublished Letters of the Ali Brothers*, ed. Shan Muhammad (Delhi: Idarah-i Adabiyat-i Delli, 1979), 276.
62. Rahman, '"We Can Leave Neither"', 265.
63. Sherman A. Jackson, *The Islamic Secular* (New York: Oxford University Press, 2024), 177.
64. Ibid, 178.
65. Tripurdaman Singh and Adeel Hussain, *Nehru: The Debates That Defined India* (London: William Collins, 2021), 65.
66. Muhammad Iqbal, *The Reconstruction of Religious Thought in Islam* (Moscow: Dodo Press, 1930), 182.
67. *Unpublished Letters*, xxi.
68. Jackson, *The Islamic Secular*, 233.
69. Andrew Hammond, *Late Ottoman Origins of Modern Islamic Thought: Turkish and Egyptian Thinkers on the Disruption of Islamic Knowledge* (New York: Cambridge University Press, 2023), 35–37.
70. Ibid, 39.
71. Jackson, *The Islamic Secular*, 52.
72. Maulana Mohamed Ali's speech at the Fourth Plenary Session of the Round Table Conference in London (19 November 1930).
73. Ali, *Life and Times*, 74.
74. Ibid.
75. Marmaduke Pickthall, 'The Muslims in the Modern World' (speech, 1936), in *Journal of the Royal Central Asian Society* 23, no. 2 (London: Taylor and Francis, 2011), 231.
76. 'Works' in *The Prince's Extraordinary World*, 197.
77. Ali, *Life and Times*, 399.
78. Zubrzycki, *The Last Nizam*, 154–155.
79. Ali, *Life and Times*, 379.

80. Ibid, 380.
81. Basheer Nafi, 'Netanyahu, Hitler, al-Mufti Al-Hussaini and the Holocaust' in *Middle East Eye*, 2 November 2015. https://www.middleeasteye.net/opinion/netanyahu-hitler-al-mufti-al-hussaini-and-holocaust
82. Peter Shambrook, 'Policy of Deceit: Britain and Palestine, 1914–1939' in *Middle East Eye*, 25 August 2023. https://www.middleeasteye.net/opinion/policy-deceit-britain-palestine–1914–1939-peter-shambrook
83. Eugene Rogan, 'The Balfour Declaration: Britain's fatal mistake in Palestine' in *Middle East Eye*, 1 November 2021. https://www.middleeasteye.net/big-story/britain-palestine-balfour-declaration-fatal-mistake
84. Philip Mattar, 'The Mufti of Jerusalem and the Politics of Palestine' in *Middle East Journal* 42, no. 2 (Washington, D.C.: Middle East Institute, 1988), 232.
85. Mohamed Ali and other members of the Indian Khilafat Delegation, letter to the prime minister of England, 10 July 1920, Paris, in *Unpublished Letters*, 204.
86. Narendra Luther, *Hyderabad: A Biography* (New Delhi: Oxford University Press, 2012), 229–230.
87. K. Humayun Ansari, 'Pickthall, Muslims of South Asia, and the British Muslim Community of the Early 1900s' in *Marmaduke Pickthall: Islam and the Modern World*, ed. Geoffrey P. Nash (Leiden and Boston: Brill, 2017), 126.
88. A.G. Noorani, *The Destruction of Hyderabad* (New Delhi: Tulika Books, 2013), 45–46.
89. Maulana Mohamed Ali's speech at the Fourth Plenary Session of the Round Table Conference in London, 19 November, 1930. https://franpritchett.com/00islamlinks/txt_muhammadali_1930.html
90. Ibid.
91. Ibid.
92. Ibid.
93. Ibid.
94. Ibid.
95. Ali, *Life and Times*, 442.
96. Ibid.
97. Ibid, 445.
98. Maoz Azaryahu; Yitzhak Reiter, 'The Geopolitics of Interment: An

Inquiry into the Burial of Muhammad Ali in Jerusalem, 1931' in *Israel Studies* 20, no. 1 (Bloomington: Indiana University Press, 2015), 36.
99. Ibid, 35.
100. Ibid, 49.
101. Ibid, 44.
102. Ibid, 48.
103. Akramul Islam. 'THE GENERAL ISLAMIC CONGRESS OF JERUSALEM RECONSIDERED' in *Muslim World* LXXXVI, no. 3–4, 1996, 246.
104. 'Matrimonial alliances between Sahibazad Azam Jah, H.E.H. the Nizam's heir apparent and the daughter of Abdul Majid, Ex Caliph of Turkey and Sahibzada Muazzam Jah, second son of the Nizam to the niece of the Ex_Caliph', 1931, *file no. 538 (Secret)*, British Library.

8. 'A DISTINGUISHED SON OF ISLAM'

1. Personal Interview.
2. Papers of Lieutenant Colonel Amiruddin, Rahnuma residence in Hyderabad.
3. Personal Interview.
4. D.F. Karaka, *Fabulous Mogul: Nizam VII of Hyderabad* (London: Derek Verschoyle Ltd, 1955), 53.
5. Personal Interview.
6. H.I.H. Prince Ali Vâsib, *Memoirs of an Ottoman Prince: What I Saw and Heard in My Homeland and in Exile*, prepared by H.I.H. Prince Osman Selaheddin, with contributions by H.I.H. Princess Ayse Gülnev and H.I.H. Prince Selim Süleyman, translated and edited by John Shakespeare Dyson (Istanbul: Timas Publishing, 2017), 403.
7. John Zubrzycki, *The Last Nizam: An Indian Prince in the Australian Outback* (Sydney: Pan Macmillan, 2006), 157–158.
8. 'Demi-Official Letter from the Hon'ble Lieutenant-Colonel T. H. Keys, C.S.I., C.M.G., C.I.E., Resident at Hyderabad, No. 96-C' in *Marriage of the Sons of HEH the Nizam to Turkish Princesses*.
9. Narendra Luther, introduction to *The Nocturnal Court: Darbaar-e-Diirbaar, The Life of a Prince of Hyderabad*, Sidq Jaisi (New Delhi: Oxford University Press, 2004), xlix.
10. Ibid.
11. 'Matrimonial alliances between Sahibazad Azam Jah, H.E.H. the

Nizam's heir apparent and the daughter of Abdul Majid, Ex Caliph of Turkey and Sahibzada Muazzam Jah, second son of the Nizam to the niece of the Ex_Caliph', *1931, file no. 538 (Secret)*, British Library.
12. Ibid.
13. K. Humayun Ansari, 'Pickthall, Muslims of South Asia, and the British Muslim Community of the Early 1900s' in *Marmaduke Pickthall: Islam and the Modern World*, ed. Geoffrey P. Nash (Leiden and Boston: Brill, 2017), 128.
14. 'Matrimonial alliances', *file no. 538 (Secret)*.
15. Ansari, 'Muslims of South Asia', 128.
16. 'Matrimonial alliances', *file no. 538 (Secret)*.
17. Ibid.
18. Ibid.
19. Ibid.
20. 'Indian Potentate's Sons to Wed Caliph's Kin; Nizam to Bestow $1,200,000 Gifts on Brides; NIZAM'S HEIR TO WED DAUGHTER OF CALIPH' in *The New York Times*, 10 November 1931, 1.
21. Zubrzycki, *The Last Nizam*, 162.
22. Murat Bardakçı, *Neslishah: The Last Ottoman Princess* (Cairo: The American University in Cairo Press, 2019), 161.
23. Vâsib, *Memoirs*, 403.
24. Ibid, 404.
25. Ibid.
26. Ibid, 104.
27. Ibid.
28. Bardakçı, *Neslishah*, 125.
29. Ibid, 127.
30. *Marriage of the Sons of HEH the Nizam to Turkish Princesses*, file no. 54, British Library.
31. Vâsib, *Memoirs*, 404.
32. 'Relative to the Activities of Maulana Shaukat Ali', Foreign Office to Resident in Hyderabad, 30 October 1931, *Matrimonial Alliances, file no. 538 (Secret)*.
33. Ibid.
34. Ibid.
35. 'Matrimonial alliances', *file no. 538 (Secret)*.
36. Ibid.
37. Ansari, 'Muslims of South Asia', 129.

38. 'Matrimonial alliances', *file no. 538 (Secret)*.
39. Ibid.
40. Ibid.
41. Ibid.
42. Ibid.
43. Ansari, 'Muslims of South Asia', 130.
44. 'Matrimonial alliances', *file no. 538 (Secret)*.
45. Ibid.
46. Ibid.
47. '*The Bombay Chronicle (Bombay)*, October 5, 1931' in *Marriage of the Sons of HEH the Nizam to Turkish Princesses*.
48. Ibid.
49. Ibid.
50. '*The Daily Express*' in *Marriage of the Sons of HEH the Nizam to Turkish Princesses*.
51. 'Islam: The Caliph's Beauteous Daughter' in *Time*, 31 August 1931. https://time.com/archive/6748107/islam-caliphs-beauteous-daughter/
52. Bardakçı, *Neslishah*, 124.
53. Vâsib, *Memoirs*, 406.
54. Bardakçı, *Neslishah*, 125.
55. Ibid, 126.
56. Vâsib, *Memoirs*, 406.
57. Bardakçı, *Neslishah*, 125.
58. 'India: Nizam's Azam and Moazzam' in *Time*, 14 September 1931. https://time.com/archive/6748197/india-nizams-azam-and-moazzam/
59. Bardakçı, *Neslishah*, 126.
60. Vâsib, *Memoirs*, 406.
61. S.A. Kirillina; A.L. Safronova; V.V. Orlov, 'Great Expectations, Lost Illusions: General Islamic Congress in Jerusalem (1931)' in *RUDN Journal of World History* 15, no. 1 (Moscow: 2023), 12.
62. Ibid, 11.
63. 'MOSLEM CONGRESS DEFENDED BY MUFTI; In Cairo He Seeks to Persuade Government That Meeting Will Benefit Faith. WOULD REVIVE CALIPHATE Sheikh Bekhit Declares He Can See No Good Reason for Convoking Conference in Jerusalem. Wants Caliphate

Restored. Wailing Wall Question' in *The New York Times*, 8 November 1931, 4.
64. Ibid.
65. Kirillina; Safronova; Orlov, 'Great Expectations, Lost Illusions', 12.
66. Ibid.
67. 'Islam: The Caliph's Beauteous Daughter'.
68. Trans. James Wrathall, purported Caliphal deed, papers of Lieutenant Colonel Amiruddin, Rahnuma residence in Hyderabad.
69. Personal Interview.
70. Personal Interview.
71. Personal Interview.
72. Murat Bardakçı, 'Hilafet sevdalılarını uyarıyorum: İngiltere'de üç gün önce yayınlanan bu belge sahtedir, bundan size ekmek çıkmaz!', *Habertürk*, 23 November 2023. https://m.haberturk.com/ozel-icerikler/murat-bardakci/3712848-hilfet-sevdalilarini-uyariyorum-ingilterede-uc-gun-once-yayinlanan-bu-belge-sahtedir-bundan-size-ekm.
73. Ibid.
74. Personal Interview.
75. Personal Interview.
76. See Muhannad Salhi, 'Written in Istanbul: Arabic, Persian, and Ottoman Calligraphy Sheets at the Library of Congress (Part 3)' in *Library of Congress Blogs*, 20 May 2021. https://blogs.loc.gov/international-collections/2021/05/written-in-istanbul-arabic-persian-and-ottoman-calligraphy-sheets-at-the-library-of-congress-part–3/; Nisha Wadhwani, 'History of Indian Calligraphy' in *Aurum Art*, 17 June 2024. https://aurum.art/history-of-indian-calligraphy/?srsltid=AfmBOor-TLh1akJ41Qdd7IvwLKQN_J96-DTsr95yAoSlVah0Dprerbya
77. Personal Interview.
78. Personal Interview.
79. Ibid.
80. Wadhwani, 'History of Indian Calligraphy'.
81. Salhi, 'Written in Istanbul'.
82. Personal Interview.
83. Personal Interview.
84. Personal Interview.
85. 'Telegram from Resident to Delhi, December 7, 1931' in 'Matrimonial alliances', *file no. 538 (Secret)*.

86. 'Telegram R. no. 1919-C, from Resident to Polindia, New Delhi, November 24, 1931' in 'Matrimonial alliances', *file no. 538 (Secret)*.
87. 'Telegram R. No. 1928, from Resident to Polindia, New Delhi, November 27 1931' in 'Matrimonial alliances', *file no. 538 (Secret)*.

9. OTTOMANS IN HYDERABAD

1. S.A. Kirillina; A.L. Safronova; V.V. Orlov, 'Great Expectations, Lost Illusions: General Islamic Congress in Jerusalem (1931)' in *RUDN Journal of World History* 15, no. 1 (Moscow: 2023), 10.
2. 'Literary notes: Palestine issue: Allama Iqbal's journey to Palestine' in *Dawn*, 10 June 2024. https://www.dawn.com/news/1839001
3. Kirillina; Safronova; Orlov, 'Great Expectations, Lost Illusions', 10.
4. Khalid Ali, *Ali Brothers: The Life and Times of Maulana Mohammed Ali and Shaukat Ali* (Karachi: Royal Book Company, 2011), 443.
5. Kirillina; Safronova; Orlov, 'Great Expectations, Lost Illusions', 10.
6. 'Allama Iqbal visits Palestine' in *Ravi Magazine*, 11 September 2017. https://www.ravimagazine.com/allama-iqbal-visits-palestine/
7. 'The Palestine Arab Congress (1919–1931)' in *Jewish Virtual Library* (American-Israeli Cooperative Enterprise). https://www.jewishvirtuallibrary.org/the-palestine-arab-congress
8. Martin Kramer, *Islam Assembled: The Advent of the Muslim Congresses* (New York: Columbia University Press, 1986), 133.
9. Ibid, 135.
10. Akramul Islam. 'THE GENERAL ISLAMIC CONGRESS OF JERUSALEM RECONSIDERED' in *Muslim World* LXXXVI, no. 3–4, 1996, 266.
11. Ibid, 265.
12. 'Literary notes: Allama Iqbal on Palestine issue' in *Dawn*, 30 October 2023. https://www.dawn.com/news/1784887/literary-notes-allama-iqbal-on-palestine-issue_
13. Ibid.
14. Islam. 'THE GENERAL ISLAMIC CONGRESS OF JERUSALEM RECONSIDERED', 261.
15. Omar Khalidi, 'Indian Muslims and Palestinian Awqaf' in *Jerusalem Quarterly* 40, Winter 2009 (Institute for Palestinian Studies). https://www.palestine-studies.org/en/node/78338
16. Ibid.

17. Kirillina; Safronova; Orlov, 'Great Expectations, Lost Illusions', 14.
18. Basheer Nafi, 'Netanyahu, Hitler, al-Mufti Al-Hussaini and the Holocaust' in *Middle East Eye*, 2 November 2015. https://www.middleeasteye.net/opinion/netanyahu-hitler-al-mufti-al-hussaini-and-holocaust
19. 'World War II: Netaji Subhash Chandra Bose and His Submarine Adventure' in *HubPages*, 29 May 2023. https://discover.hubpages.com/education/The-Submarine-Adventure-of-Subhash-Chandra-Bose
20. Kirillina; Safronova; Orlov, 'Great Expectations, Lost Illusions', 19.
21. 'Dedicating the Palestinian Flag to the Indian Leader Shaukat Ali, 1931' in *The Palestinian Museum Digital Archive* https://palarchive.org/index.php/Detail/objects/9119/lang/en_US
22. 'Hyderabad's history of support and solidarity with Palestine' in *The Hindu*, 21 October 2023. https://www.thehindu.com/news/cities/Hyderabad/hyderabads-history-of-support-and-solidarity-with-palestine/article67443412.ece
23. Kirillina; Safronova; Orlov, 'Great Expectations, Lost Illusions', 16.
24. Telegram from 'Resident to Delhi, December 7, 1931' in 'Matrimonial alliances between Sahibazad Azam Jah, H.E.H. the Nizam's heir apparent and the daughter of Abdul Majid, Ex Caliph of Turkey and Sahibzada Muazzam Jah, second son of the Nizam to the niece of the Ex_Caliph', *1931, file no. 538 (Secret)*, British Library.
25. 'Marriage of the sons of HEH the Nizam to Turkish princesses', 24 February 1932, file no. 54, British Library.
26. H.I.H. Prince Ali Vâsib, *Memoirs of an Ottoman Prince: What I Saw and Heard in My Homeland and in Exile*, prepared by H.I.H. Prince Osman Selaheddin, with contributions by H.I.H. Princess Ayse Gülnev and H.I.H. Prince Selim Süleyman, translated and edited by John Shakespeare Dyson (Istanbul: Timas Publishing, 2017), 406.
27. Ibid, 410.
28. Ibid, 417.
29. 'Revealed: Mahatma Gandhi had big impact on Princess Niloufer' in *Deccan Chronicle*, 16 January 2016. https://www.deccanchronicle.com/current-affairs/170116/revealed-mahatma-gandhi-had-big-impact-on-princess-niloufer.html
30. 'Demi-Official Letter from the Hon'ble Lieutenant-Colonel T. H. Keys, C.S.I., C.M.G., C.I.E., Resident at Hyderabad, No. 96-C, dated the 21st January 1932' in *C. File No. 54 of 1932, Hyderabad Residency, Subject:*

Marriage of the Sons of HEH the Nizam to Turkish Princesses, file no. 54, British Library.
31. John Zubrzycki, *The Last Nizam: An Indian Prince in the Australian Outback* (Sydney: Pan Macmillan, 2006), 166.
32. '29 Jan' in *Marriage of the Sons of HEH the Nizam to Turkish Princesses.*
33. Conrad Corfield, *The Princely India I Knew, from Reading to Mountbatten* (Madras: Indo British Historical Society, 1975), 58.
34. 'From the Resident at Hyderabad, No. 1-C/, dated the 1st January 1932' in *File No. 34-P (Secret), Fortnightly Reports on the Internal Situation in the Hyderabad State for 1931*, British Library.
35. 'T. H. Keys, No. 96-C, 21st January 1932' in *Marriage of the Sons of H.E.H. the Nizam to Turkish Princesses.*
36. Ibid.
37. Ibid.
38. Ibid.
39. '24.2.1932' in 'T. H. Keys, No. 96-C, 21st January 1932' in *Marriage of the Sons of H.E.H. the Nizam to Turkish Princesses.*
40. Ibid.
41. Murat Bardakçı, *Neslishah: The Last Ottoman Princess* (Cairo: The American University in Cairo Press, 2019), 131.
42. Vâsib, *Memoirs*, 425.
43. Ibid, 503.
44. 'T. H. Keys, No. 96-C, 21st January 1932' in *Marriage of the Sons of H.E.H. the Nizam to Turkish Princesses.*
45. Personal Interview.
46. Ibid.
47. Durru Shehvar Azam Jah, 'Life of an Eastern Princess: From Turkey to Hyderabad' in *Nottingham Evening News*, June 6, 1933.
48. Ibid.
49. Ibid.
50. Elizabeth Cooper, *The Harim and the Purdah* (New York: The Century Company, 1915), 168.
51. Ibid, 161–162.
52. Ibid, 162.
53. Ibid, 163.
54. Arthur Cunningham Lothian, *Kingdoms of Yesterday* (London: Butler & Tanner Ltd, 1951), 179.
55. Cemil Kutluturk, 'Princess Durrusehvar Sultan's Selfless Struggle

for Uplifting the Social Status of Hyderabadi Women' in *Cogent Social Sciences* 9 Vol.1 (Digital: Taylor & Francis, 2023), 7.
56. Ibid.
57. Ibid, 10.
58. Bardakçı, *Neslishah*, 156.
59. Ibid, 127.
60. Ibid, 128.
61. Ibid.
62. Ibid.
63. Ibid, 129.
64. Lothian, *Kingdoms*, 179.
65. Corfield, *The Princely India I Knew*, 57.
66. Ibid, 58.
67. Ibid, 59.
68. Personal Interview.
69. Sidq Jaisi, *The Nocturnal Court: Darbaar-e-Diirbaar, The Life of a Prince of Hyderabad* (New Delhi: Oxford University Press, 2004), 11.
70. Ibid, 41.
71. Ibid.
72. Ibid, 42.
73. Ibid, 13.
74. Ibid, 25–27.
75. Ibid, 13–14.
76. Ibid, 14–15.
77. Ustad Farid Ayaz and Ustad Abu Muhammad, 'Shab e Hijr Voh Dam ba Dam Yaad Aaye' in *The Dream Journey*, 22 June 2018. https://www.youtube.com/watch?v=aa8onCQryfQ
78. Adnan Mahmud and Imran Mulla, trans., 'Shab e Hijr Wo Dam Ba Dam Yaad Aaye' by Shahji (date unknown).
79. Jaisi, *The Nocturnal Court*, 45–46.
80. Zubrzycki, *The Last Nizam*, 167.
81. Ibid, 168.
82. Personal Interview.

10. THE CALIPHAL SUCCESSION

1. Personal Interview.
2. Khalid Ali, *Ali Brothers: The Life and Times of Maulana Mohammed Ali and Shaukat Ali* (Karachi: Royal Book Company, 2011), 479.

3. Ibid, 481.
4. Ibid, 486.
5. Ibid, 496.
6. Ibid.
7. Ibid, 497.
8. Ibid.
9. Trans. Deniz Erdem, Salih Keramet Nigâr, *Caliph Abdülmecid II* (Kerestecibaşı Library; additional collections, Istanbul: İnkılap ve Aka Publishing House, 1964), 42.
10. Murat Bardakçı, *Neslishah: The Last Ottoman Princess* (Cairo: The American University in Cairo Press, 2019), 203.
11. 'Bombay Chronicle, "Ex-Khalifa Dies of Shock in Paris," October 16, 1944' in *File No. 297, 1944, Matters Concerning the Ex-Khalifa, Father of Her Highness the Princess of Berar*, British Library.
12. Nigâr, *Caliph Abdülmecid II*, 46.
13. 'Bombay Chronicle' in *Matters Concerning the Ex-Khalifa*.
14. Nigâr, *Caliph Abdülmecid II*, 53.
15. Bardakçı, *Neslishah*, 202.
16. Ibid, 203.
17. Ibid, 204–205.
18. Ibid, 203.
19. 'Telegram from Crown Rep to Secretary of State, 13 October' in *Matters Concerning the Ex-Khalifa*.
20. 'Telegram from Durrushehvar to Nizam, 14th Oct 1944' in *Matters Concerning the Ex-Khalifa*.
21. 'Lothian to LCL Griffin, Secretary to HE the Crown Representative, New Delhi, 16th October' in *Matters Concerning the Ex-Khalifa*.
22. 'Letter from Nizam' in *Matters Concerning the Ex-Khalifa*.
23. 'Someone Jung to Major ACK Maunsell Secretary to the Resident at Hyderabad, 2nd January' in *Matters Concerning the Ex-Khalifa*.
24. See John Zubrzycki, *The Last Nizam: An Indian Prince in the Australian Outback* (Sydney: Pan Macmillan, 2006).
25. H.I.H. Prince Ali Vâsib, *Memoirs of an Ottoman Prince: What I Saw and Heard in My Homeland and in Exile*, prepared by H.I.H. Prince Osman Selaheddin, with contributions by H.I.H. Princess Ayse Gülnev and H.I.H. Prince Selim Süleyman, translated and edited by John Shakespeare Dyson (Istanbul: Timas Publishing, 2017), 510.
26. Ibid, 525.

27. Ibid, 526.
28. 'Telegram from Durrushehvar to Nizam' in *Matters Concerning the Ex-Khalifa*.
29. 'Lothian to LCL Griffin' in *Matters Concerning the Ex-Khalifa*.
30. Ibid.
31. Ibid.
32. Trans. James Wrathall, Nawab Dr. Sir Hafiz Muhammad Ahmed Saeed Khan Chhatari, *Yaad-e-Ayyam*, vol. 3 (Aligarh: Privately published, 1974), 172–173.
33. Ibid.
34. Ibid.
35. Personal interview.
36. Bardakçı, *Neslishah*, 202.
37. Extract from a private and secret letter dated 1st February 1946 from the Secretary of State to H.E. the Viceroy, in the National Archives of India. A copy was shown to the author by Ayub Khan.
38. Ibid.
39. Ibid.
40. Trans. Adnan Mahmud, Muhammad Abdul Hai, *Gulistan-E-Khuldabad* (Maharashtra: Privately Published, 2001), 381–383.
41. Ibid.
42. Ibid.
43. Ibid.
44. Ibid.
45. Zubrzycki, *The Last Nizam*, 170–171.
46. Ibid, 181.
47. Ibid, 184.
48. Philip Mason, *A Shaft of Sunlight: Memories of a Varied Life* (Chatham: W&J Mackay Limited, 1978), 208.
49. Ibid, 205.
50. Ibid, 204.
51. Mason, *A Shaft of Sunlight*, 203.
52. Rosita Forbes, *India of the Princes* (London: Ebenezer Baylis and Son Ltd, 1939), 226–227.
53. Ibid, 227.
54. Ibid, 225.
55. Ibid, 224.
56. Ibid, 227.

57. Ayesha Jalal, *The Sole Spokesman: Jinnah, the Muslim League, and the Demand for Pakistan* (Cambridge: Cambridge University Press, 1985), 4.
58. *The Lahore Resolution*, 1940. https://historypak.com/lahore-resolution–1940/.
59. Sunil Purushotham, 'Federating the Raj: Hyderabad, Sovereign Kingship, and Partition' in *Modern Asian Studies* 54, no. 1 (Cambridge, Cambridge University Press, 2019), 168.
60. Narendra Luther, *Hyderabad: A Biography* (New Delhi: Oxford University Press, 2012), 222.
61. Zubrzycki, *The Last Nizam*, 180.
62. A.G. Noorani, *The Destruction of Hyderabad* (New Delhi: Tulika Books, 2013), 60.
63. Purushotham, 'Federating the Raj', 186.
64. Ibid, 187.
65. John Zubrzycki, *Dethroned: The Downfall of India's Princely States* (London: C Hurst & Co Publishers Ltd, 2023), 91.
66. Barney White-Spunner, *Partition: The Story of Indian Independence and the Creation of Pakistan in 1947* (London: Simon & Schuster, 2017), 191.
67. Sir William Barton, *The Princes of India* (London: Nisbet & Co Ltd, 1934), 209.
68. White-Spunner, *Partition*, 191.
69. Noorani, *The Destruction of Hyderabad*, 130.
70. 'Jinnah and the Nizam of Hyderabad—a tragic liaison' in *Business Recorder*, 23 March 2009.
71. White-Spunner, *Partition*, 195.
72. Zubrzycki, *Dethroned*, 92.
73. Ibid, 93.
74. 'Jinnah and the Nizam of Hyderabad'.
75. D.F. Karaka, *Fabulous Mogul: Nizam VII of Hyderabad* (London: Derek Verschoyle Ltd, 1955), 24.
76. Taylor C. Sherman, 'Migration, Citizenship and Belonging in Hyderabad (Deccan), 1946–1956' in *Modern Asian Studies* 45, no. 1 (London: Cambridge University Press, 2011), 88.
77. Eric Lewis Beverly, *Hyderabad, British India, and the World: Muslim Networks and Minor Sovereignty, c.1830–1959* (Cambridge: Cambridge University Press, 2015), 179.
78. Taylor C. Sherman, *Muslim Belonging in Secular India: Negotiating*

Citizenship in Postcolonial Hyderabad (Cambridge: Cambridge University Press, 2015), 24.
79. Zubrzycki, *The Last Nizam*, 192.
80. Ibid, 193.
81. Karaka, *Fabulous Mogul*, 257.
82. Sherman, *Muslim Belonging*, 23.
83. Arthur Cunningham Lothian, *Kingdoms of Yesterday* (London: Butler & Tanner Ltd, 1951), 186.
84. Sherman, *Muslim Belonging*, 24.
85. Zubrzycki, *Dethroned*, 182–183.
86. Noorani, *The Destruction of Hyderabad*, xx.
87. Ibid, 218.
88. Ibid. xx.
89. Zubrzycki, *Dethroned*, 185.
90. Ibid, 191.
91. Ibid, 192.
92. Ibid.
93. Mason, *A Shaft of Sunlight*, 214.
94. Personal Interview.
95. Zubrzycki, *Dethroned*, 192.
96. Ibid, 193.
97. Noorani, *The Destruction of Hyderabad*, 239.
98. Zubrzycki, *Dethroned*, 194.
99. Noorani, *The Destruction of Hyderabad*, 238.
100. Zubrzycki, *Dethroned*, 192.
101. Sherman, 'Migration, Citizenship and Belonging', 91.
102. Ibid, 92.
103. Noorani, *The Destruction of Hyderabad*, 246.
104. Noorani, *The Destruction of Hyderabad*.
105. Ibid, 215.
106. Personal Interview.
107. Syed Sirajuddin, 'For Better and for Verse' in *The Untold Charminar: Writings on Hyderabad*, ed. Syeda Imam (Delhi: Penguin Random House India, 2008), 112.
108. Zubrzycki, *The Last Nizam*, 214–215.
109. Ibid, 215.
110. Ibid, 229–230.
111. Bardakçı, *Neslishah*, 129.

112. Zubrzycki, *The Last Nizam*, 229–230.
113. Ibid, 213.
114. Ibid, 229–230.
115. Nigâr, *Caliph Abdülmecid II*, 27–28.
116. Ibid, 58–63.
117. Ibid, 64–67.
118. Ibid, 69.
119. Ibid, 75.
120. Ibid, 75–76.
121. Ibid, 75.
122. Ibid.
123. Ibid.

EPILOGUE

1. John Zubrzycki, *The Last Nizam: An Indian Prince in the Australian Outback* (Sydney: Pan Macmillan, 2006), 219.
2. Ibid, 225.
3. Ibid, 228.
4. Zubrzycki, *The Last Nizam*, 238–239.
5. Ibid.
6. Ibid, 241.
7. Ibid, 249.
8. John Zubrzycki, *Dethroned: The Downfall of India's Princely States* (London: C Hurst & Co Publishers Ltd, 2023), 258.
9. Ibid, 269.
10. Ibid, 274.
11. 'HEH Nizam VIII Mir Barkat Ali Siddiqui Khan Bahadur Moves from 2 BR Flat in Türkiye to 2 Square Yards Eternal Home in Hyderabad' in *Beyond Headlines*, 19 January 2023. https://beyondheadlines.in/2023/01/heh-nizam-viii-mir-barkat-ali-siddiqui-khan-bahadur-moves-from–2-br-flat-in-turkiye-to–2-square-yards-eternal-home-in-hyderabad/
12. Zubrzycki, *The Last Nizam*, 276.
13. Narendra Luther, introduction to *The Nocturnal Court: Darbaar-e-Diirbaar, The Life of a Prince of Hyderabad*, Sidq Jaisi (New Delhi: Oxford University Press, 2004), iii.
14. Luther, introduction to *The Nocturnal Court*, iii.

15. 'Niloufer The Most Beautiful Ottoman Princess: Married to Junior Prince Moazzam Jah of Hyderabad. Not A Fairytale End' in *Colours of Rainbow: Blogs of Engr Maqbool Akram.* https://www.myishasmehfil.com/2022/05/n.html
16. Personal Interview.
17. Personal Interview.
18. 'The British cemetery home to Middle East poets, politicians and princes' in *Middle East Eye*, 28 January 2021. https://www.middleeasteye.net/discover/britain-london-brookwood-cemetery-middle-east-poets-politicians
19. Personal Interview.
20. Personal Interview.
21. 'Glimpses of the history' in *Deccan Chronicle*, 7 December 2019. https://www.deccanchronicle.com/lifestyle/viral-and-trending/081219/glimpses-of-the-history.html
22. James Onley, 'The Raj Reconsidered: British India's Informal Empire and Spheres of Influence in Asia and Africa' in *Asian Affairs* 40, no. 1 (Sharjah: Taylor & Francis, 2009), 54.
23. See Gurbachan Singh, 'India at the Rabat Islamic Summit (1969)' in *Indian Foreign Affairs Journal* 1, no. 2 (Print Publications PVT. Ltd, 2006).

BIBLIOGRAPHY

Ahmed, Yakoob. *The Role of the Ottoman Sunni Ulema During the Constitutional Revolution of 1908-1909/1326-1327 and the Ottoman Constitutional Debates.* SOAS, 2019.

Ahmed, Shahab. *What Is Islam? The Importance of Being Islamic.* Princeton: Princeton University Press, 2016.

Alam, Muzaffar, and Sanjay Subrahmanyam. "A View from Mecca: Notes on Gujarat, the Red Sea, and the Ottomans, 1517–39/923–946H." In *Modern Asian Studies* 51, no. 2, Special Issue: *New Directions in Social and Economic History: Essays in Honour of David Washbrook*, 293–318. Cambridge: Cambridge University Press, 2017.

Ali, Khalid. *Ali Brothers: The Life and Times of Maulana Mohammed Ali and Shaukat Ali.* Karachi: Royal Book Company, 2011.

Alper, Cenk. "Foreword." In *The Prince's Extraordinary World: Abdülmecid Efendi*, edited by Nazan Ölcer, 8–11. Istanbul: Sabancı University/Sakıp Sabancı Museum, 2022.

Baer, Marc David. *The Ottomans: Khans, Caesars and Caliphs.* New York: Basic Books, 2021.

Bardakçı, Murat. *Neslishah: The Last Ottoman Princess.* Cairo: The American University in Cairo Press, 2019.

Barkey, Karen. *Empire of Difference: The Ottomans in Comparative Perspective.* New York: Cambridge University Press, 2008.

Beverly, Eric Lewis. *Hyderabad, British India, and the World: Muslim Networks and Minor Sovereignty, c.1830–1959.* Cambridge: Cambridge University Press, 2015.

De Courcy, Anne. *Chanel's Riviera: Glamour, Decadence, and Survival in Peace and War, 1930–1944.* New York: St Martin's Press, 2019.

Devji, Faisal. *Muslim Zion: Pakistan as a Political Idea.* Cambridge, Massachusetts: Harvard University Press, 2013.

Edhem Eldem, "From *The History Lesson* to *Beethoven in the Harem*: An Ambitious and Bourgeois Prince." in *The Prince's Extraordinary*

World: Abdülmecid Efendi, edited by Nazan Ölcer. Istanbul: Sabancı University/Sakıp Sabancı Museum, 2022.

Enginün, İnci. "Abdulmecid Efendi and Literature." In *The Prince's Extraordinary World: Abdülmecid Efendi*, edited by Nazan Ölcer. Istanbul: Sabancı University/Sakıp Sabancı Museum, 2022.

Faroqhi, Suraiya. *The Ottoman and Mughal Empires: Social History in the Early Modern World*. London: I.B. Tauris, 2019.

Gawrych, George W. *Atatürk: Father of the Republic of Turkey*. London: I.B. Tauris, 2023.

Hammond, Andrew. *Late Ottoman Origins of Modern Islamic Thought: Turkish and Egyptian Thinkers on the Disruption of Islamic Knowledge*. New York: Cambridge University Press, 2023.

Hodgson, Marshall G.S. *The Venture of Islam: Conscience and History in a World Civilization*. Vol. 1. Chicago and London: The University of Chicago Press, 1974.

Jaffrelot, Christophe. *Hindu Nationalism: A Reader*. Princeton: Princeton University Press, 2007.

———. *The Hindu Nationalist Movement and Indian Politics, 1925 to the 1990s: Strategies of Identity-Building, Implantation and Mobilisation*. London: Hurst & Company, 1996.

Kutlay, Evren. "The Ottoman Caliph Who Painted (His) History: Şahâne-i Üstâd Abdülmecid Efendi." In *The Prince's Extraordinary World: Abdülmecid Efendi*, edited by Nazan Ölcer. Istanbul: Sabancı University/Sakıp Sabancı Museum, 2022.

Leonard, Karen. "Political Players: Courtesans of Hyderabad." *The Indian Economic and Social History Review* 50, no. 4 (2013): 509–531.

Patel, Aakar. *Our Hindu Rashtra: What It Is. How We Got Here*. Chennai: Westland Publications, 2020.

Quella-Villéger, Alain. "Pierre Loti and Abdülmecid: A Little-Known Franco-Turkish Friendship." In *The Prince's Extraordinary World: Abdülmecid Efendi*, edited by Nazan Ölcer. Istanbul: Sabancı University/Sakıp Sabancı Museum, 2022.

Satan, Ali. "Abdülmecid Efendi: From the National Struggle to the Caliphate." In *The Prince's Extraordinary World: Abdülmecid Efendi*, edited by Nazan Ölcer, 80–91. Istanbul: Sabancı University/Sakıp Sabancı Museum, 2022.

Truschke, Audrey. *The Language of History: Sanskrit Narratives of Indo-Muslim Rule*. New York: Columbia University Press, 2021.

BIBLIOGRAPHY

White-Spunner, Barney. *Partition: The Story of Indian Independence and the Creation of Pakistan in 1947*. London: Simon & Schuster, 2017.

Articles

Abu-Manneh, Butrus. "The Islamic Roots of the Gülhane Rescript." *Die Welt des Islams*, New Series 34, no. 2 (1994): 173–203.

Akramul, Islam. "The General Islamic Congress of Jerusalem Reconsidered." *Muslim World* 86, no. 3–4 (1996).

Ansari, K. Humayun. "Pickthall, Muslims of South Asia, and the British Muslim Community of the Early 1900s." In *Marmaduke Pickthall: Islam and the Modern World*, edited by Geoffrey P. Nash, 93–111. Leiden and Boston: Brill, 2017.

Aracı, Emre. "Giuseppe Donizetti at the Ottoman Court: A Levantine Life." *The Musical Times* 143, no. 1880 (2002): 49–52.

Azaryahu, Maoz, and Yitzhak Reiter. "The Geopolitics of Interment: An Inquiry into the Burial of Muhammad Ali in Jerusalem, 1931." *Israel Studies* 20, no. 1 (Bloomington: Indiana University Press, 2015).

Cemil, Kutlutürk. "Princess Durrusehvar Sultan's Selfless Struggle for Uplifting the Social Status of Hyderabadi Women." *Cogent Social Sciences* 9, no. 1 (Digital: Taylor & Francis, 2023).

Devji, Faisal. "Islam and British Imperial Thought." In *Islam and the European Empires*, edited by David Motadel, 203–222. Oxford: Oxford University Press, 2014.

Farooqi, Mehr Afshan. "Will Gujarat Mourn Adil Mansuri?" *Outlook*, 20 November 2008. https://www.outlookindia.com/books/will-gujarat-mourn-adil-mansuri-news-238983.

Farooqi, N.R. "Six Ottoman Documents on Mughal-Ottoman Relations During the Reign of Akbar." *Journal of Islamic Studies* 7, no. 1 (1996): 39–57.

Hearst, David, "Why the West cannot afford to ignore political Islam." *Middle East Eye*, 11 November 2016. https://www.middleeasteye.net/opinion/why-west-cannot-afford-ignore-political-islam.

Inanc, Yusuf Selman, "Abdulmecid II: Artist, musician and the last caliph of Islam." *Middle East Eye*, 18 March 2022. https://www.middleeasteye.net/discover/turkey-ottoman-Abdulmecid-ii-last-caliph-islam-artist-musician.

Khalidi, Omar. "The Caliph's Daughter." *Cornucopia* 31 (2004).

BIBLIOGRAPHY

Luther, Narendra. Introduction to *The Nocturnal Court: Darbaar-e-Diirbaar, The Life of a Prince of Hyderabad*, by Sidq Jaisi. New Delhi: Oxford University Press, 2004.

Minault, Gail. "Urdu Political Poetry during the Khilafat Movement." *Modern Asian Studies* 8, no. 4 (1974): 459–471.

Moaveni, Azadeh, "The Lingering Dream of an Islamic State." *The New York Times*, 12 January 2018. https://www.nytimes.com/2018/01/12/opinion/sunday/post-isis-muslim-homeland.html.

Murad, Abdal Hakim. "Marmaduke Pickthall: A Brief Biography." Masud, 6 January 2015. http://masud.co.uk/marmaduke-pickthall-a-brief-biography/.

Olson, Robert W., and William F. Tucker. "The Sheikh Sait Rebellion in Turkey (1925): A Study in the Consolidation of a Developed Uninstitutionalized Nationalism and the Rise of Incipient (Kurdish) Nationalism." *Die Welt des Islams* 18, no. 3/4 (1978).

Pernau-Reifield, Margrit. "Reaping the Whirlwind: Nizam and the Khilafat Movement." *Economic and Political Weekly* 34, no. 38 (18–24 September 1999): 2741–2750.

Rahman, M. Raisur. "'We Can Leave Neither': Mohamed Ali, Islam and Nationalism in Colonial India." *South Asian History and Culture* 3, no. 2 (2012): 157–173.

Sen Gupta, Abhijit. "Rabindranath Tagore Loved Hyderabad So Much That He Wanted to Make City His Second Home." *The Siasat Daily*, 6 May 2023.

Sherman, Taylor C. "Migration, Citizenship and Belonging in Hyderabad (Deccan), 1946–1956." *Modern Asian Studies* 45, no. 1 (2011): 81–108.

Sims-Williams, Ursula. "Curzon's Durbars and the Alqabnamah: The Persian Gulf as Part of the Indian Empire." *Asian and African Studies Blog*, 30 December 2014. https://blogs.bl.uk/asian-and-african/2014/12/curzons-durbars-and-the-alqabnamah-the-persian-gulf-as-part-of-the-indian-empire.html.

Primary Sources

Abdul Hai, Muhammad. *Gulistan-E-Khuldabad*. Maharashtra: Privately Published, 2001.

"Angora Bans the Name of Caliph in Prayers; Government Orders Clergy to Substitute a Plea to Allah to Favour the Republic." *The New York Times*, 10 March 1924.

"Angora Moves to Drive Caliph Into Exile; Police Act to Prevent His Taking Treasures." *The New York Times*, 3 March 1924.

Barton, William. *The Princes of India*. London: Nisbet & Co Ltd, 1934.

Chaudhari, K.K., ed. *Khilafat Movement (1920–1921)*. Vol. 10 of *Source Material for a History of Freedom Movement in India*. Mumbai: Government of Maharashtra, 1982.

"CALIPH APPEALS TO MOSLEM WORLD; Calls for an Inter-Islamic Conference to Consider Action Concerning His Exile." *The New York Times*, 12 March 1924.

"CALIPH'S HAREM IN PLIGHT; His Departure in Exile Leaves Women Penniless." *The New York Times*, 7 March 1924.

Chhatari, Nawab Dr Sir Hafiz Muhammad Ahmed Saeed Khan. *Yaad-eAyyam*, vol. 3. Aligarh: Privately published, 1974.

Cooper, Elizabeth. *The Harim and the Purdah*. New York: The Century Company, 1915.

Corfield, Conrad. *The Princely India I Knew, From Reading to Mountbatten*. Madras: Indo British Historical Society, 1975.

"DISSENT IN TURKEY." *The New York Times*, 11 April 1923.

"EX-CALIPH NEEDS MONEY; So He Is Painting and Composing, Hoping to Sell His Work." *The New York Times*, 20 April 1924.

"Fortnightly Reports on the Internal Situation in the Hyderabad State." In *British Library File No. 34-P, 1931, Secret*.

Jah, Durru Shehvar. "Life of an Eastern Princess: From Turkey to Hyderabad." *Nottingham Evening News*, 6 June 1933.

Jaisi, Sidq, *The Nocturnal Court: Darbaar-e-Diirbaar, The Life of a Prince of Hyderabad* (New Delhi: Oxford University Press, 2004)

Karaka, D.F. *Fabulous Mogul: Nizam VII of Hyderabad*. London: Derek Verschoyle Ltd, 1955.

Lothian, Arthur Cunningham. *Kingdoms of Yesterday*. London: Butler & Tanner Ltd, 1951.

"Marriage of the Sons of H.E.H. the Nizam to Turkish Princesses." In *British Library File No. 54, 1931*.

Mason, Philip. *A Shaft of Sunlight: Memories of a Varied Life*. Chatham: W&J Mackay Limited, 1978.

"Matrimonial Alliances Between Sahibzada Azam Jah, H.E.H. the Nizam's Heir Apparent, and the Daughter of Abdul Majid, Ex-Caliph of

Turkey, and Sahibzada Muazzam Jah, Second Son of the Nizam, to the Niece of the Ex-Caliph." In *British Library File No. 538, 1931, Secret.*

"Matters Concerning the Ex-Khalifa, Father of Her Highness the Princess of Berar." In *British Library File No. 297, 1944.*

Muhammad, Shan, ed. *Unpublished Letters of the Ali Brothers.* Delhi: Idarah-i Adabiyat-i Delli, 1979.

Nigâr, Salih Keramet. Trans. Deniz Erdem. *Caliph Abdülmecid II.* Istanbul: İnkılap ve Aka Publishing House, 1964.

Pickthall, Marmaduke. "The Muslims in the Modern World." Speech, 1936. *Journal of the Royal Central Asian Society* 23, no. 2. London: Taylor and Francis, 2011.

Seydi Ali Reis, *The Travels and Adventures of the Turkish Admiral Sidi Ali Reïs in India, Afghanistan, Central Asia, and Persia, During the Years 1553–1556.* Trans. A. Vambery. London: Forgotten Books, 2010 [1899].

"The Nizam of Hyderabad." *Time*, 22 February 1973. https://content.time.com/time/covers/0,16641,19370222,00.html.

Vâsib, Ali, H.I.H. Prince. *Memoirs of an Ottoman Prince: What I Saw and Heard in My Homeland and in Exile.* Prepared by H.I.H. Prince Osman Selaheddin, with contributions by H.I.H. Princess Ayse Gülnev and H.I.H. Prince Selim Süleyman. Translated and edited by John Shakespeare Dyson. Istanbul: Timas Publishing, 2017.

INDEX

Abbas Syed, Nawab Akram, 149, 182–3, 186
Abbasid Caliphate, 15, 99
Abdul Bari, Maulana, 57–9
Abdul Hai, Mohammad, 201
Abdul Haq, Moulvi, 126
Abdulaziz I (Sultan), 11, 13, 20
Abdulhamid II (Sultan), 10, 12, 21, 22, 73, 130, 133–4
Abdulhamid, Amid, 23
Abdulmejid I, 19, 21
Abdulmejid II (Caliph), 2, 44, 48–52, 69, 85, 90, 129, 147, 150, 176–7, 192–3, 196–9
    Abdulmejid finance, 104–6
    Caliphate of, 76–9
    Durrushehvar's marriage, 157–8, 159–60
    exile, 3–4
    in Jerusalem, 148
    leaving Istanbul, 90–1
    Loti's meeting with, 9–10
    new Caliphate, 74–6
    newspapers on, 82–5
    paintings, 11–14
    political fallout, 96–9
    Shaukat Ali's designs, 166–8
    Swiss territory, journey to, 92–5
    Turkey's independence, 79–82
    See also Durrushehvar (Princess); Pasha, Mustafa Kemal
Abu Dhabi, 114, 221
Academy of Fine Arts, 11
Adana, 35
Adile (Princess), 134, 155, 176
Aegean coast, 49
Aegean Sea, 48
al-Afghani, Jamal al-Din, 114
Afghanistan, 15, 66
Africa, 2, 132
Aga Khan III, 122
Aga Khan, 35, 55, 56, 82, 100
Ahmed Khan, Nawab Syed, 149, 163, 166
Ahmed, Maulana Haji, 59
Ahmed, Yakoob, 24
Ahmedabad, 59, 112
Akbar (Mughal Emperor), 18
Akhlaq-i Jalali (Davvani), 17
Alamgir, Aurangzeb (Emperor), 111, 201
al-Aqsa Mosque, 146–7, 169
al-Azhar seminary, 161
Algeria, 133
Ali Khan, Mir Shujaat, 151
Ali, Ahmed, 165–6
Ali, Choudhary Rahmat, 206
Ali, Khalid, 30

INDEX

Ali, Mohamed, 27, 28–9, 33–5, 39, 65–7, 141
   British betrayal and Palestinian struggle, 141–3
   European tour, 60–5
   fight the law, 41–3
   Khilafatists, 57–60
   separate electorates, 135–9
   Sultanate, abolition of, 70–2
   See also Azad, Maulana Abdul Kalam; Shaukat Ali, Maulana
Ali, Syed Sajid Hussain, 187
Aligarh, 28, 35, 57–8, 100
All-India Muslim Parties Conference, 139
al-Qaeda, 2–3
Amir Ali, Sayyid, 35, 37, 55, 82, 83–4, 100, 105–6, 129
Amiruddin Khan, Syed Mohammed (colonel), 149, 163, 186
Amritsar, 44
Anatolia, 35, 43, 44, 49–50, 57, 64, 221
Aney, Madhav, 192
Ankara, 51, 70, 72–4, 101, 173
   new Caliphate, 74–6
   Turkey's independence, 79–82
Arab National Charter, 172
Arab Revolt (1936), 171–2
Arab Sharif of Mecca, 22
Arafat, Yasser, 172
Archbishop of Canterbury, 61
Aristotle, 17
Armenia, 52
Armenian Women's Association, 25

Armenian Women's Union, 13
Armistice of Mudros, 77
Arnold, Billy, 134
Asad, Muhammad, 115
Asaf Jahi dynasty, 5, 112–13, 114, 116, 135, 152, 162, 167–8
Asia Minor. *See* Anatolia
Asia, 2
Askeshir, 80
Associated Press (news agency), 192
Atatürk, Mustafa Kemal, 81, 117, 222
Attlee, Clement, 206
Aurangabad, 1, 118
Australia, 48, 143
Azad, Maulana Abdul Kalam, 33–4, 54, 137, 206
Aziz, Abdul, 59–60
Azzam, Abd al-Rahman, 170

Baghdad, 15, 99
Bahadur, Nawab Jeng, 154
Bahrain, 114, 221
Bakhit, Sheikh Mohammed, 161
Bakr, Abu, 14
Baldwin, Stanley, 144
Balfour, Arthur, 142
Balkan Wars (1912–13), 25, 34–5, 221
Balkans, 35
Bangladesh, 221
Banjara Hills, 183, 218
Bardakçı, Murat, 164
Barelvis, 35
Bari, Maulana Abdul, 38, 54
Barton, William, 113
Beethoven in the Harem (painting), 12

INDEX

Begum, Abadi Bano, 27, 42–3, 65
Begum, Dulhan Pasha, 122, 150, 152
Begum, Gowher, 122
Begum, Leila, 122
Benedetti (Count), 134
Benedict XV (Pope), 63–4
Bengal, 138
Ben-Gurion, David, 143
Berar, 110
Berlin, 48
Bey, Ahmed Riza, 34
Bey, Asad Fuad, 64, 77, 97–8, 154, 161
Bey, Ferd, 156
Bey, Haydar, 89–90
Bey, Hikmet, 86
Bey, Lutfi Fikri, 82
Bey, Osman Zeki, 77
Bey, Remzi, 72
Bey, Sadeddin, 89–90
Bey, Shevket, 13
Bey, Tevfik, 36
Bey, Vassif, 89
Bi Amma. *See* Begum, Abadi Bano
Blunt, Wilfred Scawen, 21
Bombay Legislative Council, 60
Bombay, 5, 54, 57, 137, 144, 167, 173
Bose, Subhas Chandra, 172
Bosphorus, 20, 25–6, 79, 103
Brig, 93
Britain, 3, 4, 27, 28, 60–1, 82, 101
    British betrayal and Palestinian struggle, 141–3
British Empire, 4, 5, 180

British India, 60, 66, 111, 112, 113, 116
British Library, 4, 195
British Mandate, 170
British Raj, 110, 221
Buchan, John, 40
Bulgaria, 34, 92
Bunsen, Maurice de, 41
Bush, George W., 2–3

Cagnes-sur-Mer, 132
Cairo, 34, 142, 161
Calcutta, 34
Cambridge, 2, 28–9, 56
Camlica district, 9
Canada, 143
Cannes, 134
Catalca, 91
Central Khilafat Committee, 54, 65, 82
Chamber of the Sacred Mantle, 75
Chamberlain, High, 86
Chanda, Mah Laqa Bai, 126
Chanel, Coco, 133
Chaplin, Charles, 11
Charles II (King), 176
Cheesewright, Maurice, 208–9
Cheney, Dick, 3
Chhatari, 196–8, 200
Chowmahalla Palace, 120, 174, 185, 218
Christianity, 61, 139
Christians, 25, 62, 63, 116, 136–7
Churchill, Winston, 21
Cimiez, 130
Ciragan, 77–8

273

INDEX

Clive, Robert, 121
Comrade, The (English paper), 31, 33, 34, 38
   Ali's article, 41
Congress Party, 42–5, 135, 139, 143, 158, 187, 204–5
   Khilafat Movement, 53–7
   See also Muslim League
Constantinople. *See* Istanbul
Cooper, Elizabeth, 110–11, 179–80
Cordoba, 69
Corfield, Conrad, 118, 181–2
Cote D'Azu, 134
'counter-extremism' programme, 3
'Cyberabad', 109

'Dagh' Dehlvi, Mirza Khan, 125
Daily Express (newspaper), 159, 208–9
Dalits, 112, 205
Dalrymple, Sam, 114
Damascus, 37
Daraz, Khwaja Banda Nawaz Gaisu, 113
Darul Uloom, 35
Daulatabad Fort, 201
Davvani, Jalal-ud-Din, 17
De Vaux, 22
Defence of India Act, 41
Dehradun, 196
'Delhi Manifesto', 139
Delhi, 53, 139
Denis, Ruth St., 117
Deobandis, 35
Depressed Classes Association, 207–8

Depressed Classes Conference, 207–8
Desai, Bhulabhai, 192
Destruction of Hyderabad, The (Noorani), 209
Devji, Faisal, 23, 55, 154
Disraeli, Benjamin, 37
Dolmabahce Palace, 48, 51, 76, 86–7
Dolmabahce, 20, 78, 79, 86, 90, 102, 131
Duke of Westminster, 133
Durrushehvar (Princess), 4, 25–6, 86–7, 90–1, 131–2, 148, 152, 154–5, 156, 175–6, 185–6
   death of, 219
   life in Hyderabad, 177–81
   marriage, 157–60
   returned to Istanbul, 199
   Swiss territory, journey to, 92–5

Eastern Roman Empire, 16
Edirne, 36
Efendi, Abdurrahim, 73
Efendi, Huseyin Kamil, 21
Efendi, Qinalizadeh Ali, 17
Efendi, Sheikh-ul-Islam Cemaleddin, 24
Efendi, Vehbi, 72–3
Egypt, 19, 94, 97, 140, 161
El Edroos, 208
Emperor of Austria, 93
'Empire of Rome', 17
'The End of the Caliphate' (*L'Illustration*), 99
England, 4, 37, 61

INDEX

Indians in, 28–30
Erud, 65
Esra (Princess), 166, 220
Essentials of Hindutva (Savarkar), 136–7
Ethiopia, 114
Eton, 56
Europe, 2, 11, 18–19, 77, 98, 129, 139
    caliphate through European eyes, 21–3
    Khilafatists, European tour, 60–5
European liberalism, 19

Faisal I of Arabia, 62
Falaknuma Palace, 121
Farrère, Claude, 98
Faruk, Omer (Prince), 25, 44, 48–9, 52, 76, 81, 130, 131, 134, 135, 160, 195
Father of the Turks, 47
Fatimid Caliphate, 15
fatwa, 35
Fawzi, Sulaiman, 171
Finley, John, 80
Firangi Mahalis, 35, 58
Fisher, John Arbuthnot, 61
Forbes, Rosita, 203–4
Forster, E.M., 37
Four Horsemen of the Apocalypse, The (film), 133
Fowler, William Warde, 29
France, 50, 98, 99, 101, 154, 157, 161
    Abdulmejid's exile, 3–4
    Caliph in, 129–32
    high society in, 132–5

Fuad, Osman (Prince), 155, 173, 176

Gallipoli, 48
Gandhi, Indira, 212, 218
Gandhi, Mahatma. *See* Gandhi, Mohandas Karamchand
Gandhi, Mohandas Karamchand, 27, 42, 54, 55–6, 67, 135, 146, 158, 174
    Khilafatists, 57–60
    Khilafatists, European tour, 60–5
    letter to Durrushehvar, 180
    support for Khilafat Movement, 217
    See also Nehru, Jawaharlal
Gangshakar, Baba Farid, 171
Garden of Allah, The (1927) (romantic drama), 133
Gasparri, Cardinal, 63
Gaza, 170
George V (King), 180
German Iron Cross, 48
Germans, 192–3
Germany, 38, 142
Gertrude, Julia, 132
al-Ghita, Mohammed Hussein Kashif, 170
Ghulam Ali, Bade, 124
Giolitti, Giovanni, 63
Glehn, Jane de, 130
Goethe in the Harem (painting), 12
Gokhale, Gopal Krishna, 33
Gothic dining hall, 29
Gough-Calthorpe, Somerset Arthur, 50

275

INDEX

Government of India, 42, 54, 60, 82
Grand Commander of the Victorian Order, 83
Grand Hotel des Alpes de Territet, 94
Grand National Assembly, 51, 70, 73, 75–6, 78, 86, 89, 100, 102, 195
Grand Vizier, 48–9, 51, 70
Great War. *See* World War I
Greece, 34, 47, 50, 52
Greenmantle (novel), 40
Gujarat, 17–18, 59, 113, 125
Gulbarga, 113
Gulhane (Rose-Chamber) Edict (1839), 19
Gulistan-e-Khuldabad (Abdul Hai), 201

Haberturk (news website), 164
Habshis, 114
Hadhramaut, 114
al-Hadi, Awni Abd, 170
Hafez, 12
Halim, Kerime, 77
Hamdard (weekly), 31
Hamid, Abdulhak, 78, 86, 104
Hanafi legal school, 113
Hanafi school of law, 40
Hanzade, 94
Hardinge (Lord), 38
Harington (General), 71
Hassan (Crown Prince), 134–5
Hejaz, 40, 98, 142, 147
hijrat, 66
Hindu Kayasthas, 116
Hindu Mahasabha, 136–8

Hindus, 33, 65, 74, 115–16, 153, 205, 207
Hindu nationalism, rise of, 135–9
Hindu-Muslim unity, 42, 55
Hyderabad, centre of Islamic power, 112–15
Hyderabad, Hindu-Muslim relations in, 115–16
Khilafat Movement, 53–7
Khilafatists, 57–60, 66–7
Hitler, Adolf, 172
Hoare, Samuel, 157, 159
Home Rule, 59
Hotel Regina, 62
House of Lords, 143
House of Osman, 2, 14, 15, 25, 27, 47, 72, 77, 85, 89, 91, 132–3, 135, 152, 153
Swiss territory, journey to, 92–5
Hugo, Victor, 9
Husain, Sayyid, 60
al-Hussaini, Mufti Haj Amin, 142–3, 146–8, 161, 170, 171–2
Hussein bin Ali, Emir, 97–8
Hussein, Imam, 218
Hydari, Akbar, 117, 144, 153, 203–4
Hydari, Amina, 177
Hyderabad Forest Department, 112
Hyderabad State Manual (1938), 112
Hyderabad, 4–5, 106, 149, 152, 172
culture, 123–7
fall of, 207–10

INDEX

Hindu-Muslim relations in, 115–16
Islamic power, centre of, 112–15
largest of princely states, 109–12
Nizam's palace, 120–3
Ottomans lifestyle in, 176–81
See also Durrushehvar (Princess)
Hyderabad, Treaty of, 153
Hyderabadis, 174
Hymne (Abdulmejid), 104

Ikdam (newspaper), 82
Imam ul-Mulk family, 163
Imam, Syed Ali, 129
India, 4, 17–18, 21, 81, 84, 94
    Hyderabad, Hindu-Muslim relations in, 115–16
    Hyderabad, Islamic power, centre of, 112–15
    Hyderabad, largest of princely states, 109–12
    India and Young Turks, 33–5
    Indians in England, 28–30
    Muslims, separate electorates, 135–40
Indian Muslim soldiers, 41
Indian Muslims, 5–6, 21, 28, 33, 36, 40–1, 43, 56, 60, 66, 74, 82–3, 136, 172, 221
Indian Ocean, 17
Indian princely state, 5
Indonesia, 94
Inebolu, 52
Ingram, Rex, 133
Iqbal, Muhammad, 5–6, 28, 33, 44–5, 56, 100–1, 125, 139–40, 143–4, 169, 171

Iran, 15, 105
Iraq, 2–3, 15, 154
Islam, 33, 47–8
    Islamic law, 14–17
    new Caliphate, 74–6
    Turkey, westernisation and modernisation, 101–4
    Turkey's independence, 79–82
Islamic Charitable Society, 13
Islamic Culture (journal), 115
Islamic Culture (magazine), 140
'Islamic State of Iraq and Syria' (ISIS), 2–3
Islamism, 140
Israelis, 188
Istanbul University, 75
Istanbul, 2, 3, 5, 9, 11, 16, 20, 22, 69, 70, 72–3, 133, 189
    Abdulmejid leaving, 90–1
    India and Young Turks, 33–5
    newspaper, 82–5
    Turkey's independence, 79–82
Italy, 4, 142
Izmir, 49–50, 70

Jah 'had, 151
Jah I, Asaf, 111
Jah, Azam (Prince), 4, 149, 150, 151–3, 155–6, 157, 173–5
Jah, Azmet (Prince), 220
Jah, Moazzam (Prince), 151, 152, 154–5, 165, 173–5, 218
    Jaisi met with, 183–5
Jah, Mukarram (Prince), 4–5, 166, 185–6, 197–8, 202–4, 213–14, 219–20
Jahangir (Emperor), 18
Jaisi, Sidq, 183–4

INDEX

Jama Masjid, 191
Jannat al-Baqi graveyard, 215
Java, 169
Jerusalem, 4, 5, 146, 147, 161, 170
Jews, 62, 142–3
Jinnah, Muhammad Ali, 28, 53–4, 57, 143–4, 146, 190, 206–7
   death of, 210
   separate electorates, 135–40
jizya (poll tax), 116
Jung I, Salar, 121

Kannengiesser, Hans, 47
Karachi, 65, 172
Karaka, Dosabhai Framji, 110, 118–20
el-Karim, Abd, 98
Kasim, Abul, 60
Kenya, 114
Keramet, Salih, 13, 91–2, 105, 214–15
Keyes, Terence, 131–2, 152–3, 157, 160, 167–8, 173–6
Khan, Ayub, 164–5, 167
Khan, Mir Himayat Ali. *See* Jah, Azam (Prince)
Khan, Sayyid Ahmed, 28, 182
Khilafat Movement, 33–4, 53–7, 61, 83, 136, 143, 190
Khuldabad, 201, 216
Kidwai, Mushir Husain, 60
King Kothi Palace, 118, 120, 122
King of Greece, 93
Kisch, Frederick, 147
Kohat, 135
Kurdish districts, 101
Kuwait, 114, 221

L'Illustration (newspaper), 69, 94, 99
Lahore Resolution, 204
Laik Ali, Mir, 208–10, 212
Lajpat Rai, Lala, 136
Lake Geneva, 94
Lansbury, George, 62
Larkana, 59
Last Nizam, The (Zubrzycki), 195
Lausanne, 79, 84
Le Populaire (newspaper), 63
Légion d'Honneur, 187–8
Lewis, Bernard, 19
Liberal Union, 82
Lincoln College, 29
Liszt, 13
Lloyd George, David, 39, 43, 61, 65, 143
London Times, The (newspaper), 96
London, 4, 5, 13, 34, 55, 84, 100, 105, 129–30, 146, 156, 180
   Ali in, 32
   Durrushehvar marriage, 157–60
   Jinnah in, 28
   Khilafatists European tour, 60–5
   Round Table Conference, 143
   view from, 35–8
Longuet, Jean, 63
Lothian, Arthur, 112, 118, 180, 195, 196–8
Loti, Pierre, 9–10, 51
Lucknow Pact (1916), 42
Lucknow, 30, 58, 189
Luther, Narendra, 116

Macbeth (Fowler), 29

INDEX

MacDonald, Ramsay, 97, 143
Mackenzie, Duncan, 196
Madras province, 65
Maharashtra, 1
Mahmud II (Sultan), 19
Mahpeyker, 154–5
Majeed Mine, 218
Majlis-e Ittehad al-Muslimin, 205, 208
Malta, 71
Manikpuri, Jaleel, 126
Mappila, 66
Marmara, 103
Marquis of Hastings, 121
Marsh, Frederick, 29
Marx, Karl, 63
Mason, Philip, 106, 116, 202–4, 210
Master of Downing College, 29
May Roses (painting), 11
McMahon, Henry, 142
Mecca Masjid, 110, 194, 220
Mecca, 72, 97, 149
Medina, 72, 215
Mehisti, Atiye, 25, 131
Mehmed the Conqueror, 75
Metcalfe (Lord), 121
Mevlevi, 23
Middle East Eye (media), 164
Middle East, 5, 37, 41, 97
Ministry of Pious Foundations, 89
Mohamed Ali, Maulana, 81, 100, 105
    Maulana's final address, 143–6
Mongols, 15
Monkhile, Emine (Princess), 156
Montenegro, 34
Morali, Seniha Sami, 90–1, 133–4

Morison, Theodore, 54
Morley (Lord), 29
Mountbatten (Lord), 214
Mourad, Kenize (Princess), 187–90, 219
Mu'awiya, 14
Mughal Empire, 4
Muhammad, Prophet, 2, 42, 56, 70–2, 81, 169, 186, 215
Muhammadan Anglo-Oriental College, 27–8
ul-Mulk IV, Imam, 149
Munim, Hussain Abdul, 177, 210
Munshi, K.M., 209
Murad V (Sultan), 10, 49–50, 187
Muslim Congress, 33–4
'Muslim League Foreign Sub-Committee', 205–6
Muslim League, 34, 42–5, 143–4, 146, 204
    defeat in elections (1937), 191
    Khilafat Movement, 53–7
    separate electorates, 135–9
Muslims, 2–6, 21–3, 30, 38–41, 113–14, 129, 158, 159
    Abdulmejid finance, 104–6
    Ali brothers, 41–3
    British betrayal and Palestinian struggle, 141–3
    Hindu nationalism, rise of, 135–9
    Hindu-Muslim unity, 42, 55, 59
    Hyderabad, Hindu-Muslim relations in, 115–16
    India and Young Turks, 33–5
    Islamic modernity, 139–41
    Khilafat Movement, 53–7

INDEX

Khilafatists European tour, 60–5
London, view from, 35–8
Maulana's final address, 143–6
new Caliph, 72–4
Ottoman Caliphate, 14–17
political fallout, 96–9
Turkey, westernisation and modernisation, 101–4
Turkey's independence, 79–82

Nadvi, Sayyid Sulaiman, 60
Naidu, Sarojini, 65, 123, 179, 204
Nakib, Hussein, 162, 173, 192–3
National Assembly of Turkey, 98
National Forces, 49
National Liberation Front, 118
Nawab of Rampur, 27
Nazime (Princess), 194
Nazis, 172
Nazm-i Jamiat, 114
Negresco, 133, 134–5, 160
Nehru Report (Motilal Nehru), 138, 139
Nehru, Jawaharlal, 28, 34, 66, 83, 191–2, 209
  clash with Jinnah, 206
  death of, 217
  Sunderlal Report suppressed by, 212
Nejla (Princess), 160
Neslishah (Princess), 52, 76–7, 94, 131–2, 155, 164, 194
New York Times (newspaper), 55, 78, 84, 97, 99–100, 117, 123
New York, 117
New Zealand, 48

Nice, 5, 130–1, 132, 133, 148, 150, 156, 160, 161–2
Nigar, Salih Keramet, 79, 129
'The Night of Parting' (Jah), 184–5
Nihad, Ahmed (Prince), 195
Niloufer (Princess), 134, 155, 160, 181–2
  death of, 218–19
  letter to Nehru, 174
9/11, attacks of, 2
Nizam al-Mulk, 111
Nizam of Hyderabad, 5, 38, 60, 106, 109, 148
Nizari Ismaili Shi, 56
'Nocturnal Court', 183
Noorani, A.G., 209, 212
Nottingham Evening News (newspaper), 177
Nude (painting), 11

Oman, 114
Opium Department, 30
Oppenheim, Baron Max von, 39
Organisation of Islamic Cooperation. *See* Organisation of the Islamic Conference
Organisation of the Islamic Conference, 172
Orient Express, 91–2, 93–4
Osman Ali Khan, Mir, 3–4, 111, 116–17, 126, 129, 149–50, 153, 167, 171, 185–6
  death of, 217–18
Osmania University, 117, 125, 144
Ottoman Baroque, 19
Ottoman dynasty, 2, 5, 9, 33, 47, 50, 61–3, 70, 99, 140, 174

INDEX

constitutional Caliphate, 23–6
Islamic law, 14–17
new Caliphate, 74–6
newspaper, 82–5
Ottomans and Indians, 17–18
Westernisation, 18–21
Ottoman Jews, 91
Ottoman Red Crescent Society, 37–8
Ottomanism, 20
Our Sacred Land:Voices of the Palestine-Israeli Conflict (Mourad), 188
Oxford education, 28

Pakistan movement, 27
Pakistan, 4, 54, 172, 188, 221
Palais Carabacel, 130, 154, 160, 161
Palestine, 77, 146, 156, 161, 162
Arab Revolt (1936), 171–2
British betrayal and Palestinian struggle, 141–3
Palestinian Arabs, 143
Palestinian Liberation Organization, 172
Palestinians, 170, 188
Panaretoff, Stephen, 102
'pan-Islamism', 22, 33, 40, 84–5
Papal Secretary of State, 63
Paris Mosque, 194, 214
Paris Peace Conference, 50, 60, 69–70
Paris, 62, 130, 155
Parsis, 116
Pasha, Ahmed Zaki, 147
Pasha, Damad Ferid, 48–50
Pasha, Damad Sherif, 90

Pasha, Dulhan, 175–6
Pasha, Enver, 154–5
Pasha, Ismet, 80, 82, 84, 89, 180–1, 199
Pasha, Mustafa Kemal, 47–8, 51, 52, 64, 67, 70, 71, 72–4, 83, 84, 94, 96–7, 100, 101–2
Turkey's independence, 79–82
Pasha, Refet, 71, 72
Pasha, Tevfik, 69
Passage to India, A (Forster), 37
Patel, Vallabhbhai, 209, 213
Patterson, S.B., 176
Pershad, Maharaja Kishen, 116, 125, 126
Persia, 154
Persian Gulf, 221
Pethick-Lawrence, Frederick, 199–200
Pickthall, Marmaduke, 37–8, 41, 61, 103–4, 115, 140, 141, 153, 160, 167, 221
Plato, 17
pluralism, 20
Police Action, 211–12
Popular Party, 89
Portuguese Goa, 207
Portuguese, 17
Proust, 56
Public Works Department, 112
Puccini, 56
Punjab, 138

Qajar dynasty, 105
Qatar, 114, 221
Qawwali masters, 126
al-Qu'aiti, Ghalib, 114–15, 118–19, 123–4, 151, 213

INDEX

Quadri, Syed Abdul Mohaimin, 150, 163–4, 165–7
Qur'an, 29–30, 90, 91, 104, 155
  Pickthall translation, 115
Quraysh, 16, 22
al-Quwatli, Shukri, 169

Rahbar-e-Deccan. See *Rahnuma Daily, The* (newspaper)
Rahnuma Daily, The (newspaper), 149
Rahnuma residence, 150
Rander, 59
Razakars, 208, 210
Reading (Lord), 58–9, 146
Red Crescent charity, 25
Red Crescent Mission, 34
Regards from the Dead Princess (Mourad), 189
Reis, Seydi Ali, 18
Republic of Turkey. *See* Turkey
Reza, Shah, 154
Rida, Rashid, 169
Roman Caesar, 16–17
Roman Catholics, 104
Rome, 77
Round Table Conference II, 158
Round Table Conference, 143, 169, 174
Rousseau, 20
Royal Gallery, 143
Rumi, 23
Russell, Charles, 151
Russia, 61
Rüstem, Ünver, 19–20

Sabiha (Princess), 48–9, 76, 94, 95, 130–1, 135, 195
Sabri, Mufti Efendi, 76
Sabri, Mufti Mustafa, 140
Sabri, Shaykh Ekrama, 172
Sahib, Hazrat Pathar Wali, 163
Said, Sheikh, 101–2
Sait, Yakub Hasan, 55
Salonica, 47
San Remo, 71, 76, 85, 133
Sanjari, Hazrat Amir Hasan, 201
Sankey, 146
Saud, Ibn, 98, 141–2
Saudi Arabia, 141–2
Savoy Hotel, 213
Scarborough, 62
Selim (Sultan), 86
Selma (Princess), 187, 189–90
Serbia, 34, 92–3
Sèvres, Treaty of, 52, 62
Shah Qajar, Ahmad, 134–5
Shambrook, Peter, 142
Shamsudin, Maulana, 59
Shattered Lands (Dalrymple), 114
Shaukat Ali, Maulana, 4, 27, 30, 35, 40, 65–7, 100, 141, 146–8, 152, 156, 158, 161, 172, 189, 190–2
  British betrayal and Palestinian struggle, 141–3
  European tour, 60–5
  fight the law, 41–3
  funeral, 146–7
  Khilafatists, 57–60
  newspaper, 82–5
  Reading on, 146
  separate electorates, 135–40
  Shaukat Ali's designs, 166–8
Shawesh, Sheikh, 141
Shawn, Ted, 117

INDEX

Sheikh-ul-Islam, 24, 34, 39, 76
Shesuvar (Lady), 9–10, 12
Sholapur, 112
Sindh, 59
Slade, Augustus, 19
Smith, Muriel, 37
Smith, Wilfred Cantwell, 212
al-Solh, Riad, 169
Somalia, 114
South Asia, 30
South Yemen, 114, 118
Spain, 98
Spielberg, Steven, 220
Spirit of Islam, The (Amir Ali), 106
St George, 130
Stokes (Colonel), 156
Stravinsky, 56
Suffolk rectory, 37
Sultan of Turkey, 54
Sultan-ul-Uloom (king of learning), 117
Sunderlal Report, 211–12
Surat, 59
Swiss Foreign Office, 99
Switzerland, 3, 64, 79, 93–5, 98
Sykes, Mark, 41
Sykes-Picot Agreement, 41
Syria, 2

Tagore, Rabindranath, 125
Tanin (newspaper), 82
Tanzimat Period (Period of Reforms), 19
Telangana, 109
Tennyson, 145
Territet, 64, 94, 95
Terry, Alice, 133
Tevhid-i Efkar (newspaper), 82

Thaalbi, Abdelaziz, 147
Thalasso, Adolphe, 13
Thirty-Nine Steps, The (Buchan), 40
Thrace, 43
TIME (magazine), 117, 124, 159
Times of India (newspaper), 30
Topkapi Palace, 20, 72, 96
Tory Party, 144
Toynbee, Arnold, 61
'The Trap of Civilisation', 171
Trinity College, 28
Tripolitania, 77
Trojans, 16
Tunisia, 77
Turkestan, 169
Turkey, 3, 4, 37, 42, 62–3, 72–4, 79–82, 92, 101, 105, 213
 independence, 79–82
 westernisation and modernisation, 101–4
 See also Abdulmejid II (Caliph) Durrushehvar (Princess); Pasha, Mustafa Kemal; Vasib, Ali (Prince)
Tyabji, Abbas, 55

Ummayad Mosque, 37
UN Declaration of Human Rights, 215
United Arab Emirates, 114, 221
United Nations Security Council, 210
United Nations, 110
United Provinces, 58

Vahideddin, Mehmed (Sultan), 44, 48, 50, 52, 62–3, 70–1, 72–4, 133, 193, 195

INDEX

Vasib, Ali (Prince), 49–50, 77, 78–9, 86, 92, 130, 132, 133, 134, 135, 154–5, 156, 173–4
Vatican, 83
Venice, 174
Venkatrao, B.S., 208
Vicaruddin, Syed, 172
Victoria (Queen), 56
Vienna, 13, 25, 131
Vikhar-ul-Omara, 121
Voltaire, 20

Wahid, Abdul, 29
Walajahi (Sultana), 177, 210–11
War Academy, 47
War of Independence, 51
War on Terror, 2–3
Wars of Religion, 139
wassiyat, 196–7
Watson, Charles, 153
Wauchope, Arthur Grenfell, 170
Wavell, Archibald, 199–200
Wilhelm II, Kaiser, 48

Willingdon (Lord), 182
Wilson, Woodrow, 81
Women in the Courtyard (painting), 11
World Islamic Congress, 148, 161, 169–72
World Muslim Congress, 142
World War I, 3, 37, 47, 60, 77, 117, 129, 142, 193, 221
World War II, 135, 181, 187, 192
Wrathall, James, 121

Yar Jung, Nawab Bahadur, 160
Yazidi minority, 2
Yemen, 114
Yılmaz, Hüseyin, 15–16
Young Turks, 23–5, 33–5, 38, 44, 63
Yugoslavia, 169

Zionism, 170
Zionist settlement, 147
Zuberi, Shahid Husain, 198–9
Zubrzycki, John, 195, 219–20